Microsoft®
MCSE
Readiness Review

Exam 70-068
Windows NT° 4.0 Server
Enterprise

Microsoft Press

PUBLISHED BY
Microsoft Press
A Division of Microsoft Corporation
One Microsoft Way
Redmond, Washington 98052-6399

Library of Congress Cataloging-in-Publication Data
Perkovich, Dave.
    MCSE Readiness Review: Exam 70-068, Windows NT 4.0 Server
Enterprise / Dave Perkovich.
      p. cm.
   ISBN 0-7356-0539-4
   1. Electronic data processing personnel--Certification.
2. Microsoft software--Examinations Study guides.   3. Microsoft
Windows NT.   I. Title.
QA76.3.P472   1999
005.4'4769--dc21   99-21358
                                        CIP

Printed and bound in the United States of America.

1 2 3 4 5 6 7 8 9 QMQM   4 3 2 1 0 9

Distributed in Canada by ITP Nelson, a division of Thomson Canada Limited.

A CIP catalogue record for this book is available from the British Library.

Microsoft Press books are available through booksellers and distributors worldwide. For further information about international editions, contact your local Microsoft Corporation office or contact Microsoft Press International directly at fax (425) 936-7329. Visit our Web site at mspress.microsoft.com.

Acquisitions Editor: Jeff Madden
Project Editor: Lynn Finnel

Contents

Objective Domain 1: Planning

Objective Domain 2: Installation and Configuration

Objective Domain 3: Managing Resources

Objective Domain 4: Connectivity

Objective Domain 5: Monitoring and Optimization

Objective Domain 6: Troubleshooting

Appendix

Welcome to Windows NT 4.0 Server Enterprise

Welcome to *MCSE Readiness Review—Exam 70-068: Windows NT 4.0 Server Enterprise*. The Readiness Review series gives you a focused, timesaving way to identify the information you need to know to pass the Microsoft Certified Professional (MCP) exams. The series combines a realistic electronic assessment with a review book to help you become familiar with the types of questions you will encounter on the MCP exam. By reviewing the objectives and sample questions, you can focus on the specific skills that you need to improve before taking the exam.

This book helps you evaluate your readiness for the MCP Exam 70-068: Implementing and Supporting Microsoft Windows NT Server 4.0 in the Enterprise. When you pass this exam, you achieve Microsoft Certified Professional status. You also earn core credit toward Microsoft Certified Systems Engineer certification, and core credit toward Microsoft Certified Systems Engineer + Internet certification.

Note You can find a complete list of MCP exams and their related objectives on the Microsoft Certified Professional Web site at http://www.microsoft.com/mcp.

The Readiness Review series lets you identify any areas in which you may need additional training. To help you get the training you need to successfully pass the certification exams, Microsoft Press publishes a complete line of self-paced training kits and other study materials. For comprehensive information about the topics covered in the Windows NT Server 4.0 in the Enterprise exam, you might want to see the corresponding training kit—*Supporting Microsoft Windows NT Server in the Enterprise Training*.

Before You Begin

This MCSE Readiness Review consists of two main parts: the Readiness Review electronic assessment on the accompanying compact disc, and this Readiness Review book.

The Readiness Review Components

The electronic assessment is a practice certification exam that helps you evaluate your skills. It provides instant scoring feedback, so you can determine areas in which additional study may be helpful before you take the certification exam. Although your score on the electronic assessment does not necessarily indicate what your score will be on the certification exam, it does give you the opportunity to answer questions that are similar to those on the actual certification exam.

The Readiness Review book is organized by the exam's objectives. Each chapter of the book pertains to one of the six primary groups of objectives on the actual exam, called the *Objective Domains*. Each Objective Domain lists the tested skills you need to master to adequately answer the exam questions. Because the certification exams focus on real-world skills, the Tested Skills and Suggested Practices lists provide suggested practices that emphasize the practical application of the exam objectives.

Within each Objective Domain, you will find the related objectives that are covered on the exam. Each objective provides you with the following:

- Key terms you must know in order to understand the objective. Knowing these terms can help you answer the objective's questions correctly.

- Several sample exam questions with the correct answers. The answers are accompanied by discussions that explain why each answer is correct or incorrect. (These questions match the questions you find on the electronic assessment.)

- Suggestions for further reading or additional resources to help you understand the objective and increase your ability to perform the task or skills specified by the objective.

You use the electronic assessment to determine the exam objectives that you need to study, and then use the Readiness Review book to learn more about those particular objectives and discover additional study materials to supplement your knowledge. You can also use the Readiness Review book to research the answers to specific sample test questions. Keep in mind that to pass the exam, you should understand not only the answer to the question, but also the concepts upon which the correct answer is based.

MCP Exam Prerequisites

In addition to your hands-on experience working with Windows NT Server 4.0, you should have working knowledge of the following tasks:

- Managing a Windows NT server.

- Configuring a computer for use on a network, including the ability to:

  - Share a folder

  - Share a printer

  - Control access to a resource based on user permissions

- Explaining the basic differences between Windows NT Server and Windows NT Workstation.

- Configuring network protocols, such as NetBEUI and TCP/IP.

Note After you have used the Readiness Review and determined that you are ready for the exam, see the "Test Registration and Fees" section in the Appendix for information on scheduling for the exam. You can schedule exams up to six weeks in advance, or as late as one working day before the exam date.

Know the Products

Microsoft's certification program relies on exams that measure your ability to perform a specific job function or set of tasks. Microsoft develops the exams by analyzing the tasks performed by people who are currently performing the job function. Therefore, the specific knowledge, skills, and abilities relating to the job are reflected in the certification exam.

Because the certification exams are based on real-world tasks, you need to gain hands-on experience with the applicable technology in order to master the exam. In a sense, you might consider hands-on experience in an organizational environment to be a prerequisite for passing an MCP exam. Many of the questions relate directly to Microsoft products or technology, so use opportunities at your organization or home to practice using the relevant tools.

Using the MCSE Readiness Review

Although you can use the Readiness Review in a number of ways, you might start your studies by taking the electronic assessment as a pretest. After completing the exam, review your results for each Objective Domain and focus your studies first on the Objective Domains where you received the lowest scores. The electronic assessment allows you to print your results, and a printed report of how you fared can be useful when reviewing the exam material in this book.

After you have taken the Readiness Review electronic assessment, use the Readiness Review book to learn more about the Objective Domains that you find difficult and to find listings of appropriate study materials that may supplement your knowledge. By reviewing why the answers are correct or incorrect, you can determine if you made a simple comprehension error or if you need to study the objective topics more.

Alternatively, you can use the Learn Now feature of the electronic assessment to review your answer to each question. This feature provides you with the correct answer and a reference to the *Supporting Microsoft Windows NT Server in the Enterprise Training* kit (purchased separately) or other resources. If you use this method and you need additional information to understand an answer, you can also reference the question in the Readiness Review book.

You can also use the Readiness Review book to focus on the exact objectives that you need to master. Each objective in the book contains several questions that help you determine if you understand the information related to that particular skill. The book is also designed for you to answer each question before turning the page to review the correct answer.

The best method to prepare for the MCP exam is to use the Readiness Review book in conjunction with the electronic assessment and other study material. Thoroughly studying and practicing the material combined with substantial real-world experience can help you fully prepare for the MCP exam.

Understanding the Readiness Review Conventions

Before you start using the Readiness Review, it is important that you understand the terms and conventions used in the electronic assessment and book.

Question Numbering System

The Readiness Review electronic assessment and book contain reference numbers for each question. Understanding the numbering format will help you use the Readiness Review more effectively. When Microsoft creates the exams, the questions are grouped by job skills called *Objectives*. These Objectives are then organized by sections known as *Objective Domains*. Each question can be identified by the Objective Domain and the Objective it covers. The question numbers follow this format:

Test Number.Objective Domain.Objective.Question Number

For example, question number 70-068.02.01.003 means this is question three (003) for the first Objective (01) in the second Objective Domain (02) of the Implementing and Supporting Microsoft Windows NT Server 4.0 in the Enterprise exam (70-068). Refer to the "Exam Objectives Summary" section later in this introduction to locate the numbers associated with particular objectives. Each question is numbered based on its presentation in the printed book. You can use this numbering system to reference questions on the electronic assessment or in the Readiness Review book. Even though the questions in the book are organized by objective, you will see questions in random order during the electronic assessment and actual certification exam.

Notational Conventions

- Characters or commands that you type appear in **bold lowercase** type.

- Variable information is *italicized. Italic* is also used to identify new terms and book titles.

- Acronyms appear in FULL CAPITALS.

Notes

Notes appear throughout the book.

- Notes marked **Note** contain supplemental information.

- Notes marked **Caution** contain information you will want to know before continuing with the book's material.

Using the Readiness Review Electronic Assessment

The Readiness Review electronic assessment is designed to provide you with an experience that simulates that of the actual MCP exam. The electronic assessment material mirrors the type and nature of the questions you will see on the certification exam. Furthermore, the electronic assessment format approximates the certification exam format and includes additional features to help you prepare for the real examination.

Each iteration of the electronic assessment consists of 60 questions covering all the objectives for the Implementing and Supporting Microsoft Windows NT Server 4.0 in the Enterprise exam. (The actual certification exams generally consist of 50 to 70 questions, although fewer questions are presented if you are taking a computer adaptive test.) Just like a real certification exam, you see questions from the objectives in random order during the practice test. Similar to the certification exam, the electronic assessment allows you to mark questions and review them after you finish the test.

Note For more information about computer adaptive testing, refer to the "Computer Adaptive Testing" section in the appendix in this book.

To increase its value as a study aid, you can take the electronic assessment multiple times. Each time you are presented with a different set of questions in a revised order; however, some questions may be repeated from exams you may have taken earlier.

If you have used one of the certification exam preparation tests available from Microsoft, then the Readiness Review electronic assessment should look familiar. The difference is that the electronic assessment covers more questions while providing you with the opportunity to learn as you take the exam.

Installing and Running the Electronic Assessment Software

Before you begin using the electronic assessment, you need to install the software. You need a computer with the following minimum configuration:

- 486 or higher Intel-based processor (486 must be running in Enhanced Mode)

- Microsoft Windows 95 or later (including Windows NT)

- 4 MB of RAM

- 15 MB of available disk space

- CD-ROM drive

- Mouse or other pointing device (recommended)

▶ **To install the electronic assessment**

1. Insert the Readiness Review compact disc into your CD-ROM drive.

2. From the root directory of the compact disc, open the Assess folder and double-click the SETUP.EXE file.

   A dialog box appears indicating you will install the MCSE Readiness Review test.

3. Click Next.

   The Select Destination Directory dialog box appears showing a default installation directory (named C:\MP068, where C: is the name assigned to your hard disk).

4. Either accept the default or change the installation directory if needed, and then click Next.

   The electronic assessment software installs.

Note These procedures describe using the electronic assessment on a computer running Windows 95, Windows 98, or Windows NT 4.0.

▶ **To start the electronic assessment**

1. From the Start menu, point to Programs, point to MCSE Readiness Review, and then click (70-068) Windows NT Server 4.0.

   The electronic assessment program starts.

2. Click Start Test, or from the main menu, double-click the test name.

   Information about the MCSE Readiness Review series appears.

3. Click Start Test.

Taking the Electronic Assessment

The Readiness Review electronic assessment consists of 60 multiple-choice questions, and as in the certification exam, you can skip questions or mark them for later review. Each exam question contains a reference number that you can use to refer back to the Readiness Review book, and if you want, you can pause and continue taking the exam at a later time.

The electronic assessment contains simulation questions that use the same simulation software as the actual certification exam. These questions test your working knowledge of the software by requiring that you start the simulation and perform a specified task. After you complete the task, you close the simulator by clicking the close button in the upper-right corner of the simulation window, or by clicking the Next or Previous button.

Before you end the electronic assessment, you should make sure to answer all the questions. When the exam is graded, unanswered questions are counted as incorrect and will lower your score. Similarly, on the actual certification exam you should complete all questions or they will be counted as incorrect. No trick questions appear on the exam. The correct answer will always be among the list of choices. Some questions may require more than one response, and this will be indicated in the question. A good strategy is to eliminate the most obvious incorrect answers first to make it easier for you to select the correct answer.

You have 90 minutes to complete the electronic assessment. During the exam you will see a timer indicating the amount of time you have remaining. This will help you to gauge the amount of time you should use to answer each question and to complete the exam. The amount of time you are given on the actual certification exam varies with each exam. Generally, certification exams take approximately 90 minutes to complete.

During the electronic assessment, you can find the answer to each question by clicking the Learn Now button as you review the question. You see the correct answer and a reference to the applicable section of the Microsoft Press *Supporting Microsoft Windows NT Server in the Enterprise Training* kit and other resources, which can be purchased separately.

Ending and Grading the Electronic Assessment

When you click the Grade Now button, you have the opportunity to review the questions you marked or left incomplete. This format is similar to the one used on the actual certification exam. When you are satisfied with your answers, click the Grade Test button. The electronic assessment is graded, and the software presents your section scores and your total score.

Note You can always end a test without grading your electronic assessment by clicking the Quit Test button.

After your electronic assessment is graded, you can view a list of Microsoft Press references by clicking the Review Incorrect Answers button. You can then click OK to view the questions you missed.

Interpreting the Electronic Assessment Results

The Section Scoring screen shows you the number of questions in each Objective Domain section, the number of questions you answered correctly, and a percentage grade for each section. You can use the Section Scoring screen to determine where to spend additional time studying. On the actual certification exam, the number of questions and passing score will depend on the exam you are taking. The electronic assessment records your score each time you grade an exam so you can track your progress over time.

▶ **To view your progress and exam records**

1. From the electronic assessment main menu, select File, then select History, and then choose View.

2. Click View History.

    Each attempt score and your total score appears.

3. Select an attempt, and then click View Details.

   The section score for each attempt appears. You can review the section score in-formation to determine which Objective Domains you should study further. You can also use the scores to determine your progress as you continue to study and prepare for the real exam.

Ordering More Questions

Self Test Software offers practice tests to help you prepare for a variety of MCP cer-tification exams. These practice tests contain hundreds of additional questions and are similar to the Readiness Review electronic assessment. For a fee, you can order exam practice tests for this exam and other Microsoft certification exams. Click on the To Order More Questions button on the electronic assessment main menu for more information.

Using the Readiness Review Book

You can use the Readiness Review book as a supplement to the Readiness Review electronic assessment, or as a stand-alone study aid. If you decide to use the book as a stand-alone study aid, review the Table of Contents or the list of objectives to find topics of interest or an appropriate starting point for you. To get the greatest benefit from the book, use the electronic assessment as a pretest to determine the Objective Domains where you should spend the most study time. Or, if you would like to re-search specific questions while taking the electronic assessment, you can use the question number located on the question screen to reference the question number in the Readiness Review book.

One way to determine areas where additional study may be helpful is to carefully review your individual section scores from the electronic assessment and note objec-tive areas where your score could be improved. The section scores correlate to the Objective Domains listed in the Readiness Review book.

Reviewing the Objectives

Each Objective Domain in the book contains an introduction and a list of practice skills. Each list of practice skills describes suggested tasks you can perform to help you understand the objectives. Some of the tasks suggest reading additional material, while others are hands-on practices with software or hardware. You should pay particu-lar attention to the hands-on suggestions, as the certification exam reflects real-world knowledge you can gain only by working with the software or technology. Increasing your real-world experience with the relevant products and technologies will greatly enhance your performance on the exam.

Once you have determined the objectives you would like to study, you can use the Table of Contents to locate the objectives in the Readiness Review book. When reviewing a specific objective, you should make sure you understand the purpose of the objective and the skill or knowledge it is measuring on the certification exam. You can study each objective separately, but you may need to understand the concepts explained in other objectives.

Make sure you understand the key terms for each objective. You will need a thorough understanding of these terms to answer the objective's questions correctly. Key term definitions are located in the Glossary of this book.

Reviewing the Questions

Each odd-numbered page contains one or two questions followed by the possible answers. After you review the question and select a probable answer, you can turn to the following page to determine if you answered the question correctly. (For information about the question numbering format, see "Question Numbering System," earlier in this introduction.)

The Readiness Review briefly discusses each possible answer and provides a specific reason why each answer is correct or incorrect. You should review the discussion of each possible answer to help you understand why the correct answer is the best answer among the choices given. You should understand not only the answer to the question, but also the concepts on which the correct answer is based. If you feel you need more information about a topic or you do not understand the answer, use the Further Reading section in each objective to learn where you can find more information.

The answers to the questions in the Readiness Review are based on current industry specifications and standards. However, the information provided by the answers is subject to change as technology improves and changes.

Exam Objectives Summary

The Windows NT Server 4.0 (70-068) certification exam measures your ability to implement, administer, and troubleshoot information systems that incorporate Microsoft Windows NT Server version 4.0 in the Enterprise. Before taking the exam, you should be proficient with the job skills presented in the following sections. The sections provide the exam objectives and the corresponding objective numbers (which you can use to reference the questions in the Readiness Review electronic assessment and book), grouped by Objective Domains.

Objective Domain 1: Planning

The objectives in Objective Domain 1 are as follows:

- Objective 1.1 (70-068.01.01)—Plan the implementation of a directory services architecture. Considerations include selecting the appropriate domain model, supporting a single logon account, and allowing users to access resources in different domains.

- Objective 1.2 (70-068.01.02)—Plan the disk drive configuration for various requirements. Requirements include choosing a fault-tolerance method.

- Objective 1.3 (70-068.01.03)—Choose a protocol for various situations. Protocols include TCP/IP, TCP/IP with DHCP and WINS, NWLink IPX/SPX Compatible Transport Protocol, Data Link Control (DLC), and AppleTalk.

Objective Domain 2: Installation and Configuration

The objectives in Objective Domain 2 are as follows:

- Objective 2.1 (70-068.02.01)—Install Windows NT Server to perform various server roles. Server roles include Primary Domain Controller (PDC), Backup Domain Controller (BDC), and member server.

- Objective 2.2 (70-068.02.02)—Configure protocols and protocol bindings. Protocols include TCP/IP, TCP/IP with DHCP and WINS, NWLink IPX/SPX Compatible Transport Protocol, DLC, and AppleTalk.

- Objective 2.3 (70-068.02.03)—Configure Windows NT Server core services. Services include Directory Replicator and Computer Browser.

- Objective 2.4 (70-068.02.04)—Configure hard disks to meet various requirements. Requirements include providing redundancy and improving performance.

- Objective 2.5 (70-068.02.05)—Configure printers. Tasks include adding and configuring a printer, implementing a printer pool, and setting print priorities.

- Objective 2.6 (70-068.02.06)—Configure a Windows NT Server computer for various types of client computers. Client computer types include Windows NT Workstation, Windows 95, and Macintosh.

Objective Domain 3: Managing Resources

The objectives in Objective Domain 3 are as follows:

- Objective 3.1 (70-068.03.01)—Manage user and group accounts. Considerations include managing Windows NT user accounts, managing Windows NT user rights, managing Windows NT groups, administering account policies, and auditing changes to the user account database.

- Objective 3.2 (70-068.03.02)—Create and manage policies and profiles for various situations. Policies and profiles include local user profiles, roaming user profiles, and system policies.

- Objective 3.3 (70-068.03.03)—Administer remote servers from various types of client computers. Client computer types include Windows 95 and Windows NT Workstation.

- Objective 3.4 (70-068.03.04)—Manage disk resources. Tasks include creating and sharing resources, implementing permissions and security, and establishing file auditing.

Objective Domain 4: Connectivity

The objectives in Objective Domain 4 are as follows:

- Objective 4.1 (70-068.04.01)—Configure Windows NT Server for interoperability with NetWare servers by using various tools. Tools include Gateway Services for NetWare and Migration Tool for NetWare.

- Objective 4.2 (70-068.04.02)—Install and configure multiprotocol routing to serve various functions. Functions include Internet router, BOOTP/DHCP Relay Agent, and IPX router.

- Objective 4.3 (70-068.04.03)—Install and configure Internet Information Server.

- Objective 4.4 (70-068.04.04)—Install and configure Internet services. Services include World Wide Web, Domain Name System (DNS), and Intranet.

- Objective 4.5 (70-068.04.05)—Install and configure Remote Access Service (RAS). Configuration options include configuring RAS communications, configuring RAS protocols, and configuring RAS security.

Objective Domain 5: Monitoring and Optimization

The objectives in Objective Domain 5 are as follows:

- Objective 5.1 (70-068.05.01)—Establish a baseline for measuring system performance. Tasks include creating a database of measurement data.

- Objective 5.2 (70-068.05.02)—Monitor performance of various functions by using Performance Monitor. Functions include monitoring the processor, memory, disk activity, and the network.

- Objective 5.3 (70-068.05.03)—Monitor network traffic by using Network Monitor. Tasks include collecting data, presenting data, and filtering data.

- Objective 5.4 (70-068.05.04)—Identify performance bottlenecks.

- Objective 5.5 (70-068.05.05)—Optimize performance for various results. Results include controlling network traffic and controlling server load.

Objective Domain 6: Troubleshooting

The objectives in Objective Domain 6 are as follows:

- Objective 6.1 (70-068.06.01)—Choose the appropriate course of action to take to resolve installation failures.

- Objective 6.2 (70-068.06.02)—Choose the appropriate course of action to take to resolve boot failures.

- Objective 6.3 (70-068.06.03)—Choose the appropriate course of action to take to resolve configuration errors. Tasks include backing up and restoring the Registry and editing the Registry.

- Objective 6.4 (70-068.06.04)—Choose the appropriate course of action to take to resolve printer problems.

- Objective 6.5 (70-068.06.05)—Choose the appropriate course of action to take to resolve RAS problems.

- Objective 6.6 (70-068.06.06)—Choose the appropriate course of action to take to resolve connectivity problems.

- Objective 6.7 (70-068.06.07)—Choose the appropriate course of action to take to resolve resource access and permission problems.

- Objective 6.8 (70-068.06.08)—Choose the appropriate course of action to take to resolve fault-tolerance failures. Fault-tolerance methods include tape backup, mirroring, and stripe set with parity.

- Objective 6.9 (70-068.06.09)—Perform advanced problem resolution. Tasks include diagnosing and interpreting a blue screen, configuring a memory dump, and using the Event Log service.

Getting More Help

A variety of resources are available to help you study for the exam. Your options include instructor-led classes, seminars, self-paced kits, or other learning materials. The materials described here are created to prepare you for MCP exams. Each training resource fits a different type of learning style and budget.

Microsoft Official Curriculum (MOC)

Microsoft Official Curriculum (MOC) courses are technical training courses developed by Microsoft product groups to educate computer professionals who use Microsoft technology. The courses are developed with the same objectives used for Microsoft certification, and MOC courses are available to support most exams for the MCSE certification. The courses are available in instructor-led, online, or self-paced formats to fit your preferred learning style.

Self-Paced Training

Microsoft Press self-paced training kits cover a variety of Microsoft technical products. The self-paced kits, which are based on MOC courses, feature self-paced lessons, hands-on practices, multimedia presentations, practice files, and demonstration software. They can help you understand the concepts and get the experience you need to prepare for the corresponding MCP exam.

To help you prepare for the Windows NT Server 4.0 (70-068) MCP exam, Microsoft has written the *Supporting Microsoft Windows NT Server in the Enterprise Training* kit. With this official self-paced training kit, you can teach yourself how to work with Windows NT Server 4.0 in an enterprise that consists of a single domain or multiple domains.

MCP Approved Study Guides

MCP Approved Study Guides, available through several organizations, are learning tools that help you prepare for MCP exams. The study guides are available in a variety of formats to match your learning style, including books, compact discs, online content, and videos. These guides come in a wide range of prices to fit your budget.

Microsoft Seminar Series

Microsoft Solution Providers and other organizations are often a source of information to help you prepare for an MCP exam. For example, many solution providers will present seminars to help industry professionals understand a particular product technology, such as networking. For information on all Microsoft-sponsored events, visit http://events.microsoft.com.

Planning

The first objective domain on the MCSE exam 70-068, *Implementing and Supporting Microsoft Windows NT Server 4.0 in the Enterprise,* is Planning. This objective focuses primarily on designing the infrastructure an organization requires, based on its needs. It covers three main areas:

- Directory services (selecting a domain model and implementing security)

- Fault tolerance (applying a RAID level)

- Network protocols (for accessing computers, networks, and special resources such as network printers)

You will need a thorough understanding of the various domain models, including the workgroup model and its limitations. In addition, you should be sure to review the different RAID (redundant array of independent disks) levels supported by Windows NT and know when each would be implemented. Remember that Windows NT Server supports only RAID levels 0, 1, and 5. However, each level differs greatly in terms of support for fault tolerance and overall performance. In addition, be sure you understand when the various network protocols, including Data Link Control (DLC), are required and which computers (client and/or server) require the protocol.

You will also need to know what the Services for Macintosh network component and the AppleTalk protocol provide when installed on a Primary Domain Controller (PDC).

Tested Skills and Suggested Practices

The skills you need to successfully master the Planning Objective Domain on the exam include:

- **Managing a single domain**.

    - Practice 1: Install Windows NT Server as a PDC. Create a user account and apply it exclusively to a share. Log in from a remote client using this user account and attempt to access the network share.

    - Practice 2: Change the permissions on the share to restrict access to the user account created in practice 1. Attempt to access the share and note the messages presented to a user who does not have permission.

- **Managing multiple domains**.

    - Practice 1: Using two Windows NT servers, create two domains, called DOMAIN1 and DOMAIN2, respectively.

    - Practice 2: Create a trust relationship between the two domains.

    - Practice 3: Create a local group in DOMAIN1 that has full access to a share. Using a global group from DOMAIN2, allow a user in DOMAIN2 to access the share in DOMAIN1.

- **Implementing fault tolerance**.

    - Practice 1: On a Windows NT server with at least two disk controllers and two disk drives, implement disk duplexing.

    - Practice 2: On a second Windows NT server, implement RAID 1 (disk mirroring) using the Disk Administrator.

    - Practice 3: Implement RAID 5 on a Windows NT server by creating a stripe set with parity using Disk Administrator.

    - Practice 4: Review the considerations for each RAID level supported by Windows NT. Be able to list circumstances in which you would use one level over another.

O B J E C T I V E   1 . 1

Plan the implementation of a directory services architecture.

Aspects of this objective include selecting the appropriate domain model, supporting a single logon account, and allowing users to access resources in different domains. When using Windows NT Server, you can implement a simple security model using a single domain or a complex environment requiring many domains. Depending on the requirements of the organization, a multiple domain solution may require trust relationships between the domains. Only when these trusts have been established can users from one domain access resources that have been shared in another.

In a single domain, all user accounts are centralized on a Primary Domain Controller and can be given appropriate access to network resources either directly or through the use of groups. However, since a user account may exist in one domain and not in another, you will need to have a good understanding of how Windows NT supports trust relationships between domains. A trust relationship is a link between domains that enables pass-through authentication, in which a trusting domain honors the logon authentications of a trusted domain. With trust relationships, a user who has only one user account in one domain can potentially access the entire network. In the event there is no security provider such as Windows NT to manage user and group accounts, you may have to implement a workgroup solution. In this case, the advanced security features that accompany domains will not be available.

To successfully answer the questions for this objective, you need a firm understanding of several key terms. For definitions of these terms, refer to the Glossary in this book.

Key Terms

- Domain trusts

- FAT (file allocation table)

- Global groups

- Local groups

- NTFS (NT file system)

- Primary Domain Controller (PDC)

- Share-level security

- User-level security

70-068.01.01.001

You are designing a Windows NT network with 2 Windows NT 4.0 Servers, 30 Windows 95 client computers, and 50 Windows NT 4.0 Workstation client computers.

The required result is central administration of users.

The first optional result is to restrict access to all files by using permissions.

The second optional result is central administration of resources.

The proposed solution is to implement a workgroup model, create FAT partitions on all servers' hard drives, remove the Full Control access from the Everyone group, and establish user/group permissions for each shared resource.

What does the proposed solution provide?

A. The required result and all optional results.

B. The required result and one optional result.

C. The required result but none of the optional results.

D. The proposed solution does not provide the required result.

70-068.01.01.001

You are designing a Windows NT network with 2 Windows NT 4.0 Servers, 30 Windows 95 client computers, and 50 Windows NT 4.0 Workstation client computers.

The required result is central administration of users.

The first optional result is to restrict access to all files by using permissions.

The second optional result is central administration of resources.

The proposed solution is to implement a workgroup model, create FAT partitions on all servers' hard drives, remove the Full Control access from the Everyone group, and establish user/group permissions for each shared resource.

What does the proposed solution provide?

▶ **Correct Answer: D**

A. **Incorrect:** Using a workgroup security model with FAT partitions does not support central administration of users or resources. In addition, it does not allow for control of resources by permission, but only by password.

B. **Incorrect:** Workgroup security does not allow for centralized administration of user accounts. In addition, neither of the optional results can be realized using this solution.

C. **Incorrect:** Only the domain model with a security provider, such as Windows NT Server, can provide centralized administration of user accounts. A workgroup model does not allow users to be managed centrally. Instead, in a workgroup, access is granted on a password, not on a per-user, basis.

D. **Correct:** A workgroup model is used when no security provider is available on the network. In this case, user accounts are not managed centrally and access to resources is based on shared passwords (share-level), not on individual permissions (user-level).

70-068.01.01.002

Examine the trust relationship diagram shown below.

A member of Domain 3 needs to access a resource on Domain 2. How must this be accomplished?

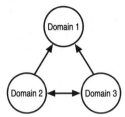

A. Resources cannot be shared because the proper trust relationship is not established.

B. On Domain 2, assign a local group with Full Access permissions to the resource. On Domain 3, create a global group and make the user a member of the group. Add the global group on Domain 3 to the local group on Domain 2.

C. On Domain 3, assign a local group with Full Access permissions to the resource. On Domain 2, create a global group and make the user a member of the group. Add the global group to the local group.

D. On Domain 2, assign a local group with Full Access permissions to the resource. On Domain 3, create a local group and make the user a member of the group. Add the local group from Domain 2 to the local group on Domain 3.

E. On Domain 3, assign a local group with Full Access permissions to the resource. On Domain 2, create a local group and make the user a member of the group. Add the local group from Domain 3 to the local group on Domain 2.

70-068.01.01.002

Examine the trust relationship diagram shown on the previous page.

A member of Domain 3 needs to access a resource on Domain 2. How must this be accomplished?

▶ **Correct Answer: B**

A. **Incorrect:** The appropriate trust relationship exists between these domains. However, the appropriate group permissions do not. In order to allow the user access to the resource, a local and a global group must be created.

B. **Correct:** Since a trust relationship already exists between these domains, a local group must be created in Domain 2 that includes the appropriate global group that is created in Domain 3.

C. **Incorrect:** The local group that is created to access the resource must exist in Domain 2, where the resource itself is located. A global group, containing the user name(s) can then be added to this local group.

D. **Incorrect:** Only global groups can be added to a local group. Therefore, a local group created in Domain 3 would not solve this problem.

E. **Incorrect:** A local group that has access to the resource cannot be created in Domain 3 because the resource is located in Domain 2. Domain 3 can create only a global group that will then be added to a local group in Domain 2 in order to provide access to the user.

70-068.01.01.003

You are implementing a Windows NT network with 5 Windows NT 4.0 Servers, 5 Windows 95 client computers, and 50 Windows NT 4.0 Workstation client computers.

The required result is central administration of users.

The first optional result is to restrict access to all files by using permissions.

The second optional result is central administration of resources.

The proposed solution is to implement a single domain model, create FAT partitions on all servers' hard drives, and establish user/group permissions for each shared resource.

What does the proposed solution provide?

A. The required result and all optional results.

B. The required result and one optional result.

C. The required result but none of the optional results.

D. The proposed solution does not provide the required result.

70-068.01.01.003

You are implementing a Windows NT network with 5 Windows NT 4.0 Servers, 5 Windows 95 client computers, and 50 Windows NT 4.0 Workstation client computers.

The required result is central administration of users.

The first optional result is to restrict access to all files by using permissions.

The second optional result is central administration of resources.

The proposed solution is to implement a single domain model, create FAT partitions on all servers' hard drives, and establish user/group permissions for each shared resource.

What does the proposed solution provide?

▶ **Correct Answer: B**

A. **Incorrect:** While the domain model provides centralized administration of the user accounts, the first optional result is also realized. Once user and group accounts exist, permissions can then be established on a particular share.

B. **Correct:** The domain model, with its user and group accounts, provides the ability to centrally administer those accounts as well as assign permissions to resources. However, until NTFS is implemented, centralized administration of resources will not be realized.

C. **Incorrect:** Since users and groups exist, permissions can now be applied to shared resources on the network. Therefore, the first optional result has been realized.

D. **Incorrect:** A domain model allows centralized management of users. Therefore, the required result has been realized.

70-068.01.01.004

A user needs to access a color laser printer on a Windows NT domain named ACCT. The user is currently a member of the MGMT domain and should retain access to the MGMT domain. No trusts have been established.

Which trust relationship and group memberships must be created to allow the user to access the color laser printer on the ACCT domain?

A. A trust relationship must be set up so that the ACCT domain trusts the MGMT domain. The user must be made a member of a local group in the MGMT domain. On the ACCT domain, a local group must be created with access to the color laser printer. The local group from the MGMT domain must be added to the ACCT domain's local group that has access to the printer.

B. A trust relationship must be set up so that the MGMT domain trusts the ACCT domain. The user must be made a member of a global group in the MGMT domain. On the ACCT domain, a local group must be created with access to the color laser printer. The global group from the MGMT domain must be added to the ACCT domain's local group that has access to the printer.

C. A trust relationship must be set up so that the ACCT domain trusts the MGMT domain. The user must be made a member of a local group in the MGMT domain. On the ACCT domain, a global group must be created with access to the color laser printer. The global group from the MGMT domain must be added to the ACCT domain's local group that has access to the printer.

D. A trust relationship must be set up so that the ACCT domain trusts the MGMT domain. The user must be made a member of a global group in the MGMT domain. On the ACCT domain, a local group must be created with access to the color laser printer. The global group from the MGMT domain must be added to the ACCT domain's local group that has access to the printer.

70-068.01.01.004

A user needs to access a color laser printer on a Windows NT domain named ACCT. The user is currently a member of the MGMT domain and should retain access to the MGMT domain. No trusts have been established.

Which trust relationship and group memberships must be created to allow the user to access the color laser printer on the ACCT domain?

▶ **Correct Answer: D**

A. **Incorrect:** Although the trust relationship in this answer is correct, the user must be added to a global group. Only global groups can be added to local groups, such as the group in the domain that owns the resource to be shared.

B. **Incorrect:** Since the ACCT domain owns the resource, this domain must trust the MGMT domain. Therefore, in this answer, the trust relationship is incorrect. The ACCT domain needs to trust the MGMT domain.

C. **Incorrect:** Although the trust relationship in this answer is correct, the user must be added to a global group in the MGMT domain. If they are added to a local group, the ACCT domain will not be able to provide access to the resource because only global groups can be added to local groups.

D. **Correct:** In this answer, the trust relationship is correct and the appropriate group types have been selected. The ACCT domain needs to trust the MGMT domain and the global group, containing the user account, can then be added to a local group that has access to the resource.

70-068.01.01.005

Your company is implementing a network consisting of 6 Windows NT 4.0 servers, 40 Windows 95 client computers, and 80 Windows NT Workstation 4.0 client computers.

The required result is to centralize administration of users.

The first optional result is to use permissions to restrict access to the \SECRET shared folder on the PDC.

The second optional result is central administration of resources.

The proposed solution is to implement a single domain model with NTFS partitions on all the servers' hard drives, create a local group with access to the \SECRET folder on the PDC, assign Read permission to the local group, remove Full Control access from the Everyone group, create a global group of users who need access to the \SECRET folder, and add the global group to the local group.

What does the proposed solution provide?

A. The required result and all optional results.

B. The required result and one optional result.

C. The required result but none of the optional results.

D. The proposed solution does not provide the required result.

70-068.01.01.005

Your company is implementing a network consisting of 6 Windows NT 4.0 servers, 40 Windows 95 client computers, and 80 Windows NT Workstation 4.0 client computers.

The required result is to centralize administration of users.

The first optional result is to use permissions to restrict access to the \SECRET shared folder on the PDC.

The second optional result is central administration of resources.

The proposed solution is to implement a single domain model with NTFS partitions on all the servers' hard drives, create a local group with access to the \SECRET folder on the PDC, assign Read permission to the local group, remove Full Control access from the Everyone group, create a global group of users who need access to the \SECRET folder, and add the global group to the local group.

What does the proposed solution provide?

▶ **Correct Answer: A**

A. **Correct:** Using a domain model, you can centrally administer user accounts. With these accounts, you can then apply the appropriate permissions to all network resources. In addition, NTFS will allow central management of resources. Thus, the required result and all optional results will be realized.

B. **Incorrect:** Using this solution, permissions have been applied to the \SECRET folder, and NTFS allows for centralized administration of resources. Therefore, both optional results are realized and this answer is incorrect.

C. **Incorrect:** Using this solution, permissions have been applied to the \SECRET folder, and NTFS allows for centralized administration of resources. Therefore, both optional results are realized and this answer is incorrect.

D. **Incorrect:** A domain model allows for the centralized creation and management of user and group accounts. Therefore, the required result has been realized. In addition, the proposed solution will also realize each of the optional results.

Further Reading

Supporting Microsoft Windows NT Server in the Enterprise Training kit. Complete Lesson 1, "Directory Architecture," of Chapter 1, "Planning the Enterprise with Microsoft Windows NT Server 4.0." In this lesson, you will learn about the various domain models supported by Windows NT.

Microsoft Windows NT Server Networking Guide. Read pages 107–110 to learn more about planning a domain.

Windows NT Server 4.0 in the Enterprise Accelerated MCSE Study Guide. Read Chapter 2, "Microsoft NT 4.0 Directory Services" to learn more about user accounts and domain management.

OBJECTIVE 1.2

Plan the disk drive configuration for various requirements.

Requirements for this objective include choosing a method for fault tolerance. Windows NT only supports three levels of RAID. These levels are:

0: disk striping with no fault tolerance

1: disk mirroring

5: disk striping with parity

RAID levels 2–4 are not supported.

You should spend time learning which levels provide the fault tolerance required by your environment.

In addition to understanding what each level of RAID provides, you should also know the basic differences between FAT and NTFS file systems. In particular, you'll need to understand what security features are provided by each file system supported by Windows NT, such as NTFS or FAT.

To successfully answer the questions for this objective, you need a firm understanding of several key terms. For definitions of these terms, refer to the Glossary in this book.

Key Terms

- FAT

- Fault tolerance

- NTFS

- RAID

- Share-level security

- User-level security

70-068.01.02.001

You are the administrator of a Windows NT 4.0 domain with a single Windows NT 4.0 Server computer. The Intel-based server computer has 10 8-GB hard drives, and you need to implement fault tolerance on the server's hard drives.

The required result is the ability to recover data in the event of a failed hard drive.

The first optional result is to secure the hard drives so only users with the appropriate permissions can access them.

The second optional result is to maximize disk utilization using fault-tolerance methods.

The proposed solution is to implement RAID 5, create NTFS partitions on all hard drives, remove Full Control access from the Everyone group, and implement the appropriate user/group permissions.

What does the proposed solution provide?

A. The required result and all optional results.

B. The required result and one optional result.

C. The required result but none of the optional results.

D. The proposed solution does not provide the required result.

70-068.01.02.001

You are the administrator of a Windows NT 4.0 domain with a single Windows NT 4.0 Server computer. The Intel-based server computer has 10 8-GB hard drives, and you need to implement fault tolerance on the server's hard drives.

The required result is the ability to recover data in the event of a failed hard drive.

The first optional result is to secure the hard drives so only users with the appropriate permissions can access them.

The second optional result is to maximize disk utilization using fault-tolerance methods.

The proposed solution is to implement RAID 5, create NTFS partitions on all hard drives, remove Full Control access from the Everyone group, and implement the appropriate user/group permissions.

What does the proposed solution provide?

▶ **Correct Answer: A**

A. **Correct:** RAID 5 will provide a solution for a drive that fails and provides maximum disk utilization. In addition, by using NTFS, complete security can be implemented based on user accounts.

B. **Incorrect:** By using RAID 5, the drives will be fully utilized as required by the first optional result. In addition, implementing NTFS will provide the level of security required for the second optional result. This solution includes support for both optional results, and therefore this answer is incorrect.

C. **Incorrect:** By using RAID 5, the drives will be fully utilized as required for the first optional result. In addition, implementing NTFS will provide the level of security required by the second optional result. This solution includes support for both optional results, and therefore this answer is incorrect.

D. **Incorrect:** RAID 5 provides the highest level of fault tolerance, resulting in the ability to rebuild the file system in the event a drive fails. Therefore, the required result will be realized by this solution.

70-068.01.02.002

A Windows NT Server Intel-based computer has 10 8-GB hard drives, and fault tolerance needs to be implemented for the server's hard drives.

The required result is the ability to recover data in the event of a failed hard drive.

The first optional result is to secure the hard drives so that only users with the appropriate permissions can access them.

The second optional result is to maximize disk utilization while still providing fault tolerance.

The proposed solution is to implement RAID 0 and create FAT partitions on all the server's hard drives.

What does the proposed solution provide?

A. The required result and all optional results.

B. The required result and one optional result.

C. The required result but none of the optional results.

D. The proposed solution does not provide the required result.

70-068.01.02.002

A Windows NT Server Intel-based computer has 10 8-GB hard drives, and fault tolerance needs to be implemented for the server's hard drives.

The required result is the ability to recover data in the event of a failed hard drive.

The first optional result is to secure the hard drives so that only users with the appropriate permissions can access them.

The second optional result is to maximize disk utilization while still providing fault tolerance.

The proposed solution is to implement RAID 0 and create FAT partitions on all the server's hard drives.

What does the proposed solution provide?

▶ **Correct Answer: D**

A. **Incorrect:** Because RAID 0 is used, there will be no fault tolerance provided. Therefore, the required result will not be realized. In addition, the FAT file system does not provide the ability to implement user-based permission on file shares. To do this, NTFS is required.

B. **Incorrect:** RAID 0 does not provide any fault tolerance; therefore the required result will not be realized. Consider RAID 1 or 5 to implement some level of fault tolerance.

C. **Incorrect:** While RAID 0 may be the most efficient use of the available drives, it provides no fault tolerance. Therefore, the required result is not realized and this answer is incorrect.

D. **Correct:** You must use RAID 1 or 5 in order to implement fault tolerance. RAID 0 does not support the required result, making this the correct answer. In addition, according to the first optional result, you would need to implement NTFS, not FAT, to support the security requirement. Also, you would need to specifically select RAID 5 to fully utilize the available drives as required by the second optional result.

70-068.01.02.003

It is necessary to optimize write performance on your domain's PDC. The PDC has 30 9-GB hard drives. Which RAID level will provide optimum write performance?

A. 0

B. 1

C. 2

D. 3

E. 4

F. 5

70-068.01.02.004

Which three RAID levels does Windows NT Server 4.0 support?

A. 0

B. 1

C. 2

D. 3

E. 4

F. 5

70-068.01.02.003

It is necessary to optimize write performance on your domain's PDC. The PDC has 30 9-GB hard drives. Which RAID level will provide optimum write performance?

▶ **Correct Answer: A**

A. **Correct:** RAID 0 provides the best performance because data is written simultaneously to different devices. RAID 1 and RAID 5 provide fault tolerance, which, while more reliable, is not as efficient.

B. **Incorrect:** RAID 1 is more reliable than RAID 0 but requires all data to be written twice. Therefore, RAID 1 is slower than RAID 0 and this answer is incorrect.

C. **Incorrect:** Windows NT does not support RAID levels 2–4.

D. **Incorrect:** Windows NT does not support RAID levels 2–4.

E. **Incorrect:** Windows NT does not support RAID levels 2–4.

F. **Incorrect:** Although RAID 5 provides the highest level of fault tolerance, it does not perform faster than RAID 0.

70-068.01.02.004

Which three RAID levels does Windows NT Server 4.0 support?

▶ **Correct Answers: A, B, and F**

A. **Correct:** RAID 0, 1, and 5 are all supported by Windows NT.

B. **Correct:** RAID 0, 1, and 5 are all supported by Windows NT.

C. **Incorrect:** Windows NT does not support RAID levels 2–4.

D. **Incorrect:** Windows NT does not support RAID levels 2–4.

E. **Incorrect:** Windows NT does not support RAID levels 2–4.

F. **Correct:** RAID 0, 1, and 5 are all supported by Windows NT.

70-068.01.02.005

What are the minimum controller and disk requirements for disk duplexing?

A. One controller and two hard disks

B. One controller and four hard disks

C. Two controllers and two hard disks

D. Two controllers and four hard disks

70-068.01.02.005

What are the minimum controller and disk requirements for disk duplexing?

▶ **Correct Answer: C**

A. **Incorrect:** While two drives are the minimum requirement for disk duplexing, a second controller is also required. Therefore, this answer is incorrect.

B. **Incorrect:** Two controllers and two drives are the minimum requirement for disk duplexing. Therefore, this answer is incorrect since another controller and two fewer drives are the minimum requirement.

C. **Correct:** In order to implement disk duplexing, you need two controllers and two drives.

D. **Incorrect:** The minimum requirement to implement disk duplexing is two controllers and two disk drives. Therefore, this answer is incorrect.

Further Reading

Supporting Microsoft Windows NT Server in the Enterprise Training kit. Complete Lesson 2, "Managing Partitions," of Chapter 1, "Planning the Enterprise with Microsoft Windows NT Server 4.0." In this lesson, Windows NT support for RAID and fault tolerance will be discussed.

Microsoft Windows NT Server Resource Guide. Read pages 155–156 to learn more about planning a fault-tolerant system.

Windows NT Server 4.0 in the Enterprise Accelerated MCSE Study Guide. Read Chapter 3, "Planning for Fault Tolerance" to learn more about how Windows NT supports hard-drive partitioning.

OBJECTIVE 1.3

Choose a protocol for various situations.

Protocols include:

- TCP/IP (Transmission Control Protocol/Internet Protocol)

- TCP/IP with DHCP (Dynamic Host Configuration Protocol) and WINS (Windows Internet Naming Service)

- NWLink IPX/SPX (Internetwork Packet Exchange/Sequenced Packet Exchange) Compatible Transport Protocol

- DLC (Data Link Control)

- AppleTalk

When planning a Windows NT Server environment, you'll need to consider the types of networks your clients require access to, such as a Novell network or the public Internet. In addition, if there are special devices on the network, such as an AS/400 or network printer, you may need to support specific protocols such as DLC. Windows NT Server provides additional features for non-Microsoft clients, such as support for Macintosh clients that need access to shared folders or printers.

At the very least, a Windows NT Server will need to have the network protocol currently in use installed in order to act as a simple file server or an advanced Primary Domain Controller. Depending on the complexity of the network, you may also need to implement WINS or DHCP in order to reduce traffic or centralize the network's management.

To successfully answer the questions for this objective, you need a firm understanding of several key terms. For definitions of these terms, refer to the Glossary in this book.

Key Terms

- AppleTalk

- DHCP

- DLC

- IPX/SPX

- NetBEUI

- NetBIOS

- PDC

- TCP/IP

- WINS

70-068.01.03.001

A Windows NT domain network has 4 Windows NT 4.0 Server computers and 30 Windows NT 4.0 Workstation client computers. You add 3 Hewlett-Packard 5SI laser printers by connecting them directly to the network. You need central administration of each printer by a Windows NT 4.0 Server computer and the ability to print from client computers.

Which computers must have the DLC protocol installed on them?

A. Only the clients

B. Only the print servers

C. All computers in the domain

D. Print servers and clients

70-068.01.03.002

You connect two Hewlett-Packard 4SI laser printers to your Windows NT domain using a network card with an RJ-45 connection. You want to administer each printer from a Windows NT Server 4.0 computer. Which protocols must be installed on the print server's client computers?

A. The domain's network protocol and TCP/IP

B. The domain's network protocol and DLC

C. The domain's network protocol and WINS

D. The domain's network protocol and DHCP

E. The domain's network protocol

70-068.01.03.001

A Windows NT domain network has 4 Windows NT 4.0 Server computers and 30 Windows NT 4.0 Workstation client computers. You add 3 Hewlett-Packard 5SI laser printers by connecting them directly to the network. You need central administration of each printer by a Windows NT 4.0 Server computer and the ability to print from client computers.

Which computers must have the DLC protocol installed on them?

▶ **Correct Answer: B**

   A. **Incorrect:** The clients do not require DLC, as the Windows NT Server will be administering the printers. Only the server itself requires the DLC protocol.

   B. **Correct:** Since the Windows NT Server will administer the printers, only the server needs the DLC protocol.

   C. **Incorrect:** Only computers that administer the printers need DLC, therefore not all computers require the protocol and this answer is incorrect.

   D. **Incorrect:** The client computers do not require the DLC protocol since the Windows NT Server will manage the printers. Therefore, only the server needs this protocol.

70-068.01.03.002

You connect two Hewlett-Packard 4SI laser printers to your Windows NT domain using a network card with an RJ-45 connection. You want to administer each printer from a Windows NT Server 4.0 computer. Which protocols must be installed on the print server's client computers?

▶ **Correct Answer: E**

   A. **Incorrect:** The DLC protocol, not TCP/IP, is required to manage the printer. Whichever network protocol being used is also required so that clients can print to the shared device.

   B. **Incorrect:** Only the domain protocol is required to be installed on the client computers. DLC is required on the server that is managing the printer.

   C. **Incorrect:** WINS is used for name resolution, not printer management. The server will require the DLC protocol. Therefore, this answer is incorrect.

   D. **Incorrect:** DHCP is used for assigning TCP/IP information to clients. The DLC protocol is used to access these network printers. Therefore, this answer is incorrect.

   E. **Correct:** The domain protocol is required on each client computer in order to communicate with the server. DLC, however, is not required on each client, only on the server. Therefore, this answer is correct.

70-068.01.03.003

A Windows NT domain has 5 Windows NT 4.0 Server computers, 2 NetWare 4.11 server computers, and 30 Windows NT 4.0 Workstation client computers. All client computers are connected to the Internet. Which protocols must be installed on the PDC for it to communicate with all computers on the network? (Choose two.)

A. DLC

B. DHCP

C. TCP/IP

D. NetBEUI

E. NWLink IPX/SPX

70-068.01.03.004

Which TCP/IP technology reduces local broadcast traffic by resolving NetBIOS names to IP addresses?

A. RIP

B. DNS

C. WINS

D. DHCP

70-068.01.03.003

A Windows NT domain has 5 Windows NT 4.0 Server computers, 2 NetWare 4.11 server computers, and 30 Windows NT 4.0 Workstation client computers. All client computers are connected to the Internet. Which protocols must be installed on the PDC for it to communicate with all computers on the network? (Choose two.)

▶ **Correct Answers: C and E**

  A. **Incorrect:** This protocol is used to manage devices such as network printers. It is not used to access Novell resources or the Internet.

  B. **Incorrect:** DHCP is used to assign TCP/IP configuration information to client computers. It is not used to access the Internet or Novell resources. In addition, if the appropriate TCP/IP information is manually configured on each client, DHCP is not required.

  C. **Correct:** TCP/IP is the protocol used by all computers on the Internet. It is therefore required to achieve the desired results.

  D. **Incorrect:** NetBEUI (NetBIOS Enhanced User Interface) is a nonroutable protocol used on a Microsoft network. It cannot be used to access Novell resources, nor can it be used on the Internet.

  E. **Correct:** The IPX/SPX protocol is required to access Novell resources. Therefore, this protocol is required to achieve the desired results.

70-068.01.03.004

Which TCP/IP technology reduces local broadcast traffic by resolving NetBIOS names to IP addresses?

▶ **Correct Answer: C**

  A. **Incorrect:** RIP (Router Information Protocol) is used when routing packets between remote networks. This protocol is typically used by routers and is not used with NetBIOS names.

  B. **Incorrect:** DNS is used to resolve Internet host names, such as www.microsoft.com, to the appropriate IP address. DNS is not used for NetBIOS names.

  C. **Correct:** WINS allows local and remote subnet NetBIOS names to be resolved to their IP address. This reduces network traffic since a database, rather than network broadcasts, is used by WINS to resolve the NetBIOS names.

  D. **Incorrect:** DHCP is used to manage and dynamically assign TCP/IP configuration information to clients on a network. It is not used to resolve NetBIOS names.

70-068.01.03.005

Your Windows NT domain environment supports 200 users running Windows NT over Ethernet 10BaseT. A Macintosh computer is added to the network. All hard disks on the primary domain controller are NTFS.

The required result is to install the AppleTalk protocol.

The first optional result is to install File Service for Macintosh.

The second optional result is to install Print Server for Macintosh.

The proposed solution is to add Services for Macintosh to the PDC.

What does the proposed solution provide?

A. The required result and all optional results.

B. The required result and one optional result.

C. The required result but none of the optional results.

D. The proposed solution does not provide the required result.

70-068.01.03.005

Your Windows NT domain environment supports 200 users running Windows NT over Ethernet 10BaseT. A Macintosh computer is added to the network. All hard disks on the primary domain controller are NTFS.

The required result is to install the AppleTalk protocol.

The first optional result is to install File Service for Macintosh.

The second optional result is to install Print Server for Macintosh.

The proposed solution is to add Services for Macintosh to the PDC.

What does the proposed solution provide?

▶ **Correct Answer: A**

A. **Correct:** Services for Macintosh will install the AppleTalk protocol and both file and printer requirements to allow the Mac client to access the Microsoft network.

B. **Incorrect:** Services for Macintosh will also install both file and printer components for the Macintosh client. Therefore, both optional results will be realized.

C. **Incorrect:** Services for Macintosh will also install both file and printer components for the Macintosh client. Therefore, both optional results will be realized.

D. **Incorrect:** Service for Macintosh will install the AppleTalk protocol, and therefore the required result will be realized.

Further Reading

Supporting Microsoft Windows NT Server in the Enterprise Training kit. Complete Lesson 3, "Network Protocols," of Chapter 1, "Planning the Enterprise with Microsoft Windows NT Server 4.0." In this lesson, the various network protocols supported by Windows NT Server will be compared and contrasted.

Supporting Microsoft Windows NT Server in the Enterprise Training kit. Complete Lesson 4, "Microsoft Windows NT Server Requirements," of Chapter 1, "Planning the Enterprise with Microsoft Windows NT Server 4.0." In this lesson, you will learn more about supporting domains with Windows NT Server.

Windows NT Server 4.0 in the Enterprise Accelerated MCSE Study Guide. Read Chapter 5, "Network Configuration," to learn more about network support provided by Windows NT Server.

Installation and Configuration

Windows NT Server can be used in many different ways on a network. Like Windows 98 or Windows NT Workstation clients, it can support file and printer sharing. However, Windows NT Server can also provide user management and logon authentication features to create a Windows NT domain environment.

This objective covers the proper Windows NT Server installation and configuration, based on the roles and functionality required by the server. In addition to choosing the appropriate feature set upon installation, this objective also includes configuring the drives available under Windows NT to create a fault-tolerant environment. Windows NT Server supports three levels of RAID (0, 1, and 5). You will need to be familiar with each level and the extent of fault tolerance that it provides.

This objective also includes questions that relate to printer configuration and services that are based on the clients being supported. For example, you will need to understand how Windows NT Server can administer a network printer. You will also need to know how to configure Windows NT Server to support both Microsoft- and non-Microsoft–based operating system clients, such as UNIX and Macintosh.

Tested Skills and Suggested Practices

The skills you need to successfully master the Installation and Configuration objective domain on the exam include:

- **Implementing a Primary Domain Controller (PDC).**

    - Practice 1: Install Windows NT Server and select the computer to be a Primary Domain Controller.

    - Practice 2: From a Windows NT server configured as a Backup Domain Controller (BDC), use the Server Manager to manually promote this server to a Primary Domain Controller.

- **Managing a member server's domain.**

  - Practice 1: Change the domain of a member server. You do not need to reinstall Windows NT Server to accomplish this task.

- **Implementing fault tolerance.**

  - Practice 1: On a new Windows NT server, implement RAID 1 (disk mirroring) using Disk Administrator.

  - Practice 2: On a Windows NT server with at least two physical drives, use Disk Administrator to create a volume set.

  - Practice 3: On a Windows NT Server with at least three physical drives, use Disk Administrator to create a stripe set with parity.

- **Managing network printers.**

  - Practice 1: Add a local printer to a Windows NT server and share it for client use.

  - Practice 2: If two or more of the same printers are available, create a printer pool. Send more than one print job to the pool and observe how the printers are used to load-balance the print requests.

O B J E C T I V E   2 . 1

Install Windows NT Server to perform various server roles.

The various roles Windows NT Server can perform include acting as a Primary Domain Controller, a Backup Domain Controller, and a member server. In order to implement centralized management of users and resources, you will need to configure a security provider and create a domain. To do this, a Windows NT server must be configured as a Primary Domain Controller when it is first installed. You cannot use an existing Windows NT server from another domain, or one that is a member server of a domain, to act as a PDC unless you reinstall the operating system.

In order to provide more efficient user authentication, and to provide redundancy in the event the PDC becomes unavailable, you can install Windows NT Server on other computers that will act as Backup Domain Controllers. If the PDC becomes unavailable, a BDC will promote itself as a temporary PDC. You can also manually promote a BDC to a PDC using Server Manager. Note, however, that promoting and demoting BDCs can be done only within a single domain. If you want to move a BDC from one domain to another, you must reinstall Windows NT Server.

The third role a Windows NT Server can play is that of a *member server*. Member servers function like other clients on the network. They can share files and printers, but cannot authenticate users. In the event you wish to use a member server to provide PDC or BDC services, you must reinstall Windows NT Server and select the appropriate option. When using a member server, you can move the computer to a new domain simply by changing the name of the domain. You do not have to reinstall Windows NT Server to move a member server from one domain to another.

To successfully answer the questions for this objective, you need a firm understanding of several key terms. For definitions of these terms, refer to the Glossary in this book.

Key Terms

- Backup Domain Controller (BDC)

- Domain

- File-level security

- Primary Domain Controller (PDC)

- Share-level security

70-068.02.01.001

A Windows NT 4.0 network has a PDC and 25 Windows 95 client computers. There are some problems with the PDC, and it has been down several times lately. When the PDC goes down, users cannot log on. What should you do to make sure users can access the network resources they need?

A. Install a second PDC.

B. Replicate the PDC's user account information to several client computers.

C. Install a BDC, and replicate the PDC's user account information to the BDC.

D. Install a member server, and replicate the PDC's user account information to the member server.

70-068.02.01.001

A Windows NT 4.0 network has a PDC and 25 Windows 95 client computers. There are some problems with the PDC, and it has been down several times lately. When the PDC goes down, users cannot log on. What should you do to make sure users can access the network resources they need?

▶ **Correct Answer: C**

A. **Incorrect:** There can be only one PDC on a Windows NT domain. In order to provide more efficient user logons or provide redundancy in the event the PDC is unavailable, implement a Backup Domain Controller.

B. **Incorrect:** Client computers cannot manage or authenticate user logons. Only a Primary Domain Controller or a Backup Domain Controller can provide this service in a Windows NT domain.

C. **Correct:** Only by installing Windows NT Server on another computer and designating it as a Backup Domain Controller can you authenticate user logons when the PDC is unavailable.

D. **Incorrect:** Member servers cannot provide user authentication to the Windows NT domain. They can authenticate only local users.

70-068.02.01.002

A company's Windows NT 4.0 domain has a PDC and 15 Windows 95 client computers.

The required result is to allow users to log on when the PDC is down.

The first optional result is to provide file-level security on the PDC.

The second optional result is to allow a user only two logon attempts before his/her account is locked.

The proposed solution is to implement another domain so that the PDC of the new domain can perform user authentication when the PDC of the original domain is not functioning, create NTFS partitions on all server's hard drives, and set policies so that a user's account will be locked out after two failed logon attempts.

What does the proposed solution provide?

A. The required result and all optional results.

B. The required result and one optional result.

C. The required result but none of the optional results.

D. The proposed solution does not provide the required result.

70-068.02.01.002

A company's Windows NT 4.0 domain has a PDC and 15 Windows 95 client computers.

The required result is to allow users to log on when the PDC is down.

The first optional result is to provide file-level security on the PDC.

The second optional result is to allow a user only two logon attempts before his/her account is locked.

The proposed solution is to implement another domain so that the PDC of the new domain can perform user authentication when the PDC of the original domain is not functioning, create NTFS partitions on all server's hard drives, and set policies so that a user's account will be locked out after two failed logon attempts.

What does the proposed solution provide?

▶ **Correct Answer: D**

A. **Incorrect:** In order to allow users to log on to a domain when the PDC is unavailable, you need to implement a Backup Domain Controller. Having a PDC in a different domain will not allow users to log on to their local domains. Therefore, this answer is incorrect.

B. **Incorrect:** A PDC in a different domain cannot authenticate users in a local domain, even if the local domain's PDC is unavailable. You must use a BDC to provide this redundancy. Therefore, the required result is not realized with this solution.

C. **Incorrect:** In order to allow users to log on to a domain when the PDC is unavailable, you need to implement a Backup Domain Controller. Therefore, the required result is not realized with this solution.

D. **Correct:** Since a PDC in a different domain cannot authenticate users in a local domain, the required result is not realized with this solution.

70-068.02.01.003

A Windows NT single domain network has one PDC, three BDCs, and five member servers. You are creating a new domain called MNGR and need to meet the following requirements:

The required result is to use one of the BDCs as the PDC for the MNGR domain.

The first optional result is to move the other BDC to the MNGR domain as a BDC.

The second optional result is to move the member servers to the MNGR domain to serve as member servers on the MNGR domain.

The proposed solution is to change the domain name of the BDCs so they are identified with the new MNGR domain, promote one of the BDCs to a PDC, and rename the member server's domain to MNGR.

What does the proposed solution provide?

A. The required result and all optional results.

B. The required result and one optional result.

C. The required result but none of the optional results.

D. The proposed solution does not provide the required result.

70-068.02.01.003

A Windows NT single domain network has one PDC, three BDCs, and five member servers. You are creating a new domain called MNGR and need to meet the following requirements:

The required result is to use one of the BDCs as the PDC for the MNGR domain.

The first optional result is to move the other BDC to the MNGR domain as a BDC.

The second optional result is to move the member servers to the MNGR domain to serve as member servers on the MNGR domain.

The proposed solution is to change the domain name of the BDCs so they are identified with the new MNGR domain, promote one of the BDCs to a PDC, and rename the member server's domain to MNGR.

What does the proposed solution provide?

▶   **Correct Answer: D**

    A. **Incorrect:** While you can use one of the BDC computers as the PDC in the new domain, you must first reinstall Windows NT and designate this computer as a PDC. You cannot promote a BDC to a PDC in a different domain. Therefore, the required result will not be realized and this answer is incorrect.

    B. **Incorrect:** A server designated as a BDC can be promoted only within its current domain to the level of a PDC. If you wish to move the BDC to a new domain, you must reinstall Windows NT Server and specify the domain to which the computer will belong. Therefore, the required result will not be realized and this answer is incorrect.

    C. **Incorrect:** The required result cannot be realized with this solution since a BDC cannot be promoted to a PDC in a different, or new, domain. Windows NT must be reinstalled on the BDC, and only then can it act as a PDC in a different domain.

    D. **Correct:** Unless Windows NT is reinstalled on the BDC, it cannot be promoted to a PDC in a new domain. Therefore, the required result will not be realized with this solution and this answer is correct.

70-068.02.01.004

A single domain network has only one Windows NT Server 4.0 computer operating as the primary domain controller for the network.

The required result is the capability to log on to the network when the PDC is not operating.

The first optional result is to provide file-level security on the PDC.

The second optional result is to allow a user only two logon attempts before his/her account is locked.

The proposed solution is to install a BDC on the domain, replicate the PDC's account information to the BDC, create NTFS partitions and permissions on all the server's hard drives, and set system policies so that two failed logon attempts will result in a user account being locked.

What does the proposed solution provide?

A. The required result and all optional results.

B. The required result and one optional result.

C. The required result but none of the optional results.

D. The proposed solution does not provide the required result.

70-068.02.01.004

A single domain network has only one Windows NT Server 4.0 computer operating as the primary domain controller for the network.

The required result is the capability to log on to the network when the PDC is not operating.

The first optional result is to provide file-level security on the PDC.

The second optional result is to allow a user only two logon attempts before his/her account is locked.

The proposed solution is to install a BDC on the domain, replicate the PDC's account information to the BDC, create NTFS partitions and permissions on all the server's hard drives, and set system policies so that two failed logon attempts will result in a user account being locked.

What does the proposed solution provide?

▶ **Correct Answer: A**

    A. **Correct:** When a BDC is installed in the domain, users will be authenticated by this server when the PDC is unavailable. Implementing NTFS will provide file-level security and configuring the system policy will limit the number of logon attempts. Therefore, the required result and all optional results will be realized.

    B. **Incorrect:** This solution will meet the required result and both optional results. Therefore, this answer is incorrect.

    C. **Incorrect:** If NTFS is used, file-level security can be implemented. Also, by configuring system policies, you can limit the number of logon attempts. Therefore, both optional results will be realized and this answer is incorrect.

    D. **Incorrect:** Implementing a Backup Domain Controller will provide redundant logon capability. In the event the PDC is unavailable, the BDC will begin providing authentication services. Therefore, the required result will be realized.

70-068.02.01.005

Computers from several domains will move to a new domain called WGP. The following computers will be moved from their domains: a BDC from the NYC domain, a BDC from the ACCT domain, two member servers from the ACE domain, and a member server from the USER domain.

The required result is to use the BDC from the NYC domain as the PDC for the WGP domain.

The first optional result is to use the BDC from the ACCT domain as a BDC for the WGP domain.

The second optional result is to use the member servers from the ACE and USER domains as member servers for the WGP domain.

The proposed solution is to use Server Manager to delete the computer accounts from the original domain, reinstall Windows NT Server 4.0 on the BDC from the NYC domain so it becomes the PDC for the WGP domain, change the domain name of the other BDC so it is identified with the new WGP domain as a BDC, and rename the member servers' domain to WGP.

What does the proposed solution provide?

A. The required result and all optional results.

B. The required result and one optional result.

C. The required result but none of the optional results.

D. The proposed solution does not provide the required result.

70-068.02.01.005

Computers from several domains will move to a new domain called WGP. The following computers will be moved from their domains: a BDC from the NYC domain, a BDC from the ACCT domain, two member servers from the ACE domain, and a member server from the USER domain.

The required result is to use the BDC from the NYC domain as the PDC for the WGP domain.

The first optional result is to use the BDC from the ACCT domain as a BDC for the WGP domain.

The second optional result is to use the member servers from the ACE and USER domains as member servers for the WGP domain.

The proposed solution is to use Server Manager to delete the computer accounts from the original domain, reinstall Windows NT Server 4.0 on the BDC from the NYC domain so it becomes the PDC for the WGP domain, change the domain name of the other BDC so it is identified with the new WGP domain as a BDC, and rename the member servers' domain to WGP.

What does the proposed solution provide?

▶ **Correct Answer: B**

A. **Incorrect:** Although reinstalling Windows NT will change the NYC BDC to the new PDC and changing the domain name of the member servers will move them to the new domain, the first optional result will not be realized with this solution. You will need to reinstall Windows NT Server on the second BDC to change its domain. Therefore, this is not the correct answer.

B. **Correct:** Both the required result and the second optional result will be realized with this proposed solution. Windows NT Server will need to be reinstalled on the second BDC to move it to the new domain. Therefore, the first optional result will not be realized, making this the correct answer.

C. **Incorrect:** Reinstalling Windows NT Server on one of the BDCs will realize the required result. However, renaming the member servers' domain will also realize the second optional result. Therefore, this answer is incorrect.

D. **Incorrect:** Reinstalling Windows NT Server on the BDC will allow it to be the PDC in a new domain. Therefore, the required result will be realized and this answer is incorrect.

70-068.02.01.006

You need to move resources from an existing domain to a new domain. Two member servers and two BDCs will be taken from the existing network domain. The new domain will be called ATLANTA.

The required result is to use one of the BDCs from the existing domain as the PDC for the ATLANTA domain.

The first optional result is to use the other BDC as a BDC for the ATLANTA domain.

The second optional result is to use the two member servers as member servers for the ATLANTA domain.

The proposed solution is to use Server Manager to delete the computer accounts from the original domain, reinstall Windows NT Server on both of the BDCs so that they become the PDC and BDC of the ATLANTA domain, and rename the member servers' domain to ATLANTA.

What does the proposed solution provide?

A. The required result and all optional results.

B. The required result and one optional result.

C. The required result but none of the optional results.

D. The proposed solution does not provide the required result.

70-068.02.01.006

You need to move resources from an existing domain to a new domain. Two member servers and two BDCs will be taken from the existing network domain. The new domain will be called ATLANTA.

The required result is to use one of the BDCs from the existing domain as the PDC for the ATLANTA domain.

The first optional result is to use the other BDC as a BDC for the ATLANTA domain.

The second optional result is to use the two member servers as member servers for the ATLANTA domain.

The proposed solution is to use Server Manager to delete the computer accounts from the original domain, reinstall Windows NT Server on both of the BDCs so that they become the PDC and BDC of the ATLANTA domain, and rename the member servers' domain to ATLANTA.

What does the proposed solution provide?

▶ **Correct Answer: A**

   A. **Correct:** Only by reinstalling Windows NT Server can the two BDCs be moved into the new AT-LANTA domain. Renaming the member servers' domain name will move them to the ATLANTA domain as well. Therefore, the required result and both optional results will be realized, making this the correct answer.

   B. **Incorrect:** Using this solution, both optional results, not just one, will be realized. Therefore, this answer is incorrect.

   C. **Incorrect:** Reinstalling Windows NT Server will allow the second BDC to be moved to the new domain. In addition, renaming the member servers' domain will move it to ATLANTA. Therefore, both optional results will be realized and this answer is incorrect.

   D. **Incorrect:** A BDC must have Windows NT Server reinstalled before it can be promoted to a PDC in a new domain. Since the proposed solution reinstalls Windows NT Server, the required result will be realized, making this answer incorrect.

70-068.02.01.007

Which action is valid to change the role of a backup domain controller?

A. Use Server Manager to convert the backup domain controller to a member server.

B. Use User Manager for Domains to convert the backup domain controller to a member server.

C. Use Server Manager to promote the backup domain controller to a primary domain controller.

D. Use User Manager for Domains to promote the backup domain controller to a primary domain controller.

E. Use Server Manager to convert the backup domain controller to a backup domain controller on another domain.

70-068.02.01.008

You are installing Windows NT Server 4.0 on a Pentium-based computer. You need the new server to be able to provide file and print resources to members of the SIMULATOR domain, but you do not want it to authenticate user logons. How should you configure the computer?

A. As a BDC in the Simulator domain

B. As the PDC in the Simulator domain

C. As a member server in the Simulator domain

70-068.02.01.007

Which action is valid to change the role of a backup domain controller?

▶ **Correct Answer: C**

A. **Incorrect:** Once a Windows NT Server has been configured as a BDC, it can be promoted only to a PDC. If you want to change its domain or change it to a member server, you will need to reinstall Windows NT Server.

B. **Incorrect:** The User Manager for Domains tool is not used to manager servers. You need to use Server Manager for this function. Therefore, this answer is incorrect.

C. **Correct:** Using the Server Manager tool, an existing BDC can be promoted to a PDC within a domain. Changing domains, or making the computer a member server, will require a reinstallation of Windows NT Server.

D. **Incorrect:** Although the BDC can be promoted to a PDC, you will need to use the Server Manager tool, not User Manager for Domains.

E. **Incorrect:** To change the domain of a BDC, you will need to reinstall Windows NT Server. The Server Manager tool can be used to promote the BDC to a PDC, but it cannot change the domain of the BDC.

70-068.02.01.008

You are installing Windows NT Server 4.0 on a Pentium-based computer. You need the new server to be able to provide file and print resources to members of the SIMULATOR domain, but you do not want it to authenticate user logons. How should you configure the computer?

▶ **Correct Answer: C**

A. **Incorrect:** A Backup Domain Controller could be used to authenticate a user logon. In addition, if the PDC were to become unavailable, the BDC might be promoted to a PDC. In either case, this would not be the correct solution.

B. **Incorrect:** A Primary Domain Controller is used to authenticate users. Therefore, this would not be the correct answer.

C. **Correct:** Member servers cannot authenticate users in a domain. However, they can share files and print devices. Therefore, this is the correct answer.

Further Reading

Supporting Microsoft Windows NT Server in the Enterprise Training kit. Complete Lesson 4, "Microsoft Windows NT Server Requirements," of Chapter 1, "Planning the Enterprise with Microsoft Windows NT Server 4.0." In this lesson, the number and size of the required domain controllers for an enterprise environment will be discussed.

Supporting Microsoft Windows NT Server in the Enterprise Training kit. Complete Lesson 1, "Configuring Server Roles," of Chapter 2, "Installation and Configuration." In this lesson, you will learn about the three roles a Windows NT Server can support.

Windows NT Server 4.0 in the Enterprise Accelerated MCSE Study Guide. Read Chapter 4, "Windows NT 4.0 Installation," to learn more about planning and implementing a Windows NT server.

OBJECTIVE 2.2

Configure protocols and protocol bindings.

The protocols covered in this objective include:

- TCP/IP

- TCP/IP with DHCP and WINS

- NWLink IPX/SPX Compatible Transport Protocol

- DLC

- AppleTalk

You will need a thorough understanding of which protocols to use on which servers and in what network environment. For instance, if the solution requires access to the Internet, TCP/IP must be used. However, if a client needs to connect to a NetWare server, the IPX/SPX protocol must be installed. In addition to selecting the appropriate protocol, you will need to understand the impact of the protocol binding order. While the order does not restrict computers from communicating, it does affect their performance. The protocol used on the server should be set as the first protocol on the client. Also, common protocols that might be installed on a client, and which are not in use by the network, should be removed in order to provide the best possible performance.

To successfully answer the questions for this objective, you need a firm understanding of several key terms. For definitions of these terms, refer to the Glossary in this book.

Key Terms

- AppleTalk

- Dynamic Host Configuration Protocol (DHCP)

- Gateway Services for NetWare (GSNW)

- Internetwork Packet Exchange/Sequenced Packet Exchange (IPX/SPX)

- Transmission Control Protocol/Internet Protocol (TCP/IP)

- Windows Internet Naming Service (WINS)

70-068.02.02.001

A new Windows NT single domain network will consist of six Windows NT 4.0 servers, two NetWare 4.11 servers, two UNIX servers, and three network printers connected directly to the network.

The required result is to use only the essential protocols so all servers can communicate with the Windows NT servers and print to the printers.

The first optional result is to set up three of the Windows NT servers so each administers one network printer.

The second optional result is to use only routable protocols.

The proposed solution is to install NetBEUI for the Windows NT computers, install TCP/IP for the UNIX computers, and install NWLink IPX/SPX for the NetWare 4.11 servers.

What does the proposed solution provide?

A. The required result and all optional results.

B. The required result and one optional result.

C. The required result but none of the optional results.

D. The proposed solution does not provide the required result.

70-068.02.02.001

A new Windows NT single domain network will consist of six Windows NT 4.0 servers, two NetWare 4.11 servers, two UNIX servers, and three network printers connected directly to the network.

The required result is to use only the essential protocols so all servers can communicate with the Windows NT servers and print to the printers.

The first optional result is to set up three of the Windows NT servers so each administers one network printer.

The second optional result is to use only routable protocols.

The proposed solution is to install NetBEUI for the Windows NT computers, install TCP/IP for the UNIX computers, and install NWLink IPX/SPX for the NetWare 4.11 servers.

What does the proposed solution provide?

▶ **Correct Answer: D**

A. **Incorrect:** NetBEUI is not required for this solution. Therefore, the required result of using only essential protocols will not be realized. This is not the correct answer.

B. **Incorrect:** The required result will not be realized if NetBEUI is used. Therefore, this is not the correct answer.

C. **Incorrect:** The required result calls for only essential protocols to be used. The inclusion of NetBEUI is not essential, therefore the required result is not realized and this answer is incorrect.

D. **Correct:** NetBEUI is not an essential protocol given this environment. Therefore, the required result will not be realized.

70-068.02.02.002

You are creating a Windows NT network. The network will consist of six Windows NT 4.0 servers, two NetWare 4.11 servers, and two UNIX servers.

The required result is to implement only the essential protocols so all servers can communicate with the Windows NT servers and print to the printers.

The first optional result is to configure three of the Windows NT servers so each of them administers one network printer.

The second optional result is to install only routable protocols.

The proposed solution is to install TCP/IP for the Windows NT and UNIX computers, connect a printer to the LPT port of each of the Windows NT servers, and install NWLink IPX/SPX on the NetWare 4.11 servers.

What does the proposed solution provide?

A. The required result and all optional results.

B. The required result and one optional result.

C. The required result but none of the optional results.

D. The proposed solution does not provide the required result.

70-068.02.02.002

You are creating a Windows NT network. The network will consist of six Windows NT 4.0 servers, two NetWare 4.11 servers, and two UNIX servers.

The required result is to implement only the essential protocols so all servers can communicate with the Windows NT servers and print to the printers.

The first optional result is to configure three of the Windows NT servers so each of them administers one network printer.

The second optional result is to install only routable protocols.

The proposed solution is to install TCP/IP for the Windows NT and UNIX computers, connect a printer to the LPT port of each of the Windows NT servers, and install NWLink IPX/SPX on the NetWare 4.11 servers.

What does the proposed solution provide?

▶ **Correct Answer: D**

A. **Incorrect:** The NWLink IPX/SPX protocol is required to be installed on the Windows NT Servers in order to meet the required result of allowing the NetWare computers access to the NT resources.

B **Incorrect:** Unless NWLink IPX/SPX is installed on the Windows NT Servers, the NetWare computers will not be able to access the NT resources. Therefore, the required result will not be realized.

C **Incorrect:** Without the NWLink IPX/SPX protocol installed on the Windows NT Servers, the NetWare computers will not be able to communicate with the Windows NT Servers. This does not meet the required result.

D **Correct:** The proposed solution must include installing the NWLink IPX/SPX protocol on the Windows NT Servers. Unless this protocol is installed, the NetWare computers will not be able to communicate with the Windows NT Servers.

70-068.02.02.003

A Windows NT single domain network will consist of 12 Windows NT 4.0 servers, 5 NetWare 4.11 servers, 3 UNIX servers, 2 Macintosh computers, and 3 printers connected directly to the network.

The required result is to use only the essential protocols on each computer so all servers can communicate with the Windows NT servers and print to the printers.

The first optional result is to set up three of the Windows NT servers to administer the network printers.

The second optional result is using only routable protocols.

The proposed solution is to use TCP/IP for the Windows NT, Macintosh, and UNIX computers, use NWLink IPX/SPX for the NetWare 4.11 servers, and install the DLC protocol on the three Windows NT servers used as print servers.

What does the proposed solution provide?

A. The required result and all optional results.

B. The required result and one optional result.

C. The required result but none of the optional results.

D. The proposed solution does not provide the required result.

70-068.02.02.003

A Windows NT single domain network will consist of 12 Windows NT 4.0 servers, 5 NetWare 4.11 servers, 3 UNIX servers, 2 Macintosh computers, and 3 printers connected directly to the network.

The required result is to use only the essential protocols on each computer so all servers can communicate with the Windows NT servers and print to the printers.

The first optional result is to set up three of the Windows NT servers to administer the network printers.

The second optional result is using only routable protocols.

The proposed solution is to use TCP/IP for the Windows NT, Macintosh, and UNIX computers, use NWLink IPX/SPX for the NetWare 4.11 servers, and install the DLC protocol on the three Windows NT servers used as print servers.

What does the proposed solution provide?

▶ **Correct Answer: D**

   A. **Incorrect:** Unless the AppleTalk protocol is installed, the Macintosh clients will not have full access to the Windows NT domain. Therefore, the required result will not be realized.

   B. **Incorrect:** The required result, which allows the Macintosh clients full access to the Windows NT domain resources, cannot be realized unless the AppleTalk protocol is first installed.

   C. **Incorrect:** In order to allow the Macintosh clients access to the Windows NT domain resources, such as the shared printers, the AppleTalk protocol must first be installed. Without this protocol, the required result cannot be realized by the proposed solution.

   D. **Correct:** The proposed solution does not include the AppleTalk protocol. In order to allow all the Macintosh clients full access to the Windows NT domain resources, such as shared printers, AppleTalk must first be installed.

70-068.02.02.004

A Windows NT domain network has a problem with too much broadcast traffic on a local subnet. The network is using the TCP/IP protocol. What can be implemented to reduce broadcast traffic?

A. RIP

B. PPP

C. SLIP

D. WINS

E. DHCP

70-068.02.02.004

A Windows NT domain network has a problem with too much broadcast traffic on a local subnet. The network is using the TCP/IP protocol. What can be implemented to reduce broadcast traffic?

▶ **Correct Answer: D**

A. **Incorrect:** Routing Information Protocol (RIP) is used to route packets from other protocols, such as IPX. This protocol uses broadcast-based communication and therefore will increase the amount of broadcast traffic. Implementing RIP will not reduce network traffic.

B. **Incorrect:** Point-to-Point Protocol (PPP) is normally used over a serial line to connect a remote computer to a network. Its use will not reduce the amount of broadcast traffic on the local subnet.

C. **Incorrect:** Serial Line Internet Protocol (SLIP) is similar to PPP in that it can be used to connect a remote computer to a network via a modem. However, SLIP is not intended to reduce broadcast traffic.

D. **Correct:** One reason a network may experience a large amount of broadcast traffic is that a computer name needs to be resolved to an IP address. Windows Internet Naming Service (WINS) is used to help resolve NetBIOS names to an IP address. This will help reduce network traffic because a database is used to resolve the names, rather than a network broadcast. Without a WINS server, each client would have to broadcast to resolve names.

E. **Incorrect:** Dynamic Host Configuration Protocol (DHCP) is used to dynamically configure a client computer for use with TCP/IP. DHCP will actually generate broadcast traffic as it sets the IP address of a client, although the increased traffic is negligible.

70-068.02.02.005

A Windows NT Workstation 4.0 client computer's network adapter has the following binding order for protocols: NetBEUI, NWLink IPX/SPX, and TCP/IP. The client computer is connected to a domain that includes five Windows NT Server domain controllers and one NetWare server. Four domain controllers use only TCP/IP, and one uses TCP/IP and NWLink.

What can you do to increase the speed of initial communication between the client computer and the Windows NT servers? (Choose two.)

A. Install NWLink IPX/SPX on the domain controllers.

B. Delete the NetBEUI protocol from the client computer.

C. Delete the NWLink IPX/SPX protocol from the client computer.

D. Configure the client computer so that TCP/IP is the first protocol in the binding list.

70-068.02.02.005

A Windows NT Workstation 4.0 client computer's network adapter has the following binding order for protocols: NetBEUI, NWLink IPX/SPX, and TCP/IP. The client computer is connected to a domain that includes five Windows NT Server domain controllers and one NetWare server. Four domain controllers use only TCP/IP, and one uses TCP/IP and NWLink.

What can you do to increase the speed of initial communication between the client computer and the Windows NT servers? (Choose two.)

▶ **Correct Answers: B and D**

    A. **Incorrect:** Installing additional protocols on the domain controllers will not increase the speed of initial communication from clients. It may even slow down the initial communication. The client computers should have their protocols set to match the configuration of the servers.

    B. **Correct:** Since none of the domain controllers are using NetBEUI, it should be removed from the client computer. Having unused protocols installed can slow down the interaction of the client and the server.

    C. **Incorrect:** Since there is a NetWare server on the network, the client must have IPX/SPX installed. Therefore, this answer is incorrect.

    D. **Correct:** Since the domain controllers all have TCP/IP installed, the performance of initial communication will be increased if the client first binds TCP/IP. If other protocols are listed first, the computer will attempt to use these when establishing the method of communication for further data transfer. Although Windows NT can support multiple protocols, you will experience better performance if the most common protocol on the network is bound first.

70-068.02.02.006

Your company's Windows NT network started with 10 computers three years ago. Due to the need to access the Internet, it was decided that the network would use TCP/IP as its only protocol.

The network has grown to 50 computers. The assignment and configuration of IP addresses for each computer is causing serious administrative problems.

Which TCP/IP component should be implemented to simplify administration of IP addresses?

A. RIP

B. DNS

C. WINS

D. DHCP

70-068.02.02.006

Your company's Windows NT network started with 10 computers three years ago. Due to the need to access the Internet, it was decided that the network would use TCP/IP as its only protocol.

The network has grown to 50 computers. The assignment and configuration of IP addresses for each computer is causing serious administrative problems.

Which TCP/IP component should be implemented to simplify administration of IP addresses?

▶ **Correct Answer: D**

A. **Incorrect:** RIP is used to allow routing of protocols such as IPX/SPX. RIP does not allow access to the Internet and will not help administer TCP/IP.

B. **Incorrect:** Domain Name System allows computers to resolve fully qualified domain names, such as www.microsoft.com, to the appropriate IP address. DNS will not help administer the application of client IP addresses. Consider using DHCP for this function.

C. **Incorrect:** WINS is used to resolve local computer names to an IP address. It is not used to help simplify the administration of TCP/IP.

D. **Correct:** DHCP is used to dynamically configure a client's TCP/IP settings. If the IP settings for the organization change—with the addition of a new gateway or DNS server, for example—administrators need only update the central DHCP server. The next time clients log in, their TCP/IP settings will be automatically updated.

70-068.02.02.007

Your company's Windows NT domain consists of six Windows NT servers, two NetWare 3.11 servers, and two NetWare 4.11 servers. NWLink IPX/SPX is the only protocol used on the network. Not all NetWare servers are being recognized by the network's PDC.

What can you do on the PDC to ensure it can communicate with all NetWare servers?

A. Install GSNW.

B. Install CSNW.

C. Install TCP/IP.

D. Edit the properties of the NWLink IPX/SPX protocol so it is configured to automatically detect frame types.

E. Edit the properties of the NWLink IPX/SPX protocol so that manual frame detection is enabled, and add each NetWare server's network number and frame type to the manual frame detection list.

70-068.02.02.007

Your company's Windows NT domain consists of six Windows NT servers, two NetWare 3.11 servers, and two NetWare 4.11 servers. NWLink IPX/SPX is the only protocol used on the network. Not all NetWare servers are being recognized by the network's PDC.

What can you do on the PDC to ensure it can communicate with all NetWare servers?

▶ **Correct Answer: E**

A. **Incorrect:** Gateway Services for NetWare is not required to allow the NetWare clients access to the PDC. GSNW is typically used to allow Microsoft clients access to Novell resources via the gateway.

B. **Incorrect:** Client Services for NetWare is not required to allow the NetWare clients access to the PDC. CSNW is typically used by a Windows NT server to act as a client to a Novell server's resources.

C. **Incorrect:** NetWare computers use IPX/SPX as their protocol. Therefore, installing TCP/IP will not resolve this problem.

D. **Incorrect:** Autodetection of the frame type is valid only when one frame type is in use on the network. In order to ensure all NetWare clients can access the PDC, the frame type must be manually set on the PDC.

E. **Correct:** Only by manually entering the network number and frame type for each client, and setting the PDC for manual frame detection, can you ensure that all NetWare clients will be able to access the PDC.

Further Reading

Supporting Microsoft Windows NT Server in the Enterprise Training kit. Complete Lesson 3, "Network Protocols," of Chapter 1, "Planning the Enterprise with Microsoft Windows NT Server 4.0." In this lesson, you will learn when to use each of the protocols covered in this objective.

Supporting Microsoft Windows NT Server in the Enterprise Training kit. Complete Lesson 1, "Managing DHCP," of Chapter 4, "Connectivity." In this lesson, you will learn how DHCP can be used to manage TCP/IP.

Supporting Microsoft Windows NT Server in the Enterprise Training kit. Complete Lesson 2, "Managing WINS," of Chapter 4, "Connectivity." In this lesson, you will learn how WINS can reduce network traffic.

Supporting Microsoft Windows NT Server in the Enterprise Training kit. Complete Lesson 4, "Configuring Routable Protocols," of Chapter 4, "Connectivity." In this lesson, the protocols that can be routed are discussed.

Windows NT Server 4.0 in the Enterprise Accelerated MCSE Study Guide. Read Chapter 5, "Network Configuration" to learn more about supporting networks with Windows NT Server.

OBJECTIVE 2.3

Configure Windows NT Server core services.

The services covered by this objective include:

- Directory Replicator

- Computer Browser

Directory replication allows a specified folder to be maintained across multiple computers. For example, you may create a logon script that all users will run when they log into the domain. In the event there is more than one domain controller that authenticates users, this script needs to be copied to each server. You could do this manually, but through the use of directory replication, the latest version of the file will be copied and maintained automatically. Windows NT computers can act as either export servers or import servers. The export server holds the original version of the folder or files. Copies are then sent to each import server. In order to support directory replication, the Directory Replication Service must be configured on each server. The service is included when you install Windows NT Server.

All Windows-based computers on a local network have their names stored in a list that is maintained by a computer called the Master Browser. The Master Browser helps reduce network traffic by resolving computer name requests rather than using network broadcasts whenever a computer needs to be located. Any Microsoft network-capable operating system can act as a Master Browser. In addition, if the number of computers grows too large, a backup browser can be selected to help load-balance requests. Determination of which computer will act as the Master Browser and which if any computers are needed to act as backup browsers occurs automatically. You can, however, configure how a computer will react to a request to become a browser. The settings are found in the following Registry location:

HKEY_LOCAL_MACHINE\System\CurrentControlSet\Services\Browser\Parameters

Use REGEDT32.EXE to set both the IsDomainMaster and MaintainServerList entry.

To successfully answer the questions for this objective, you need a firm understanding of several key terms. For definitions of these terms, refer to the Glossary in this book.

Key Terms

- Directory replication

- Master Browser

70-068.02.03.001

Which Windows NT computers can be export servers for directory replication? (Choose all that apply.)

A. Windows NT 4.0 Workstation

B. Windows NT 4.0 Server, PDC

C. Windows NT 4.0 Server, BDC

D. Windows NT 3.51 Workstation

E. Windows NT 4.0 Server, member server

70-068.02.03.002

A Windows NT domain has 4 Windows NT 4.0 Server computers, 30 Windows NT 4.0 Workstation computers, 20 Windows 95 computers, 15 Windows for Workgroups computers, 2 NetWare 4.11 servers, and 1 Macintosh client computer.

Which computers can be browsers for the Windows NT domain? (Choose all that apply.)

A. A Macintosh computer

B. A Windows 95 computer

C. A NetWare 4.11 computer

D. A Windows for Workgroups computer

E. A Windows NT 4.0 Workstation computer

70-068.02.03.001

Which Windows NT computers can be export servers for directory replication? (Choose all that apply.)

► **Correct Answers: B, C, and E**

A. **Incorrect:** Windows NT Server is required to allow for directory replication. Windows NT 4.0 Workstation does not support this feature.

B. **Correct:** Windows NT Server is required to support directory replication. In addition, the computer can be a PDC, BDC, or a member server.

C. **Correct:** Windows NT Server is required to support directory replication. In addition, the computer can be a PDC, BDC, or a member server.

D. **Incorrect:.** Windows NT 3.51 Workstation does not support directory replication. Windows NT Server 4.0 is required.

E. **Correct:** Windows NT Server is required to support directory replication. In addition, the computer can be a PDC, BDC, or a member server.

70-068.02.03.002

A Windows NT domain has 4 Windows NT 4.0 Server computers, 30 Windows NT 4.0 Workstation computers, 20 Windows 95 computers, 15 Windows for Workgroups computers, 2 NetWare 4.11 servers, and 1 Macintosh client computer.

Which computers can be browsers for the Windows NT domain? (Choose all that apply.)

► **Correct Answers: B, D, and E**

A. **Incorrect:** Only Microsoft operating systems can browse a Windows NT domain.

B. **Correct:** Windows 95 can be a Windows NT domain browser.

C. **Incorrect:** Only Microsoft operating systems, starting with Windows 95, can be Windows NT domain browsers.

D. **Correct:** Only Microsoft operating systems can be Windows NT domain browsers.

E. **Correct:** Windows NT 4.0 Workstations can be Windows NT domain browsers.

70-068.02.03.003

What is the Windows NT Server 4.0 default Registry key setting for the Browser service?

A. NO

B. YES

C. AUTO

70-068.02.03.004

What is the Windows NT Workstation 4.0 default Registry key setting for the Browser service?

A. NO

B. YES

C. AUTO

70-068.02.03.003

What is the Windows NT Server 4.0 default Registry key setting for the Browser service?

▶ **Correct Answer: B**

A. **Incorrect:** The default Registry key setting is YES.

B. **Correct:** By default, the Registry key setting is YES. The Browser service is enabled on a Windows NT Server.

C. **Incorrect:** The Browser service is enabled by default. Therefore, the default Registry key setting is YES.

70-068.02.03.004

What is the Windows NT Workstation 4.0 default Registry key setting for the Browser service?

▶ **Correct Answer: C**

A. **Incorrect:** By default, a Windows NT 4.0 Workstation can act as a browser. The initial Registry key setting is AUTO.

B. **Incorrect:** Unlike Windows NT Server, Windows NT Workstation is not configured to be a browser by default. However, Windows NT Workstation can be a browser if required, and therefore the default setting is AUTO.

C. **Correct:** Windows NT Workstation can act as a computer browser if needed. However, by default, it is configured as AUTO, rather than YES, like a Windows NT server.

Further Reading

Supporting Microsoft Windows NT Server in the Enterprise Training kit. Complete Lesson 2, "Browsing in the Enterprise," of Chapter 2, "Installation and Configuration." In this lesson, you will learn how to manage browsers.

Supporting Microsoft Windows NT Server in the Enterprise Training kit. Complete Lesson 6, "Managing Shared Resources," of Chapter 3, "Managing Enterprise Resources." In this lesson, you will learn how to implement directory replication.

Windows NT Server 4.0 in the Enterprise Accelerated MCSE Study Guide. Read Chapter 6, "Network Services" to learn more about directory replication.

OBJECTIVE 2.4

Configure hard disks to meet various requirements.

When configuring a server's hard drives, you will need to consider the fault-tolerance requirements (providing redundancy) and the effects on read/write performance. Windows NT Server supports three levels of RAID. The first level supported, RAID 0, actually provides no fault tolerance. If a drive fails, the server must be re-started from a backup. However, since the data is written to all the available devices at the same time, the read and write performance is better than any other RAID level. RAID level 1, sometimes referred to as *disk mirroring*, is the next level supported by Windows NT Server. All data is written to two drives, providing fault tolerance. However, this is slower than RAID level 0 and requires twice the drive space. RAID levels 2–4 are not supported by Windows NT Server. The final RAID level supported by Windows NT is RAID level 5. This level saves all data with parity, which provides complete fault tolerance. If a drive fails, it can be removed from the system while continuing to provide server operations.

In addition to specifying a RAID level, hard drives can be configured in volume sets or stripe sets. A volume set allows you to select free space on one or more disks and configure it as a single drive. A stripe set provides better performance, as the data is written and read across multiple physical disks. A stripe set uses at least two drives. Another option is to create a stripe set with parity. When a stripe set with parity is used, the highest level of fault tolerance is created. Since all the data and parity information is written across at least three drives, if one fails, it can be removed from the system. The remaining drives can then rebuild the lost data from the parity information.

To successfully answer the questions for this objective, you need a firm understanding of several key terms. For definitions of these terms, refer to the Glossary in this book.

Key Terms

- Fault tolerance

- Redundant array of independent disks (RAID)

- Stripe set

- Stripe set with parity

- Volume set

70-068.02.04.001

You must set up a Windows NT Server computer so it will optimize hard drive write performance. The Intel-based computer has 20 8.4-GB hard drives. Which RAID level should be implemented on the Windows NT Server computer?

A. 0

B. 1

C. 2

D. 3

E. 4

F. 5

70-068.02.04.001

You must set up a Windows NT Server computer so it will optimize hard drive write performance. The Intel-based computer has 20 8.4-GB hard drives. Which RAID level should be implemented on the Windows NT Server computer?

▶ **Correct Answer: A**

A. **Correct:** For optimal write performance, RAID level 0 uses the devices simultaneously to save data. In addition, since this level does not implement redundancy, the data is written only once.

B. **Incorrect:** RAID level 1 must write the data to the drives more than once, in order to create a redundant, fault-tolerant environment. This does not provide for the best write performance and is therefore not the correct answer.

C. **Incorrect:** Windows NT does not support RAID level 2.

D. **Incorrect:** Windows NT does not support RAID level 3.

E. **Incorrect:** Windows NT does not support RAID level 4.

F. **Incorrect:** RAID level 5 creates a complete fault-tolerant environment that allows a drive that fails to be removed from the system while the system continues to run. While this provides a more stable environment than RAID 0 does, it does so at the expense of the performance when data is saved. Therefore, to optimize write speed, this RAID level is not the correct choice.

70-068.02.04.002

A Windows NT Server 4.0 computer is being configured as a member server.

Your required result is to optimize write speed of the disk by implementing the fastest available Windows NT Server RAID level.

The first optional result is to optimize disk space utilization.

The second optional result is to provide for continued server operations if a hard disk fails.

The proposed solution is to implement RAID 0 on the server.

What does the proposed solution provide?

A. The required result and all optional results.

B. The required result and one optional result.

C. The required result but none of the optional results.

D. The proposed solution does not provide the required result.

70-068.02.04.002

A Windows NT Server 4.0 computer is being configured as a member server.

Your required result is to optimize write speed of the disk by implementing the fastest available Windows NT Server RAID level.

The first optional result is to optimize disk space utilization.

The second optional result is to provide for continued server operations if a hard disk fails.

The proposed solution is to implement RAID 0 on the server.

What does the proposed solution provide?

▶ **Correct Answer: B**

A. **Incorrect:** Although the required and the first optional result will be realized, the second optional result will not. If a drive fails using RAID level 0, the data must be restored from a backup. In this case, write speed is obtained at the expense of redundancy and fault tolerance.

B. **Correct:** RAID level 0 provides the fastest write performance and best optimization of disk space since the data is only written once. However, this solution requires the system to be taken down if the drive fails.

C. **Incorrect:** The required result will be realized with this solution, but so will the first optional result. RAID level 0 provides the best write performance and disk utilization. Therefore, this answer is incorrect.

D. **Incorrect:** Using RAID level 0, the write performance will be optimized. No redundancy of data is provided, nor is the data saved with parity. Therefore, fault tolerance will not be available. However, the write performance and use of drive space will be optimized.

70-068.02.04.003

A Windows NT single domain network has 10 domain controllers, a member server, and 1,000 Windows NT Workstation 4.0 client computers. The member server is accessed by all users for storing data.

Your required result is to optimize write speed of the disk on the member server by implementing the fastest available Windows NT Server RAID level.

The first optional result is to optimize disk space utilization.

The second optional result is to provide for continued server operations if a hard disk fails.

The proposed solution is to implement RAID 5 on the server.

What does the proposed solution provide?

A. The required result and all optional results.

B. The required result and one optional result.

C. The required result but none of the optional results.

D. The proposed solution does not provide the required result.

70-068.02.04.003

A Windows NT single domain network has 10 domain controllers, a member server, and 1,000 Windows NT Workstation 4.0 client computers. The member server is accessed by all users for storing data.

Your required result is to optimize write speed of the disk on the member server by implementing the fastest available Windows NT Server RAID level.

The first optional result is to optimize disk space utilization.

The second optional result is to provide for continued server operations if a hard disk fails.

The proposed solution is to implement RAID 5 on the server.

What does the proposed solution provide?

▶ **Correct Answer: D**

A. **Incorrect:** RAID level 5 does not provide the best write performance, since it has to save the data with parity. Therefore, while RAID level 5 provides a high degree of fault tolerance, it does not meet the required result. In addition, only one of the optional results, continued server operations, will be realized using RAID level 5.

B. **Incorrect:** Although one optional result, continued server operations, will be realized by this solution, RAID level 5 does not provide the best write performance. Therefore, this solution does not meet the required result and this answer is incorrect.

C. **Incorrect:** RAID level 5 does not provide the best write performance. To obtain the required result, you will need to use RAID level 0. Therefore, this is not the correct answer.

D. **Correct:** Only RAID level 0 can provide the required result. However, since this level does not provide fault tolerance, if the drive fails, the system will need to be rebuilt from a backup.

70-068.02.04.004

Examine the disk configuration shown below.

What is the largest NTFS volume set you can create?

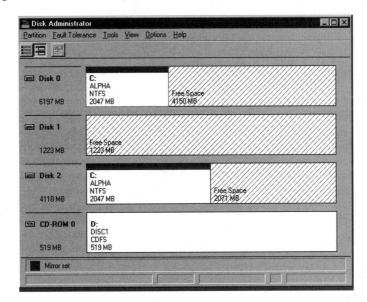

A. 2446 MB

B. 3294 MB

C. 3669 MB

D. 7444 MB

70-068.02.04.004

Examine the disk configuration shown on the previous page.

What is the largest NTFS volume set you can create?

▶ **Correct Answer: D**

    A. **Incorrect:** An NTFS volume set can use all available free space. Therefore, the correct answer is 7444 MB, not 2446.

    B. **Incorrect:** An NTFS volume set can use all available free space. Therefore, the correct answer is 7444 MB, not 3294.

    C. **Incorrect:** An NTFS volume set can use all available free space. Therefore, the correct answer is 7444 MB, not 3669.

    D. **Correct:** When creating an NTFS volume set, you can optionally use all available free space, in this case 7444 MB.

70-068.02.04.005

Examine the disk configuration shown below.

What is the maximum usable disk space a stripe set with parity can contain based on the given information?

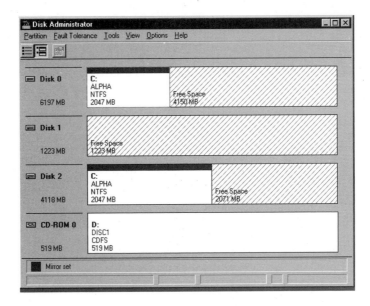

A. 2446 MB

B. 3294 MB

C. 3669 MB

D. 7444 MB

E. You cannot create a stripe set with parity because there is a mirror set in place on the drives, and only one fault-tolerance method can be implemented per disk drive.

70-068.02.04.005

Examine the disk configuration shown on the previous page.

What is the maximum usable disk space a stripe set with parity can contain based on the given information?

▶ **Correct Answer: A**

A. **Correct:** A stripe set with parity requires at least three devices. In addition, the space used on each is restricted by the smallest stripe, which is 1223 MB in this case. Once the stripe has been created, it will use 3669 MB, but have only 2446 MB of usable space.

B. **Incorrect:** A stripe set with parity requires at least three devices. This answer used only the free space from disk 1 and disk 2. Therefore, 3294 MB is not correct.

C. **Incorrect:** Using all three devices, the minimum required for a stripe set with parity, the total space required will be 3669 MB. However, due to the support for parity, only 2446 MB are available as usable space.

D. **Incorrect:** A stripe set is limited to using the maximum space from the smallest stripe, in this case 1223 MB. Therefore, you cannot use all the available space on each drive.

E. **Incorrect:** A stripe set with parity can be implemented on this system. A stripe set with parity requires three physical devices, each with available space. The existence of a mirror set does not affect whether or not a stripe set can be created.

Further Reading

Supporting Microsoft Windows NT Server in the Enterprise Training kit. Complete Lesson 2, "Managing Partitions," of Chapter 1, "Planning the Enterprise with Microsoft Windows NT Server 4.0." In this lesson, you will learn how to implement fault tolerance.

Supporting Microsoft Windows NT Server in the Enterprise Training kit. Complete Lesson 1, "Server Analysis and Optimization Basics," of Chapter 5, "Server Monitoring and Optimization." In this lesson, you will learn how to use Performance Monitor to optimize the system.

Windows NT Server 4.0 in the Enterprise Accelerated MCSE Study Guide. Read Chapter 3, "Planning for Fault Tolerance" to learn more about configuring drives for redundancy and backup.

OBJECTIVE 2.5

Configure printers.

The following tasks are covered by this objective:

- Adding and configuring a printer

- Implementing a printer pool

- Setting print priorities

Windows NT Server provides print server capability. As a print server, Windows NT can administer advanced printers that connect directly to the network, called *network printers*. The appropriate driver needs to be installed on the Windows NT server and, in the case of a Hewlett-Packard printer, the DLC protocol as well. Clients can then print to the network printer via the Windows NT server.

In addition to acting as a print server, Windows NT can be used to create a printer pool. A printer pool allows multiple printers of the same type to be load-balanced. This allows many document requests to be printed as quickly as possible. All the printers share a single driver, and a maximum of eight printers can be used in a single printer pool. When preparing for this objective, you will also need to understand how setting the print priority of a job affects the overall print queue.

To successfully answer the questions for this objective, you need a firm understanding of several key terms. For definitions of these terms, refer to the Glossary in this book.

Key Terms

- Line printer remote (LPR)

- NET USE

- Network printer

- Print priority

- Print queue

- Printer pool

70-068.02.05.001

It is tax season, and the ACCT domain users are printing tax documents on three HP LaserJet 5SI network print devices. The load on the printers is very heavy, and the print queue is always full.

Which action should you take to decrease the time a document waits in the print queue?

A. Implement a printer pool for one printer consisting of the three print devices.

B. Implement print spooling.

C. Change the priority of the print jobs.

D. Change the size of the print queues.

70-068.02.05.001

It is tax season, and the ACCT domain users are printing tax documents on three HP LaserJet 5SI network print devices. The load on the printers is very heavy, and the print queue is always full.

Which action should you take to decrease the time a document waits in the print queue?

▶ **Correct Answer: A**

A. **Correct:** Using a printer pool, you can load-balance multiple printers of the same type. This will solve the problem by sending documents to the next available printer.

B. **Incorrect:** Print spooling is implemented automatically by Windows. It will not decrease the time a document has to wait in the print queue.

C. **Incorrect:** Changing the priority of a print job will affect how quickly an individual document will be printed. It does not reduce the amount of time all the documents are waiting in queue.

D. **Incorrect:** Changing the size of the queue will not reduce the wait time for a document. The bottleneck is the utilization of the printers themselves. By implementing a printer pool, the printers will be load-balanced for optimal performance.

70-068.02.05.002

You have an HP LaserJet 3SI printer connected to a network hub. The printer is managed by a Windows NT Server 4.0 print server. Users of both Windows 95 and Windows NT Workstation 4.0 client computers print to this printer. You download a new driver from Hewlett-Packard's Web site.

On which computers must you install the new driver so that all computers can print to the printer using the new driver?

A. Only the print server

B. Only Windows 95 and Windows NT computers

C. Only Windows NT computers and the print server

D. Only Windows 95 computers and the print server

E. Windows 95 and Windows NT computers, and the print server

70-068.02.05.003

A UNIX server needs to print to a Hewlett-Packard 5SI printer controlled by a Windows NT Server 4.0 computer. Which utility enables a UNIX computer to print to a shared network printer?

A. LPT

B. LPR

C. CAPTURE

D. NET USE

70-068.02.05.002

You have an HP LaserJet 3SI printer connected to a network hub. The printer is managed by a Windows NT Server 4.0 print server. Users of both Windows 95 and Windows NT Workstation 4.0 client computers print to this printer. You download a new driver from Hewlett-Packard's Web site.

On which computers must you install the new driver so that all computers can print to the printer using the new driver?

▶ **Correct Answer: A**

   A. **Correct:** The new driver needs to be installed on only the Windows NT server that is administering the printer. The next time a client attempts to print, the updated driver will be installed on the client automatically.

   B. **Incorrect:** Only the Windows NT server needs the printer driver installed. The clients will receive the new driver automatically when they connect to the printer.

   C. **Incorrect:** The only Windows NT machine that requires the printer driver installed is the server. The Windows NT Workstation clients do not need the new driver installed.

   D. **Incorrect:** Only the Windows NT server requires the new driver installed. All clients, including the Windows 95 users, will receive the driver automatically the next time they connect to the printer.

   E. **Incorrect:** Only the Windows NT server requires the new driver installed. All clients, including the Windows 95 users, will receive the driver automatically the next time they connect to the printer.

70-068.02.05.003

A UNIX server needs to print to a Hewlett-Packard 5SI printer controlled by a Windows NT Server 4.0 computer. Which utility enables a UNIX computer to print to a shared network printer?

▶ **Correct Answer: B**

   A. **Incorrect:** LPT refers to a local printer and is not a utility used to allow UNIX computers to access the printer.

   B. **Correct:** Line printer remote (LPR) is used to allow UNIX clients access to a shared printer.

   C. **Incorrect:** CAPTURE is the feature of Network Monitor for observing network data. It is not used to allow clients to access a shared printer.

   D. **Incorrect:** NET USE is used to map devices to a local computer. It is not used to allow UNIX clients access to a shared printer. You need to use the LPR utility in order to support this functionality.

70-068.02.05.004

Your company's network has 2 Windows NT Server 4.0 domain controllers, a NetWare 4.11 server, a Macintosh computer, 30 Windows NT Workstation 4.0 client computers, 10 Windows 95 client computers, a UNIX server, and 3 Windows for Workgroup client computers. One of the Windows NT Workstation client computers shares a color laser printer.

Assuming the appropriate protocols, services, rights, and permissions have been established, which computers will be able to print to this color laser printer? (Choose all that apply.)

A. The Macintosh computer

B. A Windows 95 computer

C. A NetWare 4.11 computer

D. A Windows NT Server computer

E. A Windows for Workgroups computer

F. A Windows NT Workstation computer

70-068.02.05.004

Your company's network has 2 Windows NT Server 4.0 domain controllers, a NetWare 4.11 server, a Macintosh computer, 30 Windows NT Workstation 4.0 client computers, 10 Windows 95 client computers, a UNIX server, and 3 Windows for Workgroup client computers. One of the Windows NT Workstation client computers shares a color laser printer.

Assuming the appropriate protocols, services, rights, and permissions have been established, which computers will be able to print to this color laser printer? (Choose all that apply.)

▶ **Correct Answers: B, D, E, and F**

   A. **Incorrect:** Only a Windows NT server can share a printer to a non-Windows operating system computer, such as a Macintosh.

   B. **Correct:** A Windows NT 4.0 Workstation can share its files and printers to a Windows 95 (or Windows 98) client.

   C. **Incorrect:** A Windows NT 4.0 Workstation can only share its resources to other Windows-based operating systems.

   D. **Correct:** A Windows NT 4.0 Workstation can share its files and printers to a Windows NT Server client.

   E. **Correct:** A Windows NT 4.0 Workstation can share its files and printers to a Windows for Workgroup client.

   F. **Correct:** A Windows NT 4.0 Workstation can share its files and printers to another Windows NT 4.0 Workstation client.

70-068.02.05.005

A LAN Manager for MS-DOS client needs to print to an HP 5SI printer controlled by a Windows NT Server 4.0 computer. Which utility enables a LAN Manager for MS-DOS client computer to connect to a shared network printer?

A. LPT

B. LPR

C. CAPTURE

D. NET USE

70-068.02.05.005

A LAN Manager for MS-DOS client needs to print to an HP 5SI printer controlled by a Windows NT Server 4.0 computer. Which utility enables a LAN Manager for MS-DOS client computer to connect to a shared network printer?

▶ **Correct Answer: D**

    A. **Incorrect:** LPT refers to a local printer and is not a utility used to allow client computers to access the printer.

    B. **Incorrect:** LPR is used to allow clients, such as UNIX, to access a shared resource. Since the client is MS-DOS based, this is not the correct utility to use.

    C. **Incorrect:** CAPTURE is used by Network Monitor and is not used to manage shared resources.

    D. **Correct:** NET USE allows clients to access both shared folders and printers.

Further Reading

Supporting Microsoft Windows NT Server in the Enterprise Training kit. Complete Lesson 6, "Managing Shared Resources," of Chapter 3, "Managing Enterprise Resources." In this lesson, file and printer resource sharing will be discussed.

Windows NT Server 4.0 in the Enterprise Accelerated MCSE Study Guide. Read Chapter 10, "Printing" to learn more about sharing and managing printers.

Configure a Windows NT Server computer for various types of client computers.

The client computers that are discussed include:

- Windows NT Workstation

- Windows 95

- Macintosh

Depending on the type of client that will be supported, you may have to implement a specific file system on the server. For example, if your Windows NT server will support file share requests from Macintosh clients, you will need to use NTFS. The file system you use will also depend on the level of security you need to implement. Both FAT16 and FAT32 support only share-level access while NTFS also provides support for file-level security.

In addition, you can use the Windows NT server tools to manage your Windows NT server, depending on the client. Windows 95, Windows 98, and Windows NT Workstation can all use the various server tools, such as User Manager for Domains and Server Manager. Of course, the user account on the client must have the appropriate permissions before these tools can be used. However, these tools can make it easier to support the network. Other network components, such as Gateway Services for NetWare, may be required if you want to support access to Novell resources.

To successfully answer the questions for this objective, you need a firm understanding of several key terms. For definitions of these terms, refer to the Glossary in this book.

Key Terms

- Dynamic Host Configuration Protocol (DHCP)

- FAT16

- FAT32

- Gateway Services for NetWare (GSNW)

- NTFS (NT file system)

- WINS

70-068.02.06.001

It is essential to provide support for a Macintosh client computer in your Windows NT domain. Which file system must the Windows NT server have in order to enable Services for Macintosh?

A. HPFS

B. NTFS

C. Apple

D. FAT16

E. FAT32

70-068.02.06.002

You want to provide Windows clients on your Windows NT 4.0 domain access to a NetWare server. Which Windows NT Server service is needed?

A. Windows Internet Naming Service (WINS)

B. Dynamic Host Configuration Protocol (DHCP)

C. Client Services for NetWare (CSNW)

D. Gateway Service for NetWare (GSNW)

E. None. The client computers can use CSNW to connect to the server.

70-068.02.06.001

It is essential to provide support for a Macintosh client computer in your Windows NT domain. Which file system must the Windows NT server have in order to enable Services for Macintosh?

▶ **Correct Answer: B**

   A. **Incorrect:** Windows NT Server does not support the High Performance File System.

   B. **Correct:** NTFS is required on the Windows NT server before a Macintosh client can access its shared files.

   C. **Incorrect:** Windows NT Server does not support the native Apple file system.

   D. **Incorrect:** Since the Macintosh client cannot read a FAT file system, this is not the correct answer. The Windows NT server must be using an NTFS file system to support Macintosh clients.

   E. **Incorrect:** Since the Macintosh client cannot read a FAT16 or FAT32 file system, this is not the correct answer. The Windows NT server must be using an NTFS file system to support Macintosh clients.

70-068.02.06.002

You want to provide Windows clients on your Windows NT 4.0 domain access to a NetWare server. Which Windows NT Server service is needed?

Correct Answer: E

   A. **Incorrect:** WINS allows a computer name to be resolved to an IP address. It is not used to access a NetWare server.

   B. **Incorrect:** DHCP dynamically configures clients' TCP/IP settings. It is not used to access a NetWare server.

   C. **Incorrect:** Client Services for NetWare allows a Windows NT Workstation client access to a NetWare server. However, CSNW installed on a Windows NT Server does not allow other clients access to the NetWare resources.

   D. **Incorrect:** Although the GSNW solves this problem, you do not have to install an additional service on Windows NT Server to solve this problem. Instead, use the Client Services for NetWare on each client to allow them access to the NetWare resources.

   E. **Correct:** By installing CSNW on each client that needs access to the NetWare server, you do not have to install the GSNW service on a Windows NT Server.

70-068.02.06.003

You are designing a local area network. The network is going to use a single domain model with a single Windows NT 4.0 Server computer serving as the PDC. The only security requirement you have is that all computers must be able to provide file-level and folder-level security for all files and folders on the network. Which operating system can you use on the client computers to fulfill the security requirement?

A. Macintosh

B. Windows 95

C. Windows 3.11

D. Windows NT Workstation 4.0

70-068.02.06.003

You are designing a local area network. The network is going to use a single domain model with a single Windows NT 4.0 Server computer serving as the PDC. The only security requirement you have is that all computers must be able to provide file-level and folder-level security for all files and folders on the network. Which operating system can you use on the client computers to fulfill the security requirement?

▶ **Correct Answer: D**

A. **Incorrect:** The Macintosh operating system does not support file-level security.

B. **Incorrect:** Windows 95 supports only the FAT16 and FAT32 file systems. Neither system supports file-level security. Windows 95 supports only share-level security. Therefore, this OS is not the correct choice.

C. **Incorrect:** Windows 3.11 does not support NTFS, which is the only file system capable of implementing file-level security.

D. **Correct:** Only Windows NT Workstation and Windows NT Server can implement NTFS. NTFS is required to use file-level security.

Further Reading

Supporting Microsoft Windows NT Server in the Enterprise Training kit. Complete Lesson 3, "Client Connectivity," of Chapter 2, "Installation and Configuration." In this lesson, you will learn how to configure Windows NT Server based on the clients being supported.

Managing Resources

This objective covers the management of users and groups on a Windows NT server, including not only the local management of users on a single server, but also the management of user requests from other servers and domains. It also includes implementing a security scheme for providing appropriate access to shared resources by users from other domains and using local and global groups to efficiently manage user access. You will need to know the impact on a single user of being a member of more than one group having access to a share. For example, if a user is a member of two groups that both have permission to a folder, but one group has the No Access permission, the No Access permission will override whatever permission is granted to the other group. You would have to consider removing the user from the group with No Access if the user required any other level of access. In addition, administering a remote Windows NT server from a Windows 95 or Windows NT Workstation client is discussed. You will also need to understand the difference between a system policy and a user profile and know how to implement each. This includes the use of mandatory profiles.

Tested Skills and Suggested Practices

The skills you need to successfully master the Managing Resources objective domain on the exam include:

- **Managing policies and profiles.**

    - Practice 1: Use the System Policy Editor to create a new policy file that will be used by Windows 95 users. Be sure to name the file CONFIG.POL.

    - Practice 2: Implement a domain system policy by copying a policy file into the NETLOGON directory.

- **Creating and managing local and global groups.**

  - Practice 1: On a network with a PDC and a member server, create a global group on the PDC and add a new user account to this group. On the member server, create a share and give a local group permission to access the share. Add the global group created on the PDC to the local group on the member server. Now, log on the PDC as the user specified in the global group and try to access the shared folder.

- **Managing a remote Windows NT server.**

  - Practice 1: Install the network administration tools onto a Windows 95, Windows 98, or Windows NT Workstation client computer. Review the different tools provided and try adding a new user account to a Windows NT server.

  - Practice 2: Using the Server Manager tool that is provided with the network administration tools, create a new share on a remote Windows NT server.

OBJECTIVE 3.1

Manage user and group accounts.

There are a number of potential management and administration tasks, including:

- Managing Windows NT user accounts

- Managing Windows NT user rights

- Managing Windows NT groups

- Administering account policies

- Auditing changes to the user account database

In preparing for this objective, you must understand how to manage permissions not only from a single Windows NT Server, but across multiple domains as well. This includes providing administrative permissions, such as the ability to back up files, as well as allowing users access to shared resources. Be sure to have a good understanding of trust relationships. Read each question carefully and diagram any trust relationships presented. One domain may trust another, but that does not mean the trust is two-way.

In addition, this objective covers auditing server activities. Have a thorough understanding of the different security event categories and know when to use each depending on what activities should be monitored.

To successfully answer the questions for this objective, you need a firm understanding of several key terms. For definitions of these terms, refer to the Glossary in this book.

Key Terms

- Auditing

- Domain

- Global group

- Local group

- Trust relationships

70-068.03.01.001

Examine the trust relationship diagram shown below.

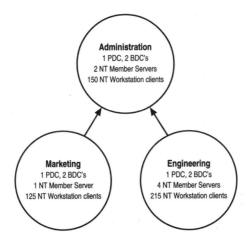

Each circle represents a domain. The Administration domain is
the master domain. Arrows represent trust relationships.

The required result is to create a group whose members will be able to back up the Primary Domain Controllers in the Administration, Marketing, and Engineering domains.

The first optional result is to allow members of the group to back up the Backup Domain Controllers and member servers in all three domains.

The second optional result is to allow members of the group to back up the Windows NT Workstation client computers in all three domains.

The proposed solution is to create a global group named Backup_all on the Primary Domain Controller in the Administration domain, add the users who need to perform backups to the group, and add the new global group to the Backup Operators local group on the Administration, Marketing, and Engineering PDCs.

What does the proposed solution provide?

A. The required result and all optional results.

B. The required result and one optional result.

C. The required result but none of the optional results.

D. The proposed solution does not provide the required result.

70-068.03.01.001

Examine the trust relationship diagram shown on the previous page.

The required result is to create a group whose members will be able to back up the Primary Domain Controllers in the Administration, Marketing, and Engineering domains.

The first optional result is to allow members of the group to back up the Backup Domain Controllers and member servers in all three domains.

The second optional result is to allow members of the group to back up the Windows NT Workstation client computers in all three domains.

The proposed solution is to create a global group named Backup_all on the Primary Domain Controller in the Administration domain, add the users who need to perform backups to the group, and add the new global group to the Backup Operators local group on the Administration, Marketing, and Engineering PDCs.

What does the proposed solution provide?

▶ **Correct Answer: C**

A. **Incorrect:** Although the required result will be realized, the Backup_all global group has to be added to the appropriate Backup Operators group to realize either of the optional results.

B. **Incorrect:** The Backup_all global group needs to be added to the Backup Operators group on the member computers and the NT Workstation clients. You will also need to add this group to the BDCs' Backup Operators group. Therefore, with this solution, neither of the optional results will be realized.

C. **Correct:** By creating a global group that is added to the Backup Operators local group on each PDC, the required result will be realized. However, this global group must then be added to each NT computer's Backup Operators group in order to realize both optional results. Therefore, this is the correct answer.

D. **Incorrect:** Since the solution creates a global group, called Backup_all, and this group is added to each Backup Operators group on each PDC, the required result will be realized. Therefore, this answer is incorrect.

70-068.03.01.002

Examine the trust relationship diagram shown below.

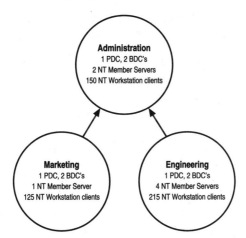

Each circle represents a domain. The Administration domain is
the master domain. Arrows represent trust relationships.

The required result is to create a group whose members will be able to back up the Primary Domain Controllers in the Administration, Marketing, and Engineering domains.

The first optional result is to allow members of the group to back up the Backup Domain Controllers and member servers in all three domains.

The second optional result is to allow members of the group to back up the Windows NT Workstation client computers in all three domains.

The proposed solution is to create a global group named Backup_all on the Primary Domain Controller in the Administration domain, add the users who need to perform backups to the group, and add the new global group to the Backup Operators local group on all Windows NT computers in each domain.

What does the proposed solution provide?

A. The required result and all optional results.

B. The required result and one optional result.

C. The required result but none of the optional results.

D. The proposed solution does not provide the required result.

70-068.03.01.002

Examine the trust relationship diagram shown on the previous page.

The required result is to create a group whose members will be able to back up the Primary Domain Controllers in the Administration, Marketing, and Engineering domains.

The first optional result is to allow members of the group to back up the Backup Domain Controllers and member servers in all three domains.

The second optional result is to allow members of the group to back up the Windows NT Workstation client computers in all three domains.

The proposed solution is to create a global group named Backup_all on the Primary Domain Controller in the Administration domain, add the users who need to perform backups to the group, and add the new global group to the Backup Operators local group on all Windows NT computers in each domain.

What does the proposed solution provide?

▶ **Correct Answer: A**

A. **Correct:** Using the global group Backup_all, the appropriate users can be given access to the Backup Operators group on each NT computer that requires backup operations to be performed. Since the solution adds this group to each computer, the required result and both optional results will be realized.

B. **Incorrect:** Although the required result will be realized with this solution, both optional results will be as well. The Backup_all global group needs to be added to each NT computer's Backup Operators local group in order to allow the users permission to conduct a backup.

C. **Incorrect:** Since the Backup_all group is added to each Backup Operators group, both optional results will be realized.

D. **Incorrect:** The creation of the global group, Backup_all, and its inclusion in each Backup Operators local group meets the required result and both optional results.

70-068.03.01.003

Examine the trust relationship diagram shown below.

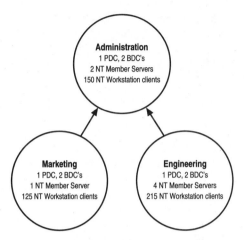

Each circle represents a domain. The Administration domain is
the master domain. Arrows represent trust relationships.

The required result is to create a group whose members will be able to back up the Primary Domain Controllers in the Administration, Marketing, and Engineering domains.

The first optional result is to allow members of the group to back up the Backup Domain Controllers and member servers in all three domains.

The second optional result is to allow members of the group to back up the Windows NT Workstation client computers in all three domains.

The proposed solution is to create a global group named Backup_all on the Primary Domain Controller in the Administration domain, add the users who need to perform backups to the group, and add the new global group to the Backup Operators local group on the PDC in the Administration domain.

What does the proposed solution provide?

A. The required result and all optional results.

B. The required result and one optional result.

C. The required result but none of the optional results.

D. The proposed solution does not provide the required result.

70-068.03.01.003

Examine the trust relationship diagram shown on the previous page.

The required result is to create a group whose members will be able to back up the Primary Domain Controllers in the Administration, Marketing, and Engineering domains.

The first optional result is to allow members of the group to back up the Backup Domain Controllers and member servers in all three domains.

The second optional result is to allow members of the group to back up the Windows NT Workstation client computers in all three domains.

The proposed solution is to create a global group named Backup_all on the Primary Domain Controller in the Administration domain, add the users who need to perform backups to the group, and add the new global group to the Backup Operators local group on the PDC in the Administration domain.

What does the proposed solution provide?

▶ **Correct Answer: D**

A. **Incorrect:** The Backup_all global group will need to be added to the local group on each PDC computer in order to realize the required result. In addition, since Backup_all will not be added to each BDC and member server or NT Workstation computer, the optional results will not be realized.

B. **Incorrect:** The Backup_all group must be added to each NT computer, whether it is a PDC or not, in order to allow the appropriate users permission to back up that computer's data. Since the solution does not include these steps, this answer is incorrect.

C. **Incorrect:** Unless Backup_all is added to each PDC's Backup Operators group, only the Administration domain can be backed up. This proposed solution does not meet the required result.

D. **Correct:** Until the Backup_all global group is added to each local Backup Operators group, the appropriate users will not be able to back up all the required data. Neither the required result nor either optional result will be realized with this solution.

70-068.03.01.004

A network consists of a master domain named Corp, and resource domains named Research and Sales. The Corp domain is trusted by both the Research and Sales domains. No other trust relationships exist. Joan has a user account in the Research domain and the Corp domain.

Which shared resources in the Corp domain will Joan be able to access when she logs on to the Research domain?

A. All resources to which the Corp\Power Users group has access.

B. All resources to which the Corp\Domain Users group has access.

C. All resources to which the Corp\Domain Guests group has access.

D. All resources to which the Corp\Domain Admins group has access.

E. No resources in the Corp domain are accessible by users in the Research domain.

70-068.03.01.004

A network consists of a master domain named Corp, and resource domains named Research and Sales. The Corp domain is trusted by both the Research and Sales domains. No other trust relationships exist. Joan has a user account in the Research domain and the Corp domain.

Which shared resources in the Corp domain will Joan be able to access when she logs on to the Research domain?

▶ **Correct Answer: E**

A. **Incorrect:** Users that have accounts in either the Research or Sales domain will not have access to resources in the Corp domain. In order to access Corp domain resources, the trust relationship will have to be changed and the user must log into the Corp domain. Otherwise, the user will need an account added to the Corp domain.

B. **Incorrect:** Because the Corp domain does not trust either the Research or Sales domain, users in these domains will not be able to access resources in the Corp domain. Reverse the trust relationship or make it a two-way trust. You could also alternatively add the user accounts to the Corp domain.

C. **Incorrect:** In order for users in the Research domain to access resources in the Corp domain, the Corp domain must be set to trust the Research domain. Currently the trust relationship is reversed; users in Corp can access resources in both Research and Sales.

D. **Incorrect:** Using the current trust relationships, users in the Research domain will not be able to access resources in the Corp domain because the trust relationship is not configured to support the direction. The Corp domain will need to trust the Research domain before those users can access the Corp domain.

E. **Correct:** Until the Corp domain trusts the Research domain, users will not be able to access Corp resources from the Research domain. The trust relationship will only allow Corp users to access Research resources.

70-068.03.01.005

Examine the trust relationship diagram shown below.

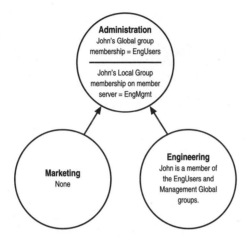

John was recently promoted from Chief Engineer to Assistant VP of Engineering. Because of his promotion, John now needs access to financial records located in a shared directory named Reports. The Reports share is located on a Windows NT member server in the Administration domain. The Administration\EngUsers global group has No Access permissions to the Reports share, while the Administration\EngMgmt local group has Read permissions.

What should you do to ensure that John has Read permissions to the Reports share?

A. Remove John from the Engineering\EngMgmt local group.

B. Remove John from the Engineering\EngUsers global group.

C. Remove John from the Administration\EngMgmt local group.

D. Remove John from the Administration\EngUsers global group.

70-068.03.01.005

Examine the trust relationship diagram shown on the previous page.

John was recently promoted from Chief Engineer to Assistant VP of Engineering. Because of his promotion, John now needs access to financial records located in a shared directory named Reports. The Reports share is located on a Windows NT member server in the Administration domain. The Administration\EngUsers global group has No Access permissions to the Reports share, while the Administration\EngMgmt local group has Read permissions.

What should you do to ensure that John has Read permissions to the Reports share?

▶ **Correct Answer: D**

A. **Incorrect:** Since the member server resides in the Administration domain, removing John from a group in the Engineering domain will not affect his access to the Reports share.

B. **Incorrect:** Removing John from the Engineering\EngUsers global group will not affect his inclusion in the Adminstration\EngUsers global group. It is the Administration group that affects his permission on the member servers in the Administration domain. Therefore, he needs to be removed from the Administation\EngUsers global group before he can access the Reports share.

C. **Incorrect:** There is no local Administration\EngMgmt group. John needs to be removed from the Administration\EngUsers global group before he can access the required folder.

D. **Correct:** Since the member server in the Administration domain contains the Reports folder, it will use the EngUsers global group created on the Administration PDC. Since John is a member of this group, which does not have access to the folder, he first needs to be removed from this group. As he is already a member of EngMgmt, the group permitted to read documents in the Reports share, he will now have the appropriate access to this folder.

70-068.03.01.006

A user is a member of the Engineering, Management, Research, and Everyone local groups on a Windows NT member server. The access permissions she receives to a shared directory named DOCS on the member server are shown below.

Engineering = Read

Management = Full Control

Research = Change

Everyone = Read

She also receives the Change permission through her NT user account.

What are her effective permissions to the DOCS directory?

A. Read

B. Change

C. Full Control

D. No Access

70-068.03.01.006

A user is a member of the Engineering, Management, Research, and Everyone local groups on a Windows NT member server. The access permissions she receives to a shared directory named DOCS on the member server are shown below.

Engineering = Read

Management = Full Control

Research = Change

Everyone = Read

She also receives the Change permission through her NT user account.

What are her effective permissions to the DOCS directory?

▶ **Correct Answer: C**

A. **Incorrect:** Since the user's account has been added to other groups that have less restrictive permissions than the Everyone group, these other permissions will be used. Because she is a member of the Management group, she will have Full Control.

B. **Incorrect:** Although the user will have Change permission, her inclusion in the Management group gives her full control of the files. Unless the No Access permission is assigned, users will receive the least restrictive permission when more than one set of permissions applies, as with multiple groups.

C. **Correct:** Since the user has been included in the Management group, which has Full Control, this is the level of permission that will be granted for the user. The only time one permission could deny access would be with the No Access permission.

D. **Incorrect:** If a user has been included in a group, or has been listed individually with No Access, this permission will override any other permissions granted. However, in this case, the user does not belong to any group that has No Access.

70-068.03.01.007

A user is a member of the Engineering, Management, Research, and Everyone local groups on a Windows NT member server. The access permissions he receives to a shared directory named DOCS on the member server are shown below.

Engineering = Read

Management = No Access

Research = Change

Everyone = Read

He also receives the Full Control permission to the share through his NT user account.

What are his effective permissions to the DOCS directory?

A. Read

B. Change

C. Full Control

D. No Access

70-068.03.01.007

A user is a member of the Engineering, Management, Research, and Everyone local groups on a Windows NT member server. The access permissions he receives to a shared directory named DOCS on the member server are shown below.

Engineering = Read

Management = No Access

Research = Change

Everyone = Read

He also receives the Full Control permission to the share through his NT user account.

What are his effective permissions to the DOCS directory?

► **Correct Answer: D**

A. **Incorrect:** Since the Management group has the No Access permission, this will override the ability to read files from the DOCS share. Therefore, this answer is incorrect.

B. **Incorrect:** The No Access permission will override any other permission granted. Therefore, while other groups may assign the user Change permission on the DOCS share, the user will ultimately not be allowed access to this share since he is also a member of the Management group.

C. **Incorrect:** Even though the user has been assigned individual Full Control permission, since he is a member of a group that has the No Access permission (the Management group), all other permissions are overridden.

D. **Correct:** Until the user is removed from the Management group, which has the No Access permission, all other permissions granted to this user will be ignored.

70-068.03.01.008

A user is a member of the Engineering, Management, Research, and Everyone local groups on a Windows NT member server. The access permissions she receives to a shared directory named DOCS on the member server are shown below.

Engineering = Read

Management = Change

Research = Change

Everyone = Read

She also receives the Read permission to the share through her NT user account.

What are her effective permissions to the DOCS directory?

A. Read

B. Change

C. Full Control

D. No Access

70-068.03.01.008

A user is a member of the Engineering, Management, Research, and Everyone local groups on a Windows NT member server. The access permissions she receives to a shared directory named DOCS on the member server are shown below.

Engineering = Read

Management = Change

Research = Change

Everyone = Read

She also receives the Read permission to the share through her NT user account.

What are her effective permissions to the DOCS directory?

▶ **Correct Answer: B**

A. **Incorrect:** Although the user will have the ability to read documents, she is also a member of a group that has Change permission. When multiple permissions apply, the least restrictive permission will be used, unless No Access is used. Therefore, the user will be able to read and change files in the DOCS share.

B. **Correct:** Unless No Access is used, the permission setting that is least restrictive is used by default. Since the user is a member of a group that has Change permission, this will be the granted level of access.

C. **Incorrect:** The user has not been granted Full Control either through a group or individually. Therefore, this level of permission will not be granted. However, since she does belong to a group that has Change access, this will be the permission applied.

D. **Incorrect:** The No Access permission will override any other permission granted to the user. However, this level of permission must first be associated with the user, either directly or through a group. Since this is not the case, the user will be able to access files in the DOCS share based on the least restrictive set of permissions, in this case Change.

70-068.03.01.009

Examine the Audit Policy screen shown below.

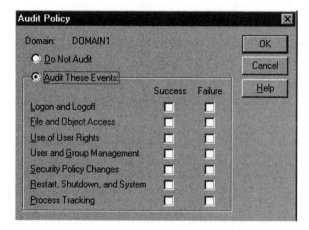

Your company recently hired two MCSEs to help you administer your network. You have given them the necessary network permissions to administer user and group accounts on the Windows NT portion of the network along with the formal authority to do so. However, you would like to audit their activities until you gain more confidence in their abilities.

Which events should you audit?

A. Process tracking

B. Use of user rights

C. File and object access

D. User and group management

70-068.03.01.009

Examine the Audit Policy screen shown on the previous page.

Your company recently hired two MCSEs to help you administer your network. You have given them the necessary network permissions to administer user and group accounts on the Windows NT portion of the network along with the formal authority to do so. However, you would like to audit their activities until you gain more confidence in their abilities.

Which events should you audit?

▶ **Correct Answer: D**

A. **Incorrect:** This option allows you to track how applications are used and other system information. It does not allow you to monitor the activities of the new administrators related to user management. Instead, consider the user and group management option.

B. **Incorrect:** Although this option will track how a user uses his granted privileges, the user and group management option is the better choice for monitoring the new administrators' activities as they relate to other users in the domain.

C. **Incorrect:** File and object access tracks access to protected objects. The new administrators have been given permissions only to manage users and groups; therefore, the user and group management option must be selected.

D. **Correct:** The user and group management option will allow you to track the activities of the new administrators as they manage security settings for users and groups.

70-068.03.01.010

Examine the Audit Policy screen shown below.

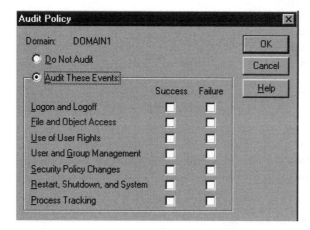

Your company recently hired two MCSEs to help you administer your network. You have given them the necessary network permissions to administer the network along with the formal authority to do so. However, you would like to audit their activities until you gain more confidence in their abilities. You are especially concerned about changes made to user rights and trust relationships.

Which events should you audit?

A. Process tracking

B. Use of user rights

C. File and object access

D. Security policy changes

70-068.03.01.010

Examine the Audit Policy screen shown on the previous page.

Your company recently hired two MCSEs to help you administer your network. You have given them the necessary network permissions to administer the network along with the formal authority to do so. However, you would like to audit their activities until you gain more confidence in their abilities. You are especially concerned about changes made to user rights and trust relationships.

Which events should you audit?

▶ **Correct Answer: D**

A. **Incorrect:** Process tracking allows you to monitor the user's activities as they relate to applications. This option does not provide you the ability to monitor how the administrators are managing user rights and trust relationships. For this you will need to select the security policy changes option.

B. **Incorrect:** The use of user Rights option allows you to monitor successful and unsuccessful uses of the permissions granted to an individual user. However, it does not help you monitor the new administrators' activities as they relate to changing other user permissions or trust relationships between domains. Consider using the security policy changes option.

C. **Incorrect:** The file and object access option will allow you to monitor access to secure objects. It will not help you monitor the new administrators' activities as they relate to user permissions or trust relationship changes. For this, you will need to use the security policy changes option.

D. **Correct:** The security policy changes option will allow you to track how the new administrators are using their permissions to manage user accounts and trust relationships between domains.

Further Reading

Supporting Microsoft Windows NT Server in the Enterprise Training kit. Complete Lesson 1, "User and Group Accounts," of Chapter 3, "Managing Enterprise Resources." In this lesson, you will learn about the differences between local and global groups.

Microsoft Windows NT Networking Guide. Page 80 lists each security event and when to use it when auditing server activity.

Create and manage policies and profiles for various situations.

The policies and profiles covered in this objective include:

- Local user profiles

- Roaming user profiles

- System policies

Windows NT Server uses both profile and policy files to allow administrators greater control over how users can interact with their computers and the network. Tools such as the System Policy Editor help administrators create these files. Having a good understanding of how to implement profiles and policies on the server is critical when preparing for this objective. You will need to know that Windows NT users use the NTCONFIG.POL policy file, while Windows 95 and Windows 98 users use the CONFIG.POL file. You will also need to know where these files must be located on the server. When using user profiles to support roaming users, where the profiles reside on the server can be customized since each user typically will have his own custom profile. Use the %Username% variable to create and manage separate folders for each user.

To successfully answer the questions for this objective, you need a firm understanding of several key terms. For definitions of these terms, refer to the Glossary in this book.

Key Terms

- User profile

- System policy

- Roaming user

70-068.03.02.001

Examine the User Environment Profile screen shown below.

You are establishing roaming personal profiles for 35 user accounts on a Windows NT domain. The profiles are located in subdirectories of the PROFILES directory on the FS1 server. Which variable should you use in the User Profile Path so that Windows NT will include the user account name at the end of the path?

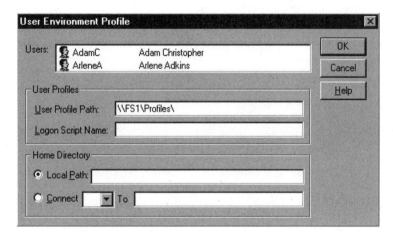

A. %Homedir%

B. %Username%

C. %Userprofile%

D. %Useraccount%

70-068.03.02.001

Examine the User Environment Profile screen shown on the previous page.

You are establishing roaming personal profiles for 35 user accounts on a Windows NT domain. The profiles are located in subdirectories of the PROFILES directory on the FS1 server. Which variable should you use in the User Profile Path so that Windows NT will include the user account name at the end of the path?

▶ **Correct Answer: B**

A. **Incorrect:** The %Homedir% variable is used to specify the home directory. It will not resolve to the user's account name.

B. **Correct:** Windows NT will substitute the user's account name for the %Username% variable in order to create unique folders in which to store each profile.

C. **Incorrect:** In order to append the user's account name to the Profiles path, you need to use the %Username% variable, not the %Userprofile% variable.

D. **Incorrect:** The correct variable name is %Username%. Windows NT will use this variable to append the user's account name to the Profiles path.

70-068.03.02.002

Examine the User Environment Profile screen shown below.

You are establishing a roaming mandatory profile for 15 user accounts on a Windows NT domain. The profiles are located in the PROFILES directory on the FS1 server. What should you place at the end of the User Profile Path to ensure that the users access the proper profile?

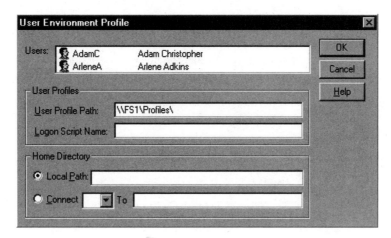

A. %Homedir%

B. NTUSER.DAT

C. NTUSER.MAN

D. %Username%

E. %Userprofile%

F. %Useraccount%

70-068.03.02.002

Examine the User Environment Profile screen shown on the previous page.

You are establishing a roaming mandatory profile for 15 user accounts on a Windows NT domain. The profiles are located in the PROFILES directory on the FS1 server. What should you place at the end of the User Profile Path to ensure that the users access the proper profile?

▶ **Correct Answer: C**

A. **Incorrect:** The %Homedir% variable is not used to implement mandatory user profiles. Instead, this variable can be used to dynamically insert the home directory as required by utilities such as logon scripts.

B. **Incorrect:** The NTUSER.DAT file represents a default user profile and is not implemented as a mandatory profile. You must rename the NTUSER.DAT file to NTUSER.MAN for a mandatory profile to be used.

C. **Correct:** When the default user profile, NTUSER.DAT, is renamed to NTUSER.MAN, the user profile becomes mandatory.

D. **Incorrect:** The %Username% variable is not used to implement mandatory user profiles.

E. **Incorrect:** The %Userprofile% variable is not used to implement mandatory user profiles.

F. **Incorrect:** The %Useraccount% variable is not used to implement mandatory user profiles.

70-068.03.02.003

How do you enable a uniform system policy for Windows NT users in a Windows NT domain?

A. Create a CONFIG.POL file using the System Policy Editor and place it in the Primary Domain Controller's POLICY shared directory.

B. Click the Enable System Policy checkbox on each user account belonging to a Windows NT user.

C. Create an NTCONFIG.POL file using the System Policy Editor and place it in the Primary Domain Controller's NETLOGON shared directory.

D. Click the Enable System Policy checkbox in the Properties box for each Windows NT computer in Server Manager.

70-068.03.02.004

How do you enable a uniform system policy for Windows 95 users in a Windows NT domain?

A. Click the Enable System Policy checkbox on each user account belonging to a Windows NT user.

B. Create a CONFIG.POL file using the System Policy Editor and place it in the Primary Domain Controller's NETLOGON shared directory.

C. Create an NTCONFIG.POL file using the System Policy Editor and place it in the Primary Domain Controller's POLICY shared directory.

D. Click the Enable System Policy checkbox in the Properties box for each Windows NT computer in Server Manager.

70-068.03.02.003

How do you enable a uniform system policy for Windows NT users in a Windows NT domain?

▶ **Correct Answer: C**

A. **Incorrect:** To implement system policies for NT users, you need to use the NTCONFIG.POL file and the NETLOGON directory, not the CONFIG.POL and POLICY folder.

B. **Incorrect:** System policies are implemented when the NTCONFIG.POL file is placed in the NETLOGON folder. User Manager for Domains does not offer the ability to enable system policies.

C. **Correct:** If NTCONFIG.POL is placed in the NETLOGON directory, the policies included will be activated when a user logs into the domain. You need to use the System Policy Editor tool in order to create this file.

D. **Incorrect:** There is no Enable System Policy checkbox in the Server Manager utility. To enable system policies, you must place the NTCONFIG.POL file in the NETLOGON folder.

70-068.03.02.004

How do you enable a uniform system policy for Windows 95 users in a Windows NT domain?

▶ **Correct Answer: B**

A. **Incorrect:** There is no Enable System Policy checkbox in User Manager for Domains. To implement policies for Windows 95 users, you must add the CONFIG.POL file to the NETLOGON directory.

B. **Correct:** Unlike NT users, who require NTCONFIG.POL, Windows 95 users require the CONFIG.POL file, which must be placed in the NETLOGON folder. Use the System Policy Editor tool in order to create the appropriate file.

C. **Incorrect:** NT users require the NTCONFIG.POL file. Windows 95 users require the CONFIG.POL file.

D. **Incorrect:** There is no Enable System Policy checkbox in the Server Manager utility. To enable system policies, you must place the CONFIG.POL file in the NETLOGON folder.

70-068.03.02.005

How should you convert an existing personal roaming profile file to a mandatory roaming profile?

A. Rename the file's extension to .MAN.

B. Modify the file's attributes to include read-only.

C. Move the file to the *servername*\PROFILES directory.

D. Open the file in System Policy Editor, and select Convert in the Options menu.

70-068.03.02.005

How should you convert an existing personal roaming profile file to a mandatory roaming profile?

▶ **Correct Answer: A**

A. **Correct:** By changing the original file extension to .MAN, you make a profile mandatory.

B. **Incorrect:** The file extension must be changed to .MAN before a profile will become mandatory. Changing the attributes will not affect whether the profile is mandatory.

C. **Incorrect:** Although the profile generally resides in the PROFILES directory, or a subdirectory of PROFILES, the file's extension controls whether the profile will be mandatory. Use the .MAN extension to implement mandatory profiles.

D. **Incorrect:** The System Policy Editor is used to create policy files. It is not used to implement mandatory profiles.

Further Reading

Supporting Microsoft Windows NT Server in the Enterprise Training kit. Complete Lesson 2, "Profiles and Policies," of Chapter 3, "Managing Enterprise Resources." In this lesson, you will learn about creating and implementing user profiles and policies.

Windows NT Server 4.0 in the Enterprise Accelerated MCSE Study Guide. Read Chapter 9, "Policies and Profiles" to learn more about supporting roaming user profiles.

OBJECTIVE 3.3

Administer remote servers from various types of client computers.

Windows 98 had not yet been released when the objective domain was created for the *Implementing and Supporting Microsoft Windows NT 4.0 in the Enterprise* exam. However, the Windows 95 configuration settings covered by this exam apply to Windows 98 clients as well. For purposes of preparing for the exam, we will refer to Windows 95 clients. The other major client discussed is Windows NT 4.0 Workstation. There are many similarities and some differences between Windows 95 and Windows NT Workstation clients in terms of administering remote Windows NT servers. To administer a remote Windows NT server, the network administration tools must first be installed, regardless of the client operating system. Although both clients can manage users and shared resources, only Windows NT Workstation clients can manage system policies on a Windows NT server. Familiar Windows NT Server utilities, such as User Manager for Domains and Server Manager, are included in the network administration tool suite.

To successfully answer the questions for this objective, you need a firm understanding of several key terms. For definitions of these terms, refer to the Glossary in this book.

Key Terms

- Network administration tools

- Server Manager

- User Manager for Domains

70-068.03.03.001

You have installed Windows NT network administration tools on both a Windows NT Workstation client computer and a Windows 95 client computer. Which administrative tasks will you be able to accomplish from either computer? (Choose two.)

A. Manage users, groups, and security policies for domains

B. Manage DHCP Service running on a Windows NT Server

C. Administer Remote Access Service on a computer running Windows NT

D. Manage shared folders and printers on computers running Windows NT

70-068.03.03.002

You have installed the Windows NT network administration tools on two Windows NT Workstation clients and two Windows 95 clients. Which client computers will you be able to use for controlling and changing Windows NT system policies?

A. Only the Windows 95 clients

B. Only the Windows NT Workstation clients

C. Both the Windows NT Workstation and Windows 95 clients

D. Neither the Windows NT Workstation nor the Windows 95 clients

70-068.03.03.001

You have installed Windows NT network administration tools on both a Windows NT Workstation client computer and a Windows 95 client computer. Which administrative tasks will you be able to accomplish from either computer? (Choose two.)

▶ **Correct Answers: A and D**

A. **Correct:** Using the network administration tools, you can run programs such as Server Manager and User Manager for Domains from client computers. User Manager for Domains allows you to manage users and groups as you normally would from a Windows NT server.

B. **Incorrect:** You cannot manage DHCP services from a Windows 95 client computer using the network administration tools. You must log on to the appropriate Windows NT server to access the current DHCP settings.

C. **Incorrect:** The network administration tools do not include support for managing RAS services on a remote Windows NT server when using a Windows 95 client.

D. **Correct:** Using the Server Manager utility, you can manage shared resources on a Windows NT server from both Windows NT Workstation and Windows 95 client computers.

70-068.03.03.002

You have installed the Windows NT network administration tools on two Windows NT Workstation clients and two Windows 95 clients. Which client computers will you be able to use for controlling and changing Windows NT system policies?

▶ **Correct Answer: B**

A. **Incorrect:** In order to manage system policies, you must be running the Windows NT Workstation operating system. Windows 95 does not support the ability to manage Windows NT policies on a remote Windows NT server.

B. **Correct:** Only clients running the Windows NT Workstation operating system can manage system policies with the network administration tools. This feature is not supported by Windows 95 clients.

C. **Incorrect:** Windows 95 does not support system policy management with the network administration tools. However, Windows NT Workstation does support this feature.

D. **Incorrect:** Although Windows 95 clients cannot support Windows NT system policy management, this feature is available to Windows NT Workstation clients.

70-068.03.03.003

You have installed the Windows NT network administration tools on two Windows NT Workstation clients and two Windows 95 clients. Which client computers will you be able to use for managing users, groups, and security policies for Windows NT–based domains and computers?

A. Only the Windows 95 clients

B. Only the Windows NT Workstation clients

C. Both the Windows NT Workstation and Windows 95 clients

D. Neither the Windows NT Workstation nor the Windows 95 clients

70-068.03.03.003

You have installed the Windows NT network administration tools on two Windows NT Workstation clients and two Windows 95 clients. Which client computers will you be able to use for managing users, groups, and security policies for Windows NT–based domains and computers?

▶ **Correct Answer: C**

    A. **Incorrect:** Once the network administration tools have been installed, you can manage a number of resources, such as users or shared folder permissions, from both Windows 95 and Windows NT Workstation clients.

    B. **Incorrect:** Both Windows 95 and Windows NT Workstation clients can manage users, groups, and security policies once the network administration tools have been installed.

    C. **Correct:** The network administration tools allow both Windows 95 and Windows NT Workstation clients access to user and group management as well as security policy administration.

    D. **Incorrect:** The network administration tools allow both Windows 95 and Windows NT Workstation clients access to user, group, and security policy management capabilities.

Further Reading

Supporting Microsoft Windows NT Server in the Enterprise Training kit. Complete Lesson 2, "Profiles and Policies," of Chapter 3, "Managing Enterprise Resources." In this lesson, you will learn about the differences between Windows 95 and Windows NT policies and profiles.

Supporting Microsoft Windows NT Server in the Enterprise Training kit. Complete Lesson 7, "Remote Management of Servers," of Chapter 3, "Managing Enterprise Resources." In this lesson, you will learn about the available tools for managing a Windows NT Server from a client computer.

Windows NT Server 4.0 in the Enterprise Accelerated MCSE Study Guide. Read Chapter 11, "Remote Administration" to learn more about using the network administration tools.

OBJECTIVE 3.4

Manage disk resources.

This objective covers the following tasks:

- Creating and sharing resources

- Implementing permissions and security

- Establishing file auditing

Windows NT Server allows its resources to be shared to users on the network. Depending on the level of security you need to implement, you may choose the Windows NT file system, NTFS. This provides the highest level of control and provides the ability to audit file access activities. These activities include general file access, file copying, and deletion of files. Together, the access control and auditing features of NTFS makes this the best file system to use in an enterprise environment.

To successfully answer the questions for this objective, you need a firm understanding of several key terms. For definitions of these terms, refer to the Glossary in this book.

Key Terms

- Auditing

- NTFS

70-068.03.04.001

Your network consists of a PDC, 2 BDCs, 1 member server, and 400 Windows NT Workstation clients. All servers' hard drives are NTFS volumes. The member server contains a directory named DOCS, which must be accessible to all users on the network. Users who are logged on locally have Full Control permission to the DOCS directory. No other computer can access it.

The required result is to give users logging in to the network from client workstations access to the DOCS directory on the Windows NT server.

The first optional result is to allow network users permission to read, execute, and modify files within the directory, but not to delete any of the files.

The second optional result is to allow users, logging in locally to the Windows NT server, to continue to have full control over the directory and files within the directory.

The proposed solution is to share the DOCS directory and assign the Everyone group Change permissions to the new share.

What does the proposed solution provide?

A. The required result and all optional results.

B. The required result and one optional result.

C. The required result but none of the optional results.

D. The proposed solution does not provide the required result.

70-068.03.04.001

Your network consists of a PDC, 2 BDCs, 1 member server, and 400 Windows NT Workstation clients. All servers' hard drives are NTFS volumes. The member server contains a directory named DOCS, which must be accessible to all users on the network. Users who are logged on locally have Full Control permission to the DOCS directory. No other computer can access it.

The required result is to give users logging in to the network from client workstations access to the DOCS directory on the Windows NT server.

The first optional result is to allow network users permission to read, execute, and modify files within the directory, but not to delete any of the files.

The second optional result is to allow users, logging in locally to the Windows NT server, to continue to have full control over the directory and files within the directory.

The proposed solution is to share the DOCS directory and assign the Everyone group Change permissions to the new share.

What does the proposed solution provide?

▶ **Correct Answer: B**

A. **Incorrect:** Although the required result will be realized with this solution, only one of the optional results will be realized. By providing the Everyone group Change permission, users will also have the right to delete files. Locally logged on users will still have Full Control permission.

B. **Correct:** By implementing this solution, all users logging into the domain will have Change access to the DOCS share. However, only the second optional result will be realized as the Change permission will allow users the right to delete files.

C. **Incorrect:** Although the required result will be realized, the second optional result will also be realized. All users that log onto the network will have Change permission, which provides the ability to delete files from the DOCS share.

D. **Incorrect:** The proposed solution will allow users that log into the domain access to the shared DOCS folder. This means the required result will be realized. In addition, locally logged on users will continue to have Full Control access, which means the second optional result will be realized as well.

70-068.03.04.002

A member server on a Windows NT domain network has an NTFS volume that contains a directory named DOCS, which must be accessible to all users on the network. Users who are logged on locally have Full Control permission to the DOCS directory. No other computer can access it.

The required result is to make the DOCS directory available to users logging onto the network from client workstations.

The first optional result is to allow network users permission only to read and execute files within the directory.

The second optional result is to modify access to locally logged on users so they have Read, Execute, and Change permissions.

The proposed solution is to assign the Everyone group Change permission for the DOCS directory. Next, share the DOCS directory, and assign the Everyone group Read permission.

What does the proposed solution provide?

A. The required result and all optional results.

B. The required result and one optional result.

C. The required result but none of the optional results.

D. The proposed solution does not provide the required result.

70-068.03.04.002

A member server on a Windows NT domain network has an NTFS volume that contains a directory named DOCS, which must be accessible to all users on the network. Users who are logged on locally have Full Control permission to the DOCS directory. No other computer can access it.

The required result is to make the DOCS directory available to users logging onto the network from client workstations.

The first optional result is to allow network users permission only to read and execute files within the directory.

The second optional result is to modify access to locally logged on users so they have Read, Execute, and Change permissions.

The proposed solution is to assign the Everyone group Change permission for the DOCS directory. Next, share the DOCS directory, and assign the Everyone group Read permission.

What does the proposed solution provide?

▶ **Correct Answer: A**

A. **Correct:** Sharing the DOCS directory will allow network users access to the folder, which meets the required result. The proposed solution will allow locally logged on users the ability to change documents in the DOCS share. This includes the ability to read and execute files. In addition, assigning the Read permission to the share will allow network users the ability to read and execute files in the DOCS share. This meets both optional requirements.

B. **Incorrect:** Although the proposed solution meets the required results it also meets both optional results. Assigning the Read permission to the share meets the first optional result and assigning the Change permission to the directory meets the second optional result.

C. **Incorrect:** By assigning the Read permission to the share and the Change permission to the directory, both optional results will be realized.

D. **Incorrect:** By sharing the DOCS directory and assigning the Read permission, users on the network will be able to access files in the folder. This meets the required result.

70-068.03.04.003

Which permissions are given to the group Everyone by default when you share a folder?

A. Read

B. Change

C. No Access

D. Full Control

70-068.03.04.004

You want to create a share and assign the minimum permissions required to run program files located in the share. Which permissions should you assign?

A. Read

B. Change

C. No Access

D. Full Control

70-068.03.04.003

Which permissions are given to the group Everyone by default when you share a folder?

▶ **Correct Answer: D**

A. **Incorrect:** The default permission granted when the Everyone group is added to a share is Full Control.

B. **Incorrect:** The default permission granted when the Everyone group is added to a share is Full Control.

C. **Incorrect:** The default permission granted when the Everyone group is added to a share is Full Control.

D. **Correct:** By default, the Everyone group is given Full Control permission to a share.

70-068.03.04.004

You want to create a share and assign the minimum permissions required to run program files located in the share. Which permissions should you assign?

▶ **Correct Answer: A**

A. **Correct:** The Read access permission will allow users to open files and execute programs, but will not allow them to change, delete, or add files.

B. **Incorrect:** The Change access permission will allow users the ability to edit and delete files in a folder.

C. **Incorrect:** This security setting will prevent users from gaining any access to the shared folder.

D. **Incorrect:** Full Access will allow users more than just the ability to read and execute files from a share. They will also be able to add new files as well as change or delete existing files.

70-068.03.04.005

Which events should you audit if you want to track users copying a file from a shared folder on an NTFS volume?

A. Read

B. Write

C. Execute

D. Change Permissions

70-068.03.04.005

Which events should you audit if you want to track users copying a file from a shared folder on an NTFS volume?

▶ **Correct Answer: B**

A. **Incorrect:** The Read event will not monitor that a file has been copied, only that it has been accessed. Therefore, you should monitor the Write event.

B. **Correct:** The Write event will monitor that a file has been copied.

C. **Incorrect:** The Execute event will not monitor that a file has been copied. For this you must use the Write event.

D. **Incorrect:** Change Permissions will not allow you to audit that a file has been copied. You must monitor the Write event to track copied files.

Further Reading

Supporting Microsoft Windows NT Server in the Enterprise Training kit. Complete Lesson 1, "User and Group Accounts," of Chapter 3, "Managing Enterprise Resources." In this lesson, you will learn about assigning permissions based on user accounts and group accounts.

Supporting Microsoft Windows NT Server in the Enterprise Training kit. Complete Lesson 6, "Managing Shared Resources," of Chapter 3, "Managing Enterprise Resources." In this lesson, you will learn about how to secure print and file resources on a network.

Connectivity

When implementing Windows NT Server, connecting the server to other computers on the network—including other Windows NT servers, client workstations, other Windows NT domains, and computers using dial-up phone line access—is a basic requirement. In addition, Novell NetWare servers and clients can also connect to a Windows NT network. In this case, the Windows NT server can act as a security provider to authenticate the Novell clients and allow them access to shared resources. A Windows NT server can also act as a gateway to allow Microsoft clients access to Novell shared resources.

In addition to these traditional server functions, Windows NT Server can act as a network router. Using the Routing Information Protocol (RIP) service, protocols such as Internetwork Packet Exchange (IPX) or Internet Protocol (IP) can be routed between networks. This extends traditional network functionality to provide organizations greater access to data and information.

Using Internet Information Server (IIS), Windows NT can act as a World Wide Web server on both the public Internet and a private intranet. One of the benefits of using IIS and Windows NT Server is that the security provided by Windows NT can be used to control access to a Web site. This allows administrators to create private, secure Web sites as well as publicly accessible sites.

Tested Skills and Suggested Practices

The skills you need to successfully master the Connectivity objective domain on the exam include:

- **Supporting Internet services.**

  - Practice 1: Install and configure Internet Information Server.

  - Practice 2: Secure the IIS site by implementing group permissions and Windows NT Challenge/Response (NTLM) authentication. Try accessing the site with a valid user name. When attempting to access the site from a computer outside the domain, you will be prompted for a valid user name and password.

  - Practice 3: Install the Domain Name System (DNS) component and attempt to use the Windows NT server as a DNS server from a Windows 95 or Windows 98 client.

  - Practice 4: Install and configure DHCP. Once it's installed, attempt to obtain IP information from the Windows NT server using a Windows 95 or Windows 98 client that has been set to obtain its TCP/IP settings automatically.

- **Supporting NetWare clients.**

  - Practice 1: Install and configure File and Print Services for NetWare (FPNW). Share a folder on the Windows NT server. Test the connection from a NetWare client computer by attempting to access resources on the Windows NT server.

  - Practice 2: If a Novell file server is available, run Migration Tool for NetWare on a Windows NT server to migrate user accounts from the Novell computer to the Windows NT server.

- **Providing dial-up services.**

  - Practice 1: Install and configure Remote Access Service (RAS) on a Windows NT server.

  - Practice 2: From a client with a modem, dial into a Windows NT server that has RAS installed. See if you can connect to shared resources on the server, and then try to access resources on the domain.

  - Practice 3: With a client connected to a RAS server, use the Windows NT RAS utilities to monitor client usage.

OBJECTIVE 4.1

Configure Windows NT Server for interoperability with NetWare servers by using various tools.

The tools for configuring Windows NT Server for interoperability with NetWare servers include:

- Gateway Services for NetWare

- Migration Tool for NetWare

Using Windows NT Server, you can provide Microsoft clients access to Novell resources by installing Gateway Services for NetWare (GSNW). GSNW can be implemented on either PDCs or member servers. You can also install File and Print Services for NetWare, which will allow Novell clients access to resources available on the Windows NT server.

If you want to use Windows NT Server as the security provider and user authentication server for Novell clients, you can use the Migration Tool for NetWare. This utility will migrate user account information from a Novell file server. Windows NT Server can then authenticate both Microsoft clients and Novell servers acting as clients. It can also centralize administration for easier network management.

To successfully answer the questions for this objective, you need a firm understanding of several key terms. For definitions of these terms, refer to the Glossary in this book.

Key Terms

- Backup Domain Controller (BDC)

- File and Print Services for NetWare (FPNW)

- Gateway Services for NetWare (GSNW)

- Member server

- Primary Domain Controller (PDC)

70-068.04.01.001

Your network consists of a single PDC, 2 BDCs, 1 Windows NT member server, a NetWare 3.12 server, and 425 Windows NT workstation and NetWare clients. All Windows NT servers use NTFS volumes. NetBEUI is the only protocol universally installed on the Windows NT servers and clients. The member server provides connectivity between the Windows NT and NetWare environments by running Gateway Services for NetWare (GSNW) and File and Print Services for NetWare (FPNW). It has NWLink installed on it. You need to simplify administration.

The required result is to merge the NetWare user accounts into Windows NT and copy all folders and files and their accompanying security information to a Windows NT server.

The first optional result is to migrate NetWare user login scripts to Windows NT.

The second optional result is to allow NetWare clients to browse all Windows NT resources.

The proposed solution is to configure GSNW and FPNW on the PDC, and use the Migration Tool for NetWare to migrate the NetWare user accounts to the PDC.

What does the proposed solution provide?

A. The required result and all optional results.

B. The required result and one optional result.

C. The required result but none of the optional results.

D. The proposed solution does not provide the required result.

70-068.04.01.001

Your network consists of a single PDC, 2 BDCs, 1 Windows NT member server, a NetWare 3.12 server, and 425 Windows NT workstation and NetWare clients. All Windows NT servers use NTFS volumes. NetBEUI is the only protocol universally installed on the Windows NT servers and clients. The member server provides connectivity between the Windows NT and NetWare environments by running Gateway Services for NetWare (GSNW) and File and Print Services for NetWare (FPNW). It has NWLink installed on it. You need to simplify administration.

The required result is to merge the NetWare user accounts into Windows NT and copy all folders and files and their accompanying security information to a Windows NT server.

The first optional result is to migrate NetWare user login scripts to Windows NT.

The second optional result is to allow NetWare clients to browse all Windows NT resources.

The proposed solution is to configure GSNW and FPNW on the PDC, and use the Migration Tool for NetWare to migrate the NetWare user accounts to the PDC.

What does the proposed solution provide?

▶ **Correct Answer: A**

A. **Correct:** With Gateway Services for NetWare and File and Print Services for NetWare installed, Novell clients will be able to access Microsoft network resources. Using the Migration Tool for NetWare, which requires Gateway Services for NetWare to be installed, allows you to move user accounts from a NetWare network. In addition, when the user accounts are migrated to the PDC, the Windows NT server will become the security provider for the NetWare clients. Therefore, this solution meets the required result and both optional result.

B. **Incorrect:** Although the required result will be realized with this solution, migrating the user accounts to the PDC and installing both Gateway Services for NetWare and File and Print Services for NetWare will realize both optional results. Therefore, this answer is incorrect.

C. **Incorrect:** The solution will realize the required result but will also meet both optional results. Therefore, this answer is incorrect.

D. **Incorrect:** When the Novell accounts are migrated to the PDC, Windows NT will merge the existing Microsoft user accounts with the Novell accounts. This will allow the PDC to become the security provider for both types of clients. Therefore, the required result will be realized and this answer is incorrect.

70-068.04.01.002

Your network consists of a single PDC, 2 BDCs, 1 Windows NT member server, a NetWare 3.12 server, and 425 Windows NT workstation and NetWare clients. All Windows NT servers use NTFS volumes. All computers use the IPX/SPX protocol. The member server provides connectivity between the Windows NT and NetWare environments by running Gateway Services for NetWare (GSNW) and File and Print Services for NetWare (FPNW). You need to simplify network administration.

The required result is to merge the NetWare user accounts into Windows NT.

The first optional result is to migrate NetWare user login scripts to Windows NT.

The second optional result is to allow NetWare clients to browse all Windows NT network resources.

The proposed solution is to promote the member server to a PDC, migrate the NetWare user accounts using the Windows NT Server Migration Tool for NetWare from the PDC, and install Client Services for NetWare (CSNW) on each NetWare client.

What does the proposed solution provide?

A. The required result and all optional results.

B. The required result and one optional result.

C. The required result but none of the optional results.

D. The proposed solution does not provide the required result.

70-068.04.01.002

Your network consists of a single PDC, 2 BDCs, 1 Windows NT member server, a NetWare 3.12 server, and 425 Windows NT workstation and NetWare clients. All Windows NT servers use NTFS volumes. All computers use the IPX/SPX protocol. The member server provides connectivity between the Windows NT and NetWare environments by running Gateway Services for NetWare (GSNW) and File and Print Services for NetWare (FPNW). You need to simplify network administration.

The required result is to merge the NetWare user accounts into Windows NT.

The first optional result is to migrate NetWare user login scripts to Windows NT.

The second optional result is to allow NetWare clients to browse all Windows NT network resources.

The proposed solution is to promote the member server to a PDC, migrate the NetWare user accounts using the Windows NT Server Migration Tool for NetWare from the PDC, and install Client Services for NetWare (CSNW) on each NetWare client.

What does the proposed solution provide?

▶ **Correct Answer: D**

   A. **Incorrect:** You cannot promote a member server to a PDC in a Windows NT domain. In order to change the member server to a PDC, you must first reinstall Windows NT. The required result will not be realized, and therefore this answer is incorrect.

   B. **Incorrect:** Since member servers cannot be promoted to PDCs, the required result cannot be realized with this solution. In addition, you need to migrate the user accounts *to* the PDC, not from the PDC.

   C. **Incorrect:** The solution presented will not realize the required result. Promoting the member server to the PDC, which requires Windows NT Server to be reinstalled, will not merge the NetWare user accounts. Therefore, this answer is incorrect.

   D. **Correct:** In order to realize the required result, the NetWare client accounts must be migrated to an existing Windows NT Server PDC. Since a PDC already exists in the domain, this-not a member server-is the computer that should be used. Administrators can run the Windows NT Server Migration Tool for NetWare to move the accounts to the PDC.

70-068.04.01.003

Your network consists of a single PDC, 2 BDCs, 1 Windows NT member server, a NetWare 3.12 server, and 425 Windows NT workstation and NetWare clients. All Windows NT servers use NTFS volumes. All computers use the IPX/SPX protocol. The member server provides connectivity between the Windows NT and NetWare environments by running Gateway Services for NetWare (GSNW) and File and Print Services for NetWare (FPNW). You need to simplify network administration.

The required result is to merge the NetWare user accounts into Windows NT.

The first optional result is to migrate NetWare user login scripts to Windows NT.

The second optional result is to allow NetWare clients to browse Windows NT network resources.

The proposed solution is to migrate the NetWare user accounts using the Windows NT Server Migration Tool for NetWare from the member server and then install a Microsoft redirector on each NetWare client.

What does the proposed solution provide?

A. The required result and all optional results.

B. The required result and one optional result.

C. The required result but none of the optional results.

D. The proposed solution does not provide the required result.

70-068.04.01.003

Your network consists of a single PDC, 2 BDCs, 1 Windows NT member server, a NetWare 3.12 server, and 425 Windows NT workstation and NetWare clients. All Windows NT servers use NTFS volumes. All computers use the IPX/SPX protocol. The member server provides connectivity between the Windows NT and NetWare environments by running Gateway Services for NetWare (GSNW) and File and Print Services for NetWare (FPNW). You need to simplify network administration.

The required result is to merge the NetWare user accounts into Windows NT.

The first optional result is to migrate NetWare user login scripts to Windows NT.

The second optional result is to allow NetWare clients to browse Windows NT network resources.

The proposed solution is to migrate the NetWare user accounts using the Windows NT Server Migration Tool for NetWare from the member server and then install a Microsoft redirector on each NetWare client.

What does the proposed solution provide?

▶ **Correct Answer: D**

   A. **Incorrect:** You can migrate NetWare client accounts from a Windows NT member server as long as that server is running Gateway Services for NetWare. However, this solution does not specify that these accounts will be migrated to the PDC, which is necessary if you want to merge the accounts from both networks. Therefore, the required result will not be realized and this answer is incorrect.

   B. **Incorrect:** Migration Tool for NetWare moves Novell user account information from a Novell file server to a Windows NT domain controller. This solution attempts to move Novell accounts from the member server, and it does not specify the appropriate domain controller to receive the accounts. Therefore, this answer is incorrect.

   C. **Incorrect:** To realize the required result, the Novell accounts must be migrated to a Windows NT Server PDC. The proposed solution attempts to migrate accounts from a Windows NT member server, and it does not specify the appropriate PDC to receive the accounts. Therefore, the required result will not be realized.

   D. **Correct:** Novell accounts can be migrated to a Windows NT PDC or from a member server, as long as the computer in question is running Gateway Services for NetWare. However, this solution does not specify that the PDC must receive the migrated accounts, which is necessary to merge account information. Therefore, the required result will not be realized, making this the correct answer.

70-068.04.01.004

Your network consists of a single PDC, 2 BDCs, 1 Windows NT member server, a NetWare 3.12 server, and 425 Windows NT Workstation and NetWare clients. All Windows NT servers use NTFS volumes. All computers use the IPX/SPX protocol. The member server provides connectivity between the Windows NT and NetWare environments by running Gateway Services for NetWare (GSNW) and File and Print Services for NetWare (FPNW). You need to simplify network administration.

The required result is to merge the NetWare user accounts into Windows NT.

The first optional result is to migrate NetWare user login scripts to Windows NT.

The second optional result is to allow NetWare clients to browse the PDC's resources.

The proposed solution is to set up GSNW and FPNW on the PDC and migrate the NetWare user accounts to the PDC using the Windows NT Server Migration Tool for NetWare.

What does the proposed solution provide?

A. The required result and all optional results.

B. The required result and one optional result.

C. The required result but none of the optional results.

D. The proposed solution does not provide the required result.

70-068.04.01.004

Your network consists of a single PDC, 2 BDCs, 1 Windows NT member server, a NetWare 3.12 server, and 425 Windows NT Workstation and NetWare clients. All Windows NT servers use NTFS volumes. All computers use the IPX/SPX protocol. The member server provides connectivity between the Windows NT and NetWare environments by running Gateway Services for NetWare (GSNW) and File and Print Services for NetWare (FPNW). You need to simplify network administration.

The required result is to merge the NetWare user accounts into Windows NT.

The first optional result is to migrate NetWare user login scripts to Windows NT.

The second optional result is to allow NetWare clients to browse the PDC's resources.

The proposed solution is to set up GSNW and FPNW on the PDC and migrate the NetWare user accounts to the PDC using the Windows NT Server Migration Tool for NetWare.

What does the proposed solution provide?

▶ **Correct Answer: A**

A. **Correct:** With Gateway Services for NetWare and File and Print Services for NetWare installed, Novell clients will be able to access Microsoft network resources. In addition, Migration Tool for NetWare allows you to migrate NetWare user login scripts to Windows NT when the server you are migrating to has File and Print Services for NetWare installed. Finally, when the user accounts are migrated to the PDC, the Windows NT server will become the security provider for the NetWare clients. Therefore, this solution meets the required result and both optional results.

B. **Incorrect:** Although the required result will be realized with this solution, migrating the user accounts to the PDC and installing both Gateway Services for NetWare and File and Print Services for NetWare will realize both optional results. Therefore, this answer is incorrect.

C. **Incorrect:** The solution will realize the required result but will also meet both optional results. Therefore, this answer is incorrect.

D. **Incorrect:** When the Novell accounts are migrated to the PDC, Windows NT will merge the existing Microsoft user accounts with the Novell accounts. This will allow the PDC to become the security provider for both types of clients. Therefore, the required result will be realized and this answer is incorrect.

70-068.04.01.005

Your network consists of a PDC, 2 BDCs, 1 Windows NT member server, 1 NetWare 3.12 server, and 425 Windows NT workstation and NetWare clients. The PDC and BDCs use NTFS volumes, while the Windows NT member server contains only a FAT volume.

IPX/SPX is the only protocol used by the NetWare server and NetWare clients. NetBEUI is the only protocol universally installed on the Windows NT servers and clients.

You need to install GSNW to allow Microsoft clients access to the NetWare server and to provide a migration path to be used in the near future. You also want to avoid any reconfiguration when performing the migration.

On which server should you install GSNW?

A. The PDC

B. One of the BDCs

C. The NetWare server

D. The Windows NT member server

70-068.04.01.005

Your network consists of a PDC, 2 BDCs, 1 Windows NT member server, 1 NetWare 3.12 server, and 425 Windows NT workstation and NetWare clients. The PDC and BDCs use NTFS volumes, while the Windows NT member server contains only a FAT volume.

IPX/SPX is the only protocol used by the NetWare server and NetWare clients. NetBEUI is the only protocol universally installed on the Windows NT servers and clients.

You need to install GSNW to allow Microsoft clients access to the NetWare server and to provide a migration path to be used in the near future. You also want to avoid any reconfiguration when performing the migration.

On which server should you install GSNW?

▶ **Correct Answer: A**

A. **Correct:** With the Gateway Services for NetWare component installed on the PDC, the server will be ready for future migration of Novell accounts. This will help reduce the need for reconfiguration when you perform the migration.

B. **Incorrect:** If Gateway Services for NetWare is installed on only one of the Backup Domain Controllers, it will have to be reinstalled on the PDC when you migrate the Novell accounts. Therefore, GSNW should be installed on the PDC to minimize having to reconfigure the servers in the future.

C. **Incorrect:** Gateway Services for NetWare is a Windows NT Server component.

D. **Incorrect:** The Windows NT member server, while able to provide gateway services, would not be the best solution for a future migration. You need to install GSNW on the PDC to begin the migration, so in the interest of reducing future reconfiguration needs, GSNW should be installed on the current PDC.

Further Reading

Supporting Microsoft Windows NT Server in the Enterprise Training kit. Complete Lesson 6, "Configuring NT Services for NetWare," of Chapter 4, "Connectivity." In this lesson, the functions of GSNW and FPNW are discussed.

Windows NT Server 4.0 in the Enterprise Accelerated MCSE Study Guide. Read Chapter 16, "NetWare Connectivity," to learn more about implementing features to support NetWare client computers.

OBJECTIVE 4.2

Install and configure multiprotocol routing to serve various functions.

The multiprotocol functions of routing include:

- Internet (IP) routing

- DHCP/BOOTP relay

- IPX routing

Although Windows NT Server can be used to manage user accounts and share resources, such as folders or printers, it can also be used to route network protocols. In order to support routing certain protocols, you will need to install the Routing Information Protocol (RIP) for either IP or IPX. Also, while not truly routable, DHCP/BOOTP information can be passed on to different networks through the use of a DHCP/BOOTP relay agent. DHCP is an enhancement of BOOTP, which configures a client's IP addresses during the boot phase, and when a DHCP/BOOTP relay agent is installed, a DHCP server implemented on one subnet can serve clients on another subnet. By default, DHCP cannot route its TCP/IP configuration information to clients on other subnets.

To successfully answer the questions for this objective, you need a firm understanding of several key terms. For definitions of these terms, refer to the Glossary in this book.

Key Terms

- BOOTP

- Data Link Control (DLC)

- Dynamic Host Configuration Protocol (DHCP)

- Router

- Routing Information Protocol (RIP)

- Service Advertising Protocol (SAP)

- Windows Internet Naming Service (WINS)

70-068.04.02.001

You are configuring a Windows NT member server to act as a router between two IP subnets (subnet A and subnet B). Once connected, both subnets will use DHCP, though a DHCP server will be implemented only on subnet A.

What should you configure on the IP router to allow hosts in subnet B to obtain IP addresses from DHCP?

A. RIP

B. SAP

C. WINS/NBNS

D. DHCP/BOOTP relay agent

70-068.04.02.002

You are configuring a Windows NT member server to act as a router between two IPX networks. What must you enable on the Windows NT server to allow it to route IPX?

A. RIP

B. SAP

C. DLC

D. WINS

70-068.04.02.001

You are configuring a Windows NT member server to act as a router between two IP subnets (subnet A and subnet B). Once connected, both subnets will use DHCP, though a DHCP server will be implemented only on subnet A.

What should you configure on the IP router to allow hosts in subnet B to obtain IP addresses from DHCP?

▶ **Correct Answer: D**

A. **Incorrect:** Although RIP (Routing Information Protocol) is designed to help route protocols, it is not designed to work with DHCP. Since the protocol to be routed is DHCP, RIP would not be the correct solution.

B. **Incorrect:** The Service Advertising Protocol is used by NetWare servers to broadcast available services. It is not used to route DHCP.

C. **Incorrect:** The Windows Internet Naming Service is Microsoft's implementation of a NetBIOS Name Server (NBNS), which helps reduce network broadcasts by maintaining a list of computer names and IP addresses. WINS is not designed to route DHCP between subnets.

D. **Correct:** The DHCP/BOOTP relay agent is a service designed to route the DHCP protocol across local area networks. Using this service, one subnet can have a DHCP server while clients in another subnet can use the dynamic configuration information provided by this server.

70-068.04.02.002

You are configuring a Windows NT member server to act as a router between two IPX networks. What must you enable on the Windows NT server to allow it to route IPX?

▶ **Correct Answer: A**

A. **Correct:** Routing Information Protocol can by used with both IP and IPX and is designed to route these protocols as necessary.

B. **Incorrect:** Service Advertising Protocol is designed to allow NetWare servers the ability to broadcast announce the services they offer. It is not designed to route protocols between networks.

C. **Incorrect:** The Data Link Control protocol is used to allow clients access to network resources such as a network printer or an AS/400 computer. DLC is not used to route protocols.

D. **Incorrect.** Windows Internet Naming Service is used to manage computer names and their IP addresses in order to reduce network broadcast traffic. It is not designed to help route protocols such as IPX.

70-068.04.02.003

You are configuring a Windows NT member server to act as a router between two IP networks. What must you enable on the Windows NT server to allow it to route TCP/IP?

A. RIP

B. SAP

C. DLC

D. WINS

E. BOOTP

70-068.04.02.003

You are configuring a Windows NT member server to act as a router between two IP networks. What must you enable on the Windows NT server to allow it to route TCP/IP?

▶ **Correct Answer: A**

A. **Correct:** Routing Information Protocol is designed to help route either IP or IPX between networks. Therefore, RIP is the correct answer.

B. **Incorrect:** Service Advertising Protocol is designed to allow NetWare servers to announce the services they offer. It is not designed to route protocols between networks.

C. **Incorrect:** The Data Link Control protocol is used to allow clients access to network resources, such as a network printer or an AS/400 computer. DLC is not used to route protocols.

D. **Incorrect:** Windows Internet Naming Service is used to manage computer names and their IP addresses in order to reduce network broadcast traffic. It is not designed to help route protocols such as IP.

E. **Incorrect:** BOOTP is a subset of DHCP and allows client computers the ability to acquire IP configuration information at startup. It does not allow routing of protocols between subnets.

Further Reading

Supporting Microsoft Windows NT Server in the Enterprise Training kit. Complete Lesson 1, "Managing DHCP," of Chapter 4, "Connectivity." In this lesson, you will learn about configuring and troubleshooting the DHCP protocol.

Supporting Microsoft Windows NT Server in the Enterprise Training kit. Complete Lesson 4, "Configuring Routable Protocols," of Chapter 4, "Connectivity." In this lesson, you will learn how to configure Windows NT as a router.

Supporting Microsoft Windows NT Server in the Enterprise Training kit. Complete Lesson 5, "Configuring Internet Information Server," of Chapter 4, "Connectivity." In this lesson, installing and configuring IIS will be discussed.

Windows NT Server 4.0 in the Enterprise Accelerated MCSE Study Guide. Read Chapter 12, "Dynamic Host Configuration Protocol," to learn more about using DHCP on a network.

OBJECTIVE 4.3

Install and configure Internet Information Server.

You can use Windows NT Server as a World Wide Web server by installing and configuring Internet Information Server. IIS is designed for enterprise Web servers that can be used on both the public Internet and a private intranet. In addition to offering large-scale Web site support, IIS uses the integrated security provided by Windows NT Server. This allows administrators to secure their Web sites using the same security model, including users and groups, that they are accustomed to in Windows NT.

Windows NT can also support multiple IP addresses associated with a single network interface card (NIC). This concept is sometimes called *multihoming*. A multihomed server can then support more than one Web site, each having its own custom security implementation. Each Web site has its own folder, and accompanying HTML content, which is associated with the appropriate IP address. This occurs even though all the IP addresses are bound to a single NIC. Windows NT Server's and Internet Information Server's support for multihoming can be used by large organizations or Internet service providers (ISPs) that wish to host more than one Web site on a single server.

To successfully answer the questions for this objective, you need a firm understanding of several key terms. For definitions of these terms, refer to the Glossary in this book.

Key Terms

- Internet Information Server (IIS)

- Multihoming

- Network interface card

- TCP/IP

70-068.04.03.001

On which computers can you install IIS? (Choose all that apply.)

A. A PDC running NetBEUI

B. A BDC running TCP/IP and NetBEUI

C. A NetWare 4.1 server running IPX/SPX

D. A Windows NT member server running TCP/IP

E. A Windows NT Workstation computer running TCP/IP and NetBEUI

70-068.04.03.002

You are installing IIS on a computer whose NetBIOS name is Jalapeno. The WWW service is configured to allow anonymous access. Which user account will be automatically created on the computer to allow anonymous users to access the Web server?

A. IIS_Jalapeno

B. IUSR_Jalapeno

C. Jalapeno_Guest

D. IISUSER_Jalapeno

70-068.04.03.001

On which computers can you install IIS? (Choose all that apply.)

▶ **Correct Answers: B and D**

A. **Incorrect:** Internet Information Server can run on a PDC, or BDC. However, IIS requires the TCP/IP protocol, not NetBEUI.

B. **Correct:** IIS can be installed on a BDC running the TCP/IP protocol. Therefore, a BDC running TCP/IP and other protocols will support IIS.

C. **Incorrect:** Internet Information Server is a Windows NT networking component that is not supported on the Novell platform.

D. **Correct:** IIS requires a Windows NT Server operating system and the TCP/IP protocol. Therefore, a member server running TCP/IP will support IIS.

E. **Incorrect:** Internet Information Server is not supported by the Windows NT Workstation operating system.

70-068.04.03.002

You are installing IIS on a computer whose NetBIOS name is Jalapeno. The WWW service is configured to allow anonymous access. Which user account will be automatically created on the computer to allow anonymous users to access the Web server?

▶ **Correct Answer: B**

A. **Incorrect:** Internet Information Server uses the IUSR prefix and the NetBIOS name to create the anonymous account. Therefore, the correct name is IUSR_Jalapeno, not IIS_Jalapeno.

B. **Correct:** Internet Information Server uses the IUSR prefix and the NetBIOS name to create the anonymous account. Therefore, IUSR_Jalapeno is the correct name.

C. **Incorrect:** IIS does not use Guest as a suffix to the NetBIOS name. It does, however, use IUSR as a prefix. Therefore, the correct name is IUSR_Jalapeno.

D. **Incorrect:** The correct prefix is IUSR, not IISUSER. Therefore, IUSR_Jalapeno is the correct name.

70-068.04.03.003

You need to provide an intranet web site for each of your company's departments on a single IIS 3.0 server. Each department's site will have its own domain name and IP address. Your network is not currently using a WINS or DHCP server. Also, all IP addresses are manually configured.

Which steps are required to allow the IIS server to host each department's intranet web site? (Choose three.)

A. Install a network interface card for each IP address required.

B. Bind each site's IP address to the IIS server's network interface card.

C. Install a DNS server, and add each department's web site IP address and domain name to the HOSTS file.

D. Install a DHCP server to maintain lease information on the IP addresses assigned to the IIS server's network interface card.

E. Create a WWW folder for each company web site hosted by the IIS server and manually assign the corresponding IP address to the folder.

70-068.04.03.003

You need to provide an intranet web site for each of your company's departments on a single IIS 3.0 server. Each department's site will have its own domain name and IP address. Your network is not currently using a WINS or DHCP server. Also, all IP addresses are manually configured.

Which steps are required to allow the IIS server to host each department's intranet web site? (Choose three.)

▶ **Correct Answers: B, C, and E**

  A. **Incorrect:** Windows NT Server can support multiple IP addresses per NIC. Therefore, you do not need to add additional network cards to solve this problem.

  B. **Correct:** Windows NT Server can support multiple IP addresses as long as each new address is first bound to the existing NIC.

  C. **Correct:** In order to allow clients the ability to find web sites by entering their domain name rather than their IP addresses, a DNS server is required. The DNS server will maintain the list of IP addresses bound to the NIC in the Windows NT server.

  D. **Incorrect:** DHCP assigns dynamic IP information to a computer on the network. Therefore, installing a DHCP server could give a Web site a new IP address every time the IIS server computer is booted. This could prevent users from being able to access the proper Web site on a network.

  E. **Correct:** Once IP addresses have been assigned to the Windows NT server and the appropriate DNS entries made for client resolution, a folder must be created on the web server. This folder will map to the appropriate IP address. It will then store the web files, such as DEFAULT.HTM, that will be associated with the individual web site. Supporting multiple IP addresses on one server is sometimes called *multihoming*.

Further Reading

Supporting Microsoft Windows NT Server in the Enterprise Training kit. Complete Lesson 3, "Managing DNS," of Chapter 4, "Connectivity." In this lesson, you will learn how to configure the Domain Name System and compare and contrast DNS to WINS.

Supporting Microsoft Windows NT Server in the Enterprise Training kit. Complete Lesson 5, "Configuring Internet Information Server," of Chapter 4, "Connectivity." In this lesson, installing and configuring IIS will be discussed.

Windows NT Server 4.0 in the Enterprise Accelerated MCSE Study Guide. Read Chapter 14, "Domain Name System," to learn more about configuring DNS for use on a network.

O B J E C T I V E   4 . 4

Install and configure Internet services.

The services covered by this objective include:

- World Wide Web

- DNS

- Intranet

In addition to supporting the World Wide Web with Internet Information Server, Windows NT Server can also provide domain name services. With the DNS service installed, a Windows NT server can respond to client requests for IP address resolution. This way, clients can use fully qualified domain names, such as www.microsoft.com in a browser, and the Windows NT server will respond by providing the correct IP address. Once DNS has been installed and configured, any Internet client, including non-Microsoft clients, can request name resolution.

To successfully answer the questions for this objective, you need a firm understanding of several key terms. For definitions of these terms, refer to the Glossary in this book.

Key Terms

- Domain Name System (DNS)

- Dynamic Host Configuration Protocol (DHCP)

- Internet Information Server

70-068.04.04.001

What must be running on a Windows NT Server computer before you install DNS?

A. IIS

B. WINS

C. DHCP

D. TCP/IP

70-068.04.04.001

What must be running on a Windows NT Server computer before you install DNS?

▶ **Correct Answer: D**

A. **Incorrect:** Internet Information Server is not required before installing the Domain Naming System service.

B. **Incorrect:** Windows Internet Naming Service is used to resolve NetBIOS names to an IP address. It can be used with DNS, but is not required before installing DNS.

C. **Incorrect:** DHCP will assign and manage dynamic IP information as requested by clients on a network. While a Windows NT server can act as both a DHCP and DNS server, DHCP is not required before installing DNS.

D. **Correct:** DNS is used to resolve Internet host names, such as www.microsoft.com, to a specific IP address. Therefore, the TCP/IP protocol must first be installed before a Windows NT Server can act as a DNS server.

70-068.04.04.002

An IIS server is hosting a company's Internet Web site, and you need to create an intranet that is not accessible to unauthorized users from the World Wide Web.

The required result is to provide an intranet that will be accessible only to company employees.

The first optional result is to secure the site from intruders who use sniffers to obtain access to the intranet.

The second optional result is to secure the site from intruders who want to view the default Web document.

The proposed solution is to create an intranet that contains private company information, create links from the default Web document to secure areas, create a group account and assign the group the permissions to allow intranet browsing, place the user accounts of the employees who need access to the intranet into the group, and set the password authentication method for the WWW service to Allow Anonymous.

What does the proposed solution provide?

A. The required result and all optional results.

B. The required result and one optional result.

C. The required result but none of the optional results.

D. The proposed solution does not provide the required result.

70-068.04.04.002

An IIS server is hosting a company's Internet Web site, and you need to create an intranet that is not accessible to unauthorized users from the World Wide Web.

The required result is to provide an intranet that will be accessible only to company employees.

The first optional result is to secure the site from intruders who use sniffers to obtain access to the intranet.

The second optional result is to secure the site from intruders who want to view the default Web document.

The proposed solution is to create an intranet that contains private company information, create links from the default Web document to secure areas, create a group account and assign the group the permissions to allow intranet browsing, place the user accounts of the employees who need access to the intranet into the group, and set the password authentication method for the WWW service to Allow Anonymous.

What does the proposed solution provide?

▶ **Correct Answer: B**

A. **Incorrect:** The solution will realize the required result by requiring users to be validated before accessing the secure Web pages. In addition, with Allow Anonymous authentication, the user's name and password are secure because they are not transmitted over the network. However, this solution does not prevent intruders from viewing the default Web document.

B. **Correct:** The solution will restrict access by allowing only employees access to the secure site. In addition, intruders will not be able to gain access to user names and passwords since Allow Anonymous authentication will be used. Therefore, this is the correct answer.

C. **Incorrect:** Although the required result will be realized, using Allow Anonymous as the authentication method will also prevent intruders from accessing user names and passwords. Therefore, the first optional result will be realized, making this an incorrect answer.

D. **Incorrect:** Using group permissions will control access to the internal Web site. This meets the required result. Therefore, this answer is incorrect.

70-068.04.04.003

An IIS server is hosting a company's Internet Web site, and you need to create an intranet that is not accessible to the World Wide Web.

The required result is to provide an intranet on the IIS server that will be readily accessible only to company employees.

The first optional result is to secure the site from intruders who use sniffers to obtain access to the intranet.

The second optional result is to secure the site from intruders who use sniffers to view web content from the intranet.

The proposed solution is to create an intranet that contains private company information, create links from the default Web document to the intranet, create a group account and assign it the permissions to allow intranet browsing, place the user accounts of each employee who needs access to the intranet into the group, and set the password authentication method for the WWW service to Allow Anonymous and Basic authentication.

What does the proposed solution provide?

A. The required result and all optional results.

B. The required result and one optional result.

C. The required result but none of the optional results.

D. The proposed solution does not provide the required result.

70-068.04.04.003

An IIS server is hosting a company's Internet Web site, and you need to create an intranet that is not accessible to the World Wide Web.

The required result is to provide an intranet on the IIS server that will be readily accessible only to company employees.

The first optional result is to secure the site from intruders who use sniffers to obtain access to the intranet.

The second optional result is to secure the site from intruders who use sniffers to view web content from the intranet.

The proposed solution is to create an intranet that contains private company information, create links from the default Web document to the intranet, create a group account and assign it the permissions to allow intranet browsing, place the user accounts of each employee who needs access to the intranet into the group, and set the password authentication method for the WWW service to Allow Anonymous and Basic authentication.

What does the proposed solution provide?

▶ **Correct Answer: C**

A. **Incorrect:** Although this solution realizes the required result, using Basic authentication will allow an intruder using a sniffer to obtain user name and password information. Therefore, neither optional result will be realized with this solution.

B. **Incorrect:** With Basic authentication, the user name and password will be sent unencrypted across the network. An intruder using a sniffer will be able to obtain this information. Therefore, neither optional result will be realized with this solution.

C. **Correct:** This solution will restrict only access to the intranet. Therefore, the required result will be realized, but neither optional result will be achieved.

D. **Incorrect:** Using group permissions will control access to the internal Web site. This meets the required result. Therefore, this answer is incorrect.

Further Reading

Supporting Microsoft Windows NT Server in the Enterprise Training kit. Complete Lesson 5, "Configuring Internet Information Server," of Chapter 4, "Connectivity." In this lesson, installing and configuring IIS is discussed.

Windows NT Server 4.0 in the Enterprise Accelerated MCSE Study Guide. Read Chapter 17, "Internet Information Server" to learn more about configuring IIS for use on an intranet or the public Internet.

OBJECTIVE 4.5

Install and configure Remote Access Service (RAS).

The configuration options covered by this objective include:

- Configuring RAS communications

- Configuring RAS protocols

- Configuring RAS security

Windows NT Server can provide connectivity to clients that use dial-up phone lines. By installing Remote Access Service (RAS), clients such as Windows 95 or Windows 98 can then use their dial-up networking features to connect to and gain access to a domain. The Windows NT server both authenticates the client and acts as a gateway to network resources. Depending on the features implemented, the RAS server can require encrypted authentication and data transfer. When these encryption options are used, the information being transferred across the phone line will be secure. Otherwise, user names and passwords, for example, might be sent as clear text, which could violate corporate security policies.

To successfully answer the questions for this objective, you need a firm understanding of several key terms. For definitions of these terms, refer to the Glossary in this book.

Key Terms

- Basic authentication

- Global group

- Local group

- Remote Access Server (RAS)

70-068.04.05.001

Most users on your Windows NT network connect using 10BaseT Ethernet, but 25 employees telecommute using their phone lines to connect directly to the RAS server. You need to implement security for RAS.

The required result is to allow only telecommuters to access the domain through RAS.

The first optional result is to make sure passwords and user names do not travel from the RAS client to the RAS server in clear text.

The second optional result is to ensure that RAS data does not travel across the phone line in clear text.

The proposed solution is to grant dial-in permissions individually to the 25 telecommuters' Windows NT user accounts. Set the Encryption settings to Require Microsoft Encrypted Authentication, and enable Multilink.

What does the proposed solution provide?

A. The required result and all optional results.

B. The required result and one optional result.

C. The required result but none of the optional results.

D. The proposed solution does not provide the required result.

70-068.04.05.001

Most users on your Windows NT network connect using 10BaseT Ethernet, but 25 employees telecommute using their phone lines to connect directly to the RAS server. You need to implement security for RAS.

The required result is to allow only telecommuters to access the domain through RAS.

The first optional result is to make sure passwords and user names do not travel from the RAS client to the RAS server in clear text.

The second optional result is to ensure that RAS data does not travel across the phone line in clear text.

The proposed solution is to grant dial-in permissions individually to the 25 telecommuters' Windows NT user accounts. Set the Encryption settings to Require Microsoft Encrypted Authentication, and enable Multilink.

What does the proposed solution provide?

▶ **Correct Answer: B**

A. **Incorrect:** Although the required result will be realized with this solution, only the first optional result will be realized. Multilink binds multiple devices together, in order to increase bandwidth over slow networks, but does not encrypt the data being sent across the phone line.

B. **Correct:** Adding each user account that requires dial-in access realizes the required result. Implementing encrypted authentication meets the requirements of the first optional result. However, unless data encryption is enabled, the second optional result will not be realized.

C. **Incorrect:** Although the required result will be realized, the solution will also achieve the first optional result. Enabling encrypted authentication will prohibit user names and passwords from being sent over phone lines as clear text.

D. **Incorrect:** By setting permissions individually, you can control which users have access to the domain via RAS. Therefore, the required result will be realized and this answer is incorrect.

70-068.04.05.002

Most users on your Windows NT network connect using 10BaseT Ethernet, but 25 employees telecommute using their phone lines to connect directly to the RAS Server. You need to implement security for RAS.

The required result is to allow only telecommuters to access the domain through RAS.

The first optional result is to make sure passwords and user names do not travel from the RAS client to the RAS server in clear text.

The second optional result is to ensure that RAS data does not travel across the phone line in clear text.

The proposed solution is to grant dial-in permissions individually to the 25 telecommuters' Windows NT user accounts. Set the Encryption settings to Require Microsoft Encrypted Authentication and Require Data Encryption.

What does the proposed solution provide?

A. The required result and all optional results.

B. The required result and one optional result.

C. The required result but none of the optional results.

D. The proposed solution does not provide the required result.

70-068.04.05.002

Most users on your Windows NT network connect using 10BaseT Ethernet, but 25 employees telecommute using their phone lines to connect directly to the RAS Server. You need to implement security for RAS.

The required result is to allow only telecommuters to access the domain through RAS.

The first optional result is to make sure passwords and user names do not travel from the RAS client to the RAS server in clear text.

The second optional result is to ensure that RAS data does not travel across the phone line in clear text.

The proposed solution is to grant dial-in permissions individually to the 25 telecommuters' Windows NT user accounts. Set the Encryption settings to Require Microsoft Encrypted Authentication and Require Data Encryption.

What does the proposed solution provide?

Correct Answer: A

A. **Correct:** This solution meets the required result and both optional results. Adding each user account that requires dial-in access satisfies the required result. Specifying encrypted authentication and data will control how information is sent across the phone line, which meets the requirements of both optional results.

B. **Incorrect:** This solution meets the requirements of both optional results. Enabling encrypted authentication and data will ensure that information will be securely sent across the phone line.

C. **Incorrect:** Although the required result will be realized, both optional results will also be achieved by this solution. Enabling encrypted authentication and data will meet the requirements of both optional results.

D. **Incorrect:** You can control which users will have dial-up permission by including their user accounts in the RAS manager. Therefore, the required result will be achieved and this answer is incorrect.

70-068.04.05.003

Most users on your Windows NT network connect using 10BaseT Ethernet, but 25 employees telecommute using the Internet and RAS. You need to implement security for RAS.

The required result is to allow only telecommuters to access the domain through RAS.

The first optional result is to make sure passwords and user names do not travel from the RAS client to the RAS server in clear text.

The second optional result is to ensure that RAS data does not pass between the client and server unencrypted.

The proposed solution is to grant dial-in permissions individually to the 25 telecommuters' Windows NT user accounts, set the Encryption settings to Require Microsoft Encrypted Authentication, and enable callback security.

What does the proposed solution provide?

A. The required result and all optional results.

B. The required result and one optional result.

C. The required result but none of the optional results.

D. The proposed solution does not provide the required result.

70-068.04.05.003

Most users on your Windows NT network connect using 10BaseT Ethernet, but 25 employees telecommute using the Internet and RAS. You need to implement security for RAS.

The required result is to allow only telecommuters to access the domain through RAS.

The first optional result is to make sure passwords and user names do not travel from the RAS client to the RAS server in clear text.

The second optional result is to ensure that RAS data does not pass between the client and server unencrypted.

The proposed solution is to grant dial-in permissions individually to the 25 telecommuters' Windows NT user accounts, set the Encryption settings to Require Microsoft Encrypted Authentication, and enable callback security.

What does the proposed solution provide?

▶ **Correct Answer: D**

A. **Incorrect:** When users connect to a RAS server via the Internet, the callback security option cannot be used. You can only use callback security when the user dials into the RAS server using a modem and a phone line. Therefore, the required result will not be realized.

B. **Incorrect:** When users connect to a RAS server via the Internet, the callback security option cannot be used. You can only use callback security when the user dials into the RAS server using a modem and a phone line. Therefore, the required result will not be realized.

C. **Incorrect:** When users connect to a RAS server via the Internet, the callback security option cannot be used. You can only use callback security when the user dials into the RAS server using a modem and a phone line. Therefore, the required result will not be realized.

D. **Correct:** When users connect to a RAS server via the Internet, the callback security option cannot be used. You can only use callback security when the user dials into the RAS server using a modem and a phone line. Therefore, the required result will not be realized and this is the correct answer.

Further Reading

Supporting Microsoft Windows NT Server in the Enterprise Training kit. Complete Lesson 7, "Managing Remote Access Servers," of Chapter 4, "Connectivity." In this lesson, you will learn about configuring RAS on Windows NT Server.

Windows NT Server 4.0 in the Enterprise Accelerated MCSE Study Guide. Read Chapter 15, "Remote Access Server" to learn more about configuring and securing a RAS dial-up server.

Monitoring and Optimization

Windows NT Server includes two important troubleshooting tools: Performance Monitor and Network Monitor. Both of these utilities can be used to gather data associated with system and network performance. This data can then be analyzed to monitor the efficiency of the environment and to troubleshoot problems.

When using Performance Monitor, you can specify what data should be monitored. The categories of data that can be tracked are called *objects.* Each object provides specific data items, such as Available Bytes or Page Faults/sec. that can be monitored. These data items, called *counters*, are added to a list that Performance Monitor will automatically track. The number of objects and counters available depends on the services installed. By default, objects such as Memory, Processor, and PhysicalDisk are provided. As you add additional services to your system, additional objects will be included automatically. For example, when you install Internet Information Server with the FTP service, new objects for Internet Information Services Global and FTP Server are made available in Performance Monitor.

Under each object, you can then select specific counters to track. In the case of the FTP Server object, you can select from counters such as Connection Attempts, Bytes Received/sec, and Bytes Sent/sec. These are just 3 of the 16 counters included with the FTP Server object alone. The Performance Monitor will then display counter statistics in a real-time chart.

In addition, a report can be generated that summarizes the data that has been collected. Performance Monitor can often provide the necessary information to troubleshoot potential problems. However, it can also be used as a starting point to help you determine where a problem exists so that you can then use a more specific tool to finish the troubleshooting process.

While Performance Monitor is a general tool that allows you to observe many network and computer performance measures, Network Monitor serves a more specific purpose. It is used only to capture and display packet-by-packet breakdowns of network traffic. Network Monitor must be added to your system by installing the Network Monitor Tools and Agent component. Note, however, that for the complete version of

Network Monitor, which includes the ability to monitor remote computers, you will need to install the version of Network Monitor included with Microsoft System Management Server.

Once it's installed, you can use Network Monitor to capture packet information from the network. When you complete the capture process, you can begin evaluating the data or save it for later analysis. The data captured will reflect network activity associated with that computer. You can then filter and sort the data based on protocol or computer address. In the case of a large enterprise, this process may provide too much data, so Network Monitor allows you to individually exclude computers from the capture so that your data collection will be more specific.

Tested Skills and Suggested Practices

The skills you need to successfully master the Monitoring and Optimization objective domain on the exam include:

- **Using Performance Monitor to analyze system performance.**

  - Practice 1: Start Performance Monitor and begin tracking data on the number of Page Faults/sec. Use the Memory: Page Faults/sec counter. Open an application and check the status of the chart.

  - Practice 2: Create an alert in Performance Monitor to notify you if the available disk space is less than 25 percent. Use the LogicalDisk: % Free Space counter. Depending on your system, you may need to raise the percentage in order to have Performance Monitor generate an alert. For practice purposes, try setting the percentage to 99 percent to guarantee an alert will be generated.

  - Practice 3: Edit the alert created in practice 2 to generate alerts every 1 second. By default, an alert will be generated every 5 seconds.

  - Practice 4: Create a Performance Monitor report that uses the Processor: % Processor Time counter.

- **Using Network Monitor to analyze network traffic.**

  - Practice 1: If you have not already done so, install the Network Monitor Tools and Agent. To do this, right-click Network Neighborhood and click Properties. Select the Services tab and click Server. Click Add and locate Network Monitor Tools and Agent in the list. Click OK to install the component.

  - Practice 2: Start a data capture using Network Monitor. Save the results to a local file for future analysis.

  - Practice 3: Using a display filter, organize the data collected by Network Monitor by protocol and computer address.

OBJECTIVE 5.1

Establish a baseline for measuring system performance.

Establishing a baseline includes creating a database of measurement data. This database can then be used as a benchmark for evaluating the system. For example, using Performance Monitor, you can gather data about your environment for analysis. This captured data can then be compared against the baseline measurement to determine if a bottleneck exists. You can view the data in a chart or report format to aid your analysis. Monitoring memory usage, processor utilization, and disk performance are just some of the capabilities of Performance Monitor.

Performance Monitor can be scheduled to gather baseline data automatically using the Windows NT AT utility. You can also allow Performance Monitor to continue gathering data over specific periods of time in order to obtain data that is representative of peak periods.

To successfully answer the questions for this objective, you need a firm understanding of several key terms. For definitions of these terms, refer to the Glossary in this book.

Key Terms

- AT Scheduler

- Backup Domain Controller (BDC)

- Performance Monitor

- Primary Domain Controller (PDC)

70-068.05.01.001

You need to create a baseline for measuring the performance of a network that consists of a PDC, a BDC, and 20 client computers.

The required result is to create a measurement baseline using Performance Monitor.

The first optional result is to include information from the enhanced RAID disk counters.

The second optional result is to automate the collection of data.

The proposed solution is to start the Schedule service and enable the disk counters with the DISKPERF –YE command. Create a Performance Monitor Workspace (.PMW) settings file specifying a time interval and counters to log for system, processor, memory, logical disk, physical disk, server, cache, and network. Set Performance Monitor to start automatically at system startup. Use centralized monitoring and the AT command to start the Performance Monitor service for collection of data during periods of peak activity over a week.

What does the proposed solution provide?

A. The required result and all optional results.

B. The required result and one optional result.

C. The required result but none of the optional results.

D. The proposed solution does not provide the required result.

70-068.05.01.001

You need to create a baseline for measuring the performance of a network that consists of a PDC, a BDC, and 20 client computers.

The required result is to create a measurement baseline using Performance Monitor.

The first optional result is to include information from the enhanced RAID disk counters.

The second optional result is to automate the collection of data.

The proposed solution is to start the Schedule service and enable the disk counters with the DISKPERF –YE command. Create a Performance Monitor Workspace (.PMW) settings file specifying a time interval and counters to log for system, processor, memory, logical disk, physical disk, server, cache, and network. Set Performance Monitor to start automatically at system startup. Use centralized monitoring and the AT command to start the Performance Monitor service for collection of data during periods of peak activity over a week.

What does the proposed solution provide?

▶ **Correct Answer: A**

A. **Correct:** The proposed solution will create a measurement baseline by capturing data at peak periods during a week's time. Using the –YE switches, enhanced counters will be enabled to include information from a RAID (redundant array of independent disks) disk. In addition, with AT Scheduler, the process of capturing measurement data will be automated. This proposed solution meets the required result and both optional results.

B. **Incorrect:** Although the required result will be realized by this solution, both optional results will also be realized. Using the –YE switches and AT Scheduler, RAID information will be captured and the process will be automated.

C. **Incorrect:** The proposed solution will meet the requirements of both optional solutions. Using –YE will enable enhanced counters for use with a RAID disk, and AT Scheduler can be used to automate the data-gathering process.

D. **Incorrect:** Using Performance Monitor to gather data over the period of a week, targeting peak periods of network use, will provide a baseline measurement of data. This baseline can then be used as a reference point with which to compare future measurements.

70-068.05.01.002

You need to create a baseline for measuring the performance of a network that consists of a PDC, a BDC, and 20 client computers.

The required result is to create a measurement baseline using Performance Monitor.

The first optional result is to include information from the enhanced RAID disk counters.

The second optional result is to automate the collection of data.

The proposed solution is to start the Schedule service and enable the disk counters with the DISKPERF –Y command. Create a Performance Monitor Workspace (.PMW) settings file specifying a time interval and counters to log for system, processor, memory, logical disk, physical disk, server, cache, and network. Set Performance Monitor to start automatically at system startup. Use centralized monitoring and the AT command to start the Performance Monitor service for collection of data during periods of peak activity over a week.

What does the proposed solution provide?

A. The required result and all optional results.

B. The required result and one optional result.

C. The required result but none of the optional results.

D. The proposed solution does not provide the required result.

70-068.05.01.002

You need to create a baseline for measuring the performance of a network that consists of a PDC, a BDC, and 20 client computers.

The required result is to create a measurement baseline using Performance Monitor.

The first optional result is to include information from the enhanced RAID disk counters.

The second optional result is to automate the collection of data.

The proposed solution is to start the Schedule service and enable the disk counters with the DISKPERF –Y command. Create a Performance Monitor Workspace (.PMW) settings file specifying a time interval and counters to log for system, processor, memory, logical disk, physical disk, server, cache, and network. Set Performance Monitor to start automatically at system startup. Use centralized monitoring and the AT command to start the Performance Monitor service for collection of data during periods of peak activity over a week.

What does the proposed solution provide?

▶ **Correct Answer: B**

    A. **Incorrect:** Although this solution will meet the required result, it will realize only the second optional result. Using the –Y switch with the DISKPERF command will enable normal disk counters when the system is restarted. In order to gather information on a RAID disk, you will need to use the –YE switches.

    B. **Correct:** The proposed solution will realize only the required result and the second optional result. Performance Monitor will automatically gather measurement data, but the solution will not provide RAID information. Therefore, this is the correct answer.

    C. **Incorrect:** Using AT Scheduler will automate the process of gathering measurement data. The proposed solution meets the required result and the second optional result, making this answer incorrect.

    D. **Incorrect:** Using Performance Monitor over a week's period to gather data during peak periods on network usage meets the required result. Therefore, this answer is incorrect.

70-068.05.01.003

You need to create a baseline for measuring the performance of your newly installed network. There are 2 domain controllers and 20 client computers.

The required result is to create a measurement baseline using Performance Monitor.

The first optional result is to include information from the enhanced RAID disk counters.

The second optional result is to automate the collection of data.

The proposed solution is to enable the disk counters with the DISKPERF –Y command. Use Performance Monitor to collect data during periods of peak activity over a week.

What does the proposed solution provide?

A. The required result and all optional results.

B. The required result and one optional result.

C. The required result but none of the optional results.

D. The proposed solution does not provide the required result.

70-068.05.01.003

You need to create a baseline for measuring the performance of your newly installed network. There are 2 domain controllers and 20 client computers.

The required result is to create a measurement baseline using Performance Monitor.

The first optional result is to include information from the enhanced RAID disk counters.

The second optional result is to automate the collection of data.

The proposed solution is to enable the disk counters with the DISKPERF −Y command. Use Performance Monitor to collect data during periods of peak activity over a week.

What does the proposed solution provide?

▶ **Correct Answer: C**

    A. **Incorrect:** Although the required result will be realized, unless the −YE switches are used and the process is automated, neither optional result will be realized.

    B. **Incorrect:** Using the −Y switch with DISKPERF command will enable normal disk counters. It does not provide enhanced counters for measuring RAID information. In addition, the use of Performance Monitor is not automated. Therefore, neither optional result will be realized, making this answer incorrect.

    C. **Correct:** Only the required result will be realized with this solution. The −YE switches are required to measure a RAID disk, and AT Scheduler must be used in order to automate the data gathering process.

    D. **Incorrect:** Capturing data from peak periods over seven days should provide a reasonable set of measurement data. Therefore, the required result will be met by this solution.

70-068.05.01.004

Which two Microsoft tools with a Windows graphical interface can be used to display data regarding the performance of a processor in a Windows NT Server system?

A. Response Probe

B. Network Monitor

C. Performance Monitor

D. Task Manager

70-068.05.01.004

Which two Microsoft tools with a Windows graphical interface can be used to display data regarding the performance of a processor in a Windows NT Server system?

▶ **Correct Answers: C and D**

A. **Incorrect:** Response Probe is used to stress-test resources on a system. Using this tool, you can monitor the results of a system before deploying it in a production environment. However, Response Probe is not used to display performance information about a processor.

B. **Incorrect:** Network monitor is used to monitor network traffic and can capture data for future review. It would not be used to gather data about a system processor.

C. **Correct:** The Windows NT Performance Monitor offers the broadest capabilities to monitor the activities of a server. You can observe the information Performance Monitor has collected about processor performance in the many counters associated with the Processor object.

D. **Correct:** Task Manager displays information about the applications, processes, and threads that are currently running on the system. Its functions include the ability to graphically present live information about system processor usage.

70-068.05.01.005

You need to create a database of measurement data on your server named TECHSRV3. There are 2 domain controllers and 19 other client computers.

The required result is to use one tool to create a measurement baseline.

The first optional result is to exclude packets from a temporary employee using computer HR_4.

The second optional result is to set an alert to appear if the total free disk space on your server falls below 30 percent.

The proposed solution is to enable the disk counters with the DISKPERF –Y command, set a capture filter for use with Network Monitor using an inclusion line of EXCLUDE TECHSRV3<-> HR_4, and use the Alert View in Performance Monitor to set an alert when LogicalDisk: % Free Space falls below 30 percent. Create a Performance Monitor Workspace (.PMW) settings file specifying a time interval and counters to log for system, processor, memory, logical disk, physical disk, server, cache, and network, and use Performance Monitor to log the data on your server.

What does the proposed solution provide?

A. The required result and all optional results.

B. The required result and one optional result.

C. The required result but none of the optional results.

D. The proposed solution does not provide the required result.

70-068.05.01.005

You need to create a database of measurement data on your server named TECHSRV3. There are 2 domain controllers and 19 other client computers.

The required result is to use one tool to create a measurement baseline.

The first optional result is to exclude packets from a temporary employee using computer HR_4.

The second optional result is to set an alert to appear if the total free disk space on your server falls below 30 percent.

The proposed solution is to enable the disk counters with the DISKPERF –Y command, set a capture filter for use with Network Monitor using an inclusion line of EXCLUDE TECHSRV3<-> HR_4, and use the Alert View in Performance Monitor to set an alert when LogicalDisk: % Free Space falls below 30 percent. Create a Performance Monitor Workspace (.PMW) settings file specifying a time interval and counters to log for system, processor, memory, logical disk, physical disk, server, cache, and network, and use Performance Monitor to log the data on your server.

What does the proposed solution provide?

▶ **Correct Answer: B**

A. **Incorrect:** You cannot exclude a specific computer when creating a baseline measurement of data using the Performance Monitor. Setting a capture filter in Network Monitor will not affect the data gathered by Performance Monitor. Therefore, the first optional result will not be realized.

B. **Correct:** Using Performance Monitor, you can create a baseline measurement of data to serve as a reference point for system and network performance. By creating an alert on LogicalDisk: % Free Space, the system will monitor the available disk space. However, the first optional result cannot be realized since the syntax for excluding HR_4 is incorrect. Therefore, only the second optional result will be realized, making this the correct answer.

C. **Incorrect:** Although the required result will be realized, if you use the Alert View in Performance Monitor, this solution also meets the second optional result. Therefore, at least one optional result will be met, making this answer incorrect.

D. **Incorrect:** Using Performance Monitor, as configured by this solution, you will obtain measurement data that can be analyzed at a later time. This meets the required result, and this answer is incorrect.

Further Reading

Supporting Microsoft Windows NT Server in the Enterprise Training kit. Complete Lesson 1, "Server Analysis and Optimization Basics," of Chapter 5, "Server Monitoring and Optimization." In this lesson, you will learn about using the Performance Monitor utility included with Windows NT Server.

Supporting Microsoft Windows NT Server in the Enterprise Training kit. Complete Lesson 2, "Implementing a Measurement Baseline," of Chapter 5, "Server Monitoring and Optimization." In this lesson, you will learn about establishing a database of measurement information.

Windows NT Server 4.0 in the Enterprise Accelerated MCSE Study Guide. Read Chapter 18, "Server Optimization," to learn more about using Performance Monitor.

OBJECTIVE   5 . 2

Monitor performance of various functions by using Performance Monitor.

The subsystems to be monitored that are covered in this objective include:

- Memory

- Processor

- Disk

- Network

As introduced under the previous objective, Performance Monitor can be used to gather data for analysis. The results of this analysis may help administrators to diagnose performance problems and system bottlenecks.

The categories of data that can be tracked in Performance Monitor are called objects. Each object provides specific data items, such as Available Bytes or Page Faults/sec, that can be monitored. These data items are called counters. This objective covers the objects belonging to each of the four major subsystems of an NT server: Memory, Processor, Disk, and Network. Use the Memory object to track memory usage. This can help determine if additional RAM is required by the system. The Processor object will report whether additional processors, or upgraded processors, are needed to support the system given its current load. The Physical Disk, Logical Disk, Network Interface, and Network Segment objects will track how the disk and network subsystems are supporting the demands made on the system. Using these objects, you can determine whether an upgrade of the current hard drive or network interface card (NIC) is required.

To successfully answer the questions for this objective, you need a firm understanding of several key terms. For definitions of these terms, refer to the Glossary in this book.

Key Terms

- Counter

- Performance Monitor

70-068.05.02.001

Your Windows NT Server environment does not use RAID. From the Primary Domain Controller, you want to log the disk performance of a client computer with a single hard disk. When you check the disk statistics using Performance Monitor, they all show a 0 (zero) reading.

Which action will likely solve this problem?

A. Start the Server service at the client computer.

B. Start the Workstation service at the client computer.

C. Activate the disk performance statistics on the client computer with the DISKPERF –Y command.

D. Activate the disk performance statistics on the client computer with the DISKPERF –YE command.

70-068.05.02.002

You want to use Performance Monitor on a Windows NT Server system installed as a member server to monitor a group of servers. What is the maximum number of servers that can be monitored simultaneously?

A. 5

B. 25

C. 256

D. Number limited only by available RAM

70-068.05.02.001

Your Windows NT Server environment does not use RAID. From the Primary Domain Controller, you want to log the disk performance of a client computer with a single hard disk. When you check the disk statistics using Performance Monitor, they all show a 0 (zero) reading.

Which action will likely solve this problem?

▶ **Correct Answer: C**

A. **Incorrect:** Disk performance statistics must be started on the client computer using the DISKPERF command. The Server service will not provide the counters that Performance Monitor requires.

B. **Incorrect:** Disk performance statistics must be started on the client computer using the DISKPERF command. The Workstation service will not provide the counters that Performance Monitor requires.

C. **Correct:** Since the client is not using RAID, the –Y switch of the DISKPERF command must run on the client.

D. **Incorrect:** If the client were using a disk configured to support RAID, the –YE switches would be required. However, in this case, the client is not using RAID, and the –Y switch should be used.

70-068.05.02.002

You want to use Performance Monitor on a Windows NT Server system installed as a member server to monitor a group of servers. What is the maximum number of servers that can be monitored simultaneously?

▶ **Correct Answer: B**

A. **Incorrect:** Performance Monitor can support more than 5 concurrent servers.

B. **Correct:** Performance Monitor can support up to 25 concurrent servers.

C. **Incorrect:** Performance Monitor can support only up to 25 servers.

D. **Incorrect:** The number of servers supported by Performance Monitor is 25. The available RAM does not limit this number.

70-068.05.02.003

You install Windows NT Server on a Pentium-based computer with a single hard disk. You want to use Performance Monitor to view logical disk object counters on a remote computer.

What should you do?

A. No action is required.

B. Run DISKPERF –Y on the remote computer.

C. Install Network Monitor Agent on the remote computer.

D. Install Network Monitor Agent and run DISKPERF –Y on the remote computer.

70-068.05.02.003

You install Windows NT Server on a Pentium-based computer with a single hard disk. You want to use Performance Monitor to view logical disk object counters on a remote computer.

What should you do?

▶ **Correct Answer: B**

A. **Incorrect:** You must first enable the disk counters on the remote computer by using DISKPERF.

B. **Correct:** Only after you enable the counters using DISKPERF –Y will you be able to monitor the computer remotely.

C. **Incorrect:** The Network Monitor Agent is not required on the remote server. Instead, you must enable the disk counters by using DISKPERF.

D. **Incorrect:** Only DISKPERF –Y is required before you can monitor a remote computer.

70-068.05.02.004

You want to monitor the performance of your Windows NT Server system, which has two processors and two hard disk drives. There is a paging file on each disk.

The required result is to monitor the usage of both processors with one object counter.

The first optional result is to monitor for a memory shortage.

The second optional result is to monitor the amount of both paging files in use with one object counter.

The proposed solution is to use Performance Monitor to chart these object counters:

> System: % Total Processor Time
> Memory: Page Faults/sec
> Paging File: % Usage [_Total]

What does the proposed solution provide?

A. The required result and all optional results.

B. The required result and one optional result.

C. The required result but none of the optional results.

D. The proposed solution does not provide the required result.

70-068.05.02.004

You want to monitor the performance of your Windows NT Server system, which has two processors and two hard disk drives. There is a paging file on each disk.

The required result is to monitor the usage of both processors with one object counter.

The first optional result is to monitor for a memory shortage.

The second optional result is to monitor the amount of both paging files in use with one object counter.

The proposed solution is to use Performance Monitor to chart these object counters:

System: % Total Processor Time
Memory: Page Faults/sec
Paging File: % Usage [_Total]

What does the proposed solution provide?

► **Correct Answer: A**

A. **Correct:** The proposed solution uses the % Total Processor Time counter to monitor all processor activity. This meets the required result. The Memory: Page Faults/sec counter will monitor potential memory shortages, and the Paging File: % Usage [_Total] counter will monitor the paging files. These counters meet the requirements of both optional results. Therefore, this is the correct answer.

B. **Incorrect:** Although the required result will be realized by the solution, using the Memory: Page Faults/sec and Paging File: % Usage [_Total] counters will meet both optional results.

C. **Incorrect:** Use of the Memory: Page Faults/sec and Paging File: % Usage [_Total] counters will meet the requirements of both optional results.

D. **Incorrect:** The System: % Total Processor Time counter will monitor all processor activity, which meets the required result. Therefore, this answer is incorrect.

70-068.05.02.005

You want to monitor the performance of your Windows NT Server system, which has two processors and two hard disk drives. There is a paging file on each disk.

The required result is to monitor the usage of both processors with one object counter.

The first optional result is to monitor for a memory shortage.

The second optional result is to monitor the amount of both paging files in use with one object counter.

The proposed solution is to use Performance Monitor to chart these object counters:

> Processor: % Processor Time
> Memory: Page Faults/sec
> Paging File: % Usage [_Total]

What does the proposed solution provide?

A. The required result and all optional results.

B. The required result and one optional result.

C. The required result but none of the optional results.

D. The proposed solution does not provide the required result.

70-068.05.02.005

You want to monitor the performance of your Windows NT Server system, which has two processors and two hard disk drives. There is a paging file on each disk.

The required result is to monitor the usage of both processors with one object counter.

The first optional result is to monitor for a memory shortage.

The second optional result is to monitor the amount of both paging files in use with one object counter.

The proposed solution is to use Performance Monitor to chart these object counters:

Processor: % Processor Time
Memory: Page Faults/sec
Paging File: % Usage [_Total]

What does the proposed solution provide?

▶ **Correct Answer: D**

A. **Incorrect:** The proposed solution will require more than one object counter to monitor the available processors. Therefore, the required result will not be realized, making this answer incorrect.

B. **Incorrect:** Since there is more than one processor in this system, the Processor: % Processor Time would not be the correct counter to monitor all processors. This does not meet the required result.

C. **Incorrect:** Using the Processor: % Processor Time counter, only one processor can be monitored. Since this system has two processors and the required result is to monitor both with one counter, this solution does not meet the required result.

D. **Correct:** The proposed solution does not meet the required result because the Processor: % Processor Time counter is used. In a multiprocessor environment, the System: % Total Processor Time counter is required to monitor all processors.

70-068.05.02.006

You want to monitor the performance of your TCP/IP-based LAN.

The required result is to monitor directory database replication.

The first optional result is to monitor WINS.

The second optional result is to monitor DHCP traffic.

The proposed solution is to install the Simple Network Management Protocol (SNMP) Service and use Performance Monitor to chart these object counters:

SMB: File name
UDP Datagrams/sec
NBT: Question Name
Frame: Total frame length

What does the proposed solution provide?

A. The required result and all optional results.

B. The required result and one optional result.

C. The required result but none of the optional results.

D. The proposed solution does not provide the required result.

70-068.05.02.006

You want to monitor the performance of your TCP/IP-based LAN.

The required result is to monitor directory database replication.

The first optional result is to monitor WINS.

The second optional result is to monitor DHCP traffic.

The proposed solution is to install the Simple Network Management Protocol (SNMP) Service and use Performance Monitor to chart these object counters:

SMB: File name
UDP Datagrams/sec
NBT: Question Name
Frame: Total frame length

What does the proposed solution provide?

▶ **Correct Answer: D**

A. **Incorrect:** To monitor directory database replication, you should observe captures in Network Monitor, not Performance Monitor. In addition, SMB: File name, NBT: Question Name, and Frame: Total frame length are not Performance Monitor counters. Consequently, attempting this solution will not allow you to monitor directory database replication and does not meet the required result.

B. **Incorrect:** The required result will not be realized using the proposed solution. To monitor directory database replication, you should observe captures in Network Monitor, not Performance Monitor.

C. **Incorrect:** Performance Monitor will not allow administrators the ability to monitor directory database replication. Therefore the required result will not be realized.

D. **Correct:** Directory database monitoring, as defined by the required result, cannot be realized by this proposed solution. To monitor directory database replication, you should observe captures in Network Monitor, not Performance Monitor.

Further Reading

Supporting Microsoft Windows NT Server in the Enterprise Training kit. Complete Lesson 1, "Server Analysis and Optimization Basics," of Chapter 5, "Server Monitoring and Optimization." In this lesson, you will learn about using Performance Monitor for server analysis.

Supporting Microsoft Windows NT Server in the Enterprise Training kit. Complete Lesson 2, "Implementing a Measurement Baseline," of Chapter 5, "Server Monitoring and Optimization." In this lesson, using a baseline to help analyze a system is discussed.

Supporting Microsoft Windows NT Server in the Enterprise Training kit. Complete Lesson 3, "Performance Analysis, Forecasting, and Record Keeping," of Chapter 5, "Server Monitoring and Optimization." In this lesson, you will learn how to characterize workload on a server.

Supporting Microsoft Windows NT Server in the Enterprise Training kit. Complete Lesson 4, "Analyze File and Print Server Performance," of Chapter 5, "Server Monitoring and Optimization." In this lesson, creating and managing a shared file and printer environment is discussed.

Supporting Microsoft Windows NT Server in the Enterprise Training kit. Complete Lesson 5, "Analyzing Application Server Performance," of Chapter 5, "Server Monitoring and Optimization." In this lesson, configuring and managing servers that share applications is discussed.

Supporting Microsoft Windows NT Server in the Enterprise Training kit. Complete Lesson 6, "Analyzing Domain Server Performance," of Chapter 5, "Server Monitoring and Optimization." In this lesson, you will learn about specific server considerations when using a domain model.

O B J E C T I V E   5 . 3

Monitor network traffic by using Network Monitor.

Tasks covered by this objective include:

- Collecting data

- Presenting data

- Filtering data

Much like Performance Monitor, the Network Monitor utility can gather and save data for future analysis. The data gathered is specific to your local subnet. Once you finish the capture, you can begin filtering and sorting the data by protocol or computer address. This allows for a detailed review of the network traffic. By default, the Network Monitor captures data that originates from or is sent to your local computer. You can elect to exclude data sent between your local system and a remote computer. However, in order to capture the information associated with a remote computer, you will need the version of Network Monitor that comes with Microsoft System Management Server.

To successfully answer the questions for this objective, you need a firm understanding of several key terms. For definitions of these terms, refer to the Glossary in this book.

Key Terms

- Capture filter

- Display filter

- Network Monitor

70-068.05.03.001

You are using Network Monitor from the Windows NT Server 4.0 retail product. You have captured 500 frames from a Windows NT Server–based computer. You want to display data originating from one specific client computer sent to the server.

How should you proceed?

A. Create a display filter based on address.

B. Create a display filter based on protocol.

C. Create a capture filter based on protocol.

D. Create a capture filter based on address.

70-068.05.03.002

You are using Network Monitor from the Windows NT Server 4.0 retail product. Your network environment includes TCP/IP with WINS and DHCP. You have captured 900 packets from a Windows NT Server–based computer. You want to display data originating from one specific client computer to your server.

Which two methods can be used to accomplish this?

A. Edit the Address table.

B. Use a display filter by address.

C. Use a display filter by protocol.

D. Sort the Network address in the Capture window.

70-068.05.03.001

You are using Network Monitor from the Windows NT Server 4.0 retail product. You have captured 500 frames from a Windows NT Server–based computer. You want to display data originating from one specific client computer sent to the server.

How should you proceed?

▶ **Correct Answer: A**

A. **Correct:** By filtering on the computer's address, you can create a view specific to that computer.

B. **Incorrect:** Filtering by protocol will show all the data associated with all computers. In this case, a specific computer needs to be filtered.

C. **Incorrect:** Since you've already captured a number of frames, you only need to create a filter. There is no need to gather more data.

D. **Incorrect:** If you create a display filter based on address, you will not need to collect more data.

70-068.05.03.002

You are using Network Monitor from the Windows NT Server 4.0 retail product. Your network environment includes TCP/IP with WINS and DHCP. You have captured 900 packets from a Windows NT Server–based computer. You want to display data originating from one specific client computer to your server.

Which two methods can be used to accomplish this?

▶ **Correct Answers: B and D**

A. **Incorrect:** Since data has already been gathered, you need to create a display filter, or sort by address, to narrow the packets that originated from a certain computer.

B. **Correct:** By implementing a display filter, you can reduce the number of computers included in the data set. However, you can also sort on the computer's address to locate all packets associated with a specific computer.

C. **Incorrect:** If you create a display filter based on protocol, all the computers included in the data set will be shown. Since you want to analyze the data based on a certain computer, you should create a display filter based on the computer's address.

D. **Correct:** By sorting on a computer's address, you can organize the data that has been collected. This would be one alternative to creating a display filter using the computer's address.

70-068.05.03.003

There is a single domain Windows NT Server environment in your startup company. Your NetBEUI ThinNet bus network is growing rapidly. You want to use Network Monitor to monitor network traffic.

The required result is to install Network Monitor.

The first optional result is to collect packets on the network.

The second optional result is to save the captured data.

The proposed solution is to open the Network Neighborhood properties and add Network Monitor Tools and Agent. Start Network Monitor and click the Start Capture button. Click the Stop Capture button after 1 hour of monitoring during a peak network load. Click Save As from the File menu, and enter a valid file name with a .CAP extension.

What does the proposed solution provide?

A. The required result and all optional results.

B. The required result and one optional result.

C. The required result but none of the optional results.

D. The proposed solution does not provide the required result.

70-068.05.03.003

There is a single domain Windows NT Server environment in your startup company. Your NetBEUI ThinNet bus network is growing rapidly. You want to use Network Monitor to monitor network traffic.

The required result is to install Network Monitor.

The first optional result is to collect packets on the network.

The second optional result is to save the captured data.

The proposed solution is to open the Network Neighborhood properties and add Network Monitor Tools and Agent. Start Network Monitor and click the Start Capture button. Click the Stop Capture button after 1 hour of monitoring during a peak network load. Click Save As from the File menu, and enter a valid file name with a .CAP extension.

What does the proposed solution provide?

▶ **Correct Answer: A**

A. **Correct:** The proposed solution will install the necessary monitoring tool. In addition, by following the steps outlined to capture and save data, both optional results will be realized.

B. **Incorrect:** The steps outlined by the solution will both capture data and save the data for future analysis. This meets the requirements of both optional results.

C. **Incorrect:** Both optional results will be realized by following the steps described by the solution. The Network Monitor utility can be used to gather and save network traffic information.

D. **Incorrect:** Network Monitor Tools and Agent can be installed via the Network Neighborhood. This meets the required result.

70-068.05.03.004

There is a single domain Windows NT Server environment in your startup company. Your NetBEUI ThinNet bus network is growing rapidly. You want to use Network Monitor to monitor network traffic.

The required result is to install Network Monitor on your computer, named NTS4SE.

The first optional result is to capture packets on the network.

The second optional result is to exclude packets from being captured at the HR_4 computer.

The proposed solution is to open the Network Neighborhood properties and add Network Monitor Tools and Agent. Set a capture filter with an inclusion line of EXCLUDE ANY<— HR_4. Start Network Monitor and click the Start Capture button. Click the Stop Capture button after 1 hour of monitoring during a peak network load.

What does the proposed solution provide?

A. The required result and all optional results.

B. The required result and one optional result.

C. The required result but none of the optional results.

D. The proposed solution does not provide the required result.

70-068.05.03.004

There is a single domain Windows NT Server environment in your startup company. Your NetBEUI ThinNet bus network is growing rapidly. You want to use Network Monitor to monitor network traffic.

The required result is to install Network Monitor on your computer, named NTS4SE.

The first optional result is to capture packets on the network.

The second optional result is to exclude packets from being captured at the HR_4 computer.

The proposed solution is to open the Network Neighborhood properties and add Network Monitor Tools and Agent. Set a capture filter with an inclusion line of EXCLUDE ANY<— HR_4. Start Network Monitor and click the Start Capture button. Click the Stop Capture button after 1 hour of monitoring during a peak network load.

What does the proposed solution provide?

▶ **Correct Answer: A**

A. **Correct:** The proposed solution will install the tools necessary to gather network traffic data. In addition, this solution will capture packets generated by the network and exclude those created by the HR_4 computer. This meets the requirements of both optional results.

B. **Incorrect:** Following the steps described by this solution, data will be captured and the HR_4 computer will be excluded. Therefore, both optional results will be realized, making this answer incorrect.

C. **Incorrect:** The Network Monitor's Start Capture command will begin gathering data about the network's traffic. In addition, the use of an exclusion command will allow packets associated with HR-4 to be exempt. This meets the requirements of both optional results. Therefore, this answer is incorrect.

D. **Incorrect:** Network Monitor Tools and Agent can be installed via the Network Neighborhood. This meets the required result.

70-068.05.03.005

There is a single domain Windows NT Server environment in your startup company. Your NetBEUI ThinNet bus network is growing rapidly. You want to use Network Monitor to evaluate the situation.

The required result is to install Network Monitor on your computer named NTS4SE.

The first optional result is to capture packets on the network.

The second optional result is to exclude packets from a computer named HR_4.

The proposed solution is to open the Network Neighborhood properties and add Network Monitor Tools and Agent. Set a capture filter with an inclusion line of EXCLUDE NTS4SE—> HR_4. Start Network Monitor and click the Start Capture button. Click the Stop Capture button after 1 hour of monitoring during a peak network load.

What does the proposed solution provide?

A. The required result and all optional results.

B. The required result and one optional result.

C. The required result but none of the optional results.

D. The proposed solution does not provide the required result.

70-068.05.03.005

There is a single domain Windows NT Server environment in your startup company. Your NetBEUI ThinNet bus network is growing rapidly. You want to use Network Monitor to evaluate the situation.

The required result is to install Network Monitor on your computer named NTS4SE.

The first optional result is to capture packets on the network.

The second optional result is to exclude packets from a computer named HR_4.

The proposed solution is to open the Network Neighborhood properties and add Network Monitor Tools and Agent. Set a capture filter with an inclusion line of EXCLUDE NTS4SE—> HR_4. Start Network Monitor and click the Start Capture button. Click the Stop Capture button after 1 hour of monitoring during a peak network load.

What does the proposed solution provide?

▶ **Correct Answer: B**

A. **Incorrect:** The proposed solution will realize the required result and the first optional result. However, the correct syntax to exclude the HR_4 computer is EXCLUDE NTS4SE<— HR_4. Therefore, the second optional result will not be realized with this solution.

B. **Correct:** The proposed solution will install the Network Monitor and will capture network traffic data. This meets the required result and the first optional result. The second optional result will not be realized since the syntax for excluding the HR_4 computer is incorrect.

C. **Incorrect:** In addition to realizing the required result, the proposed solution will gather network data by using the Start Capture command. This meets the requirements of the first optional result. Therefore, this answer is incorrect.

D. **Incorrect:** Network Monitor Tools and Agent can be installed via the Network Neighborhood. This meets the required result.

Further Reading

Supporting Microsoft Windows NT Server in the Enterprise Training kit. Complete Lesson 1, "Network Analysis and Optimization Basics," of Chapter 6, "Network Monitoring and Optimization." In this lesson, the various types of network traffic that should be analyzed are described.

Supporting Microsoft Windows NT Server in the Enterprise Training kit. Complete Lesson 2, "Analyzing Client Initialization Traffic," of Chapter 6, "Network Monitoring and Optimization." In this lesson, you will learn about analyzing traffic generated by functions such as DHCP and WINS.

Supporting Microsoft Windows NT Server in the Enterprise Training kit. Complete Lesson 3, "Analyzing and Optimizing Client to Server Traffic," of Chapter 6, "Network Monitoring and Optimization." In this lesson, you will learn about analyzing traffic generated by client browsers, DNS, and intranet browsing.

Supporting Microsoft Windows NT Server in the Enterprise Training kit. Complete Lesson 4, "Analyzing Server to Server traffic," of Chapter 6, "Network Monitoring and Optimization." In this lesson, traffic generated by interserver communication, such as WINS or directory replication, is discussed.

Supporting Microsoft Windows NT Server in the Enterprise Training kit. Complete Lesson 5, "Predicting Network Traffic," of Chapter 6, "Network Monitoring and Optimization." In this lesson, guidelines used for predicting network traffic are presented.

O B J E C T I V E   5 . 4

Identify performance bottlenecks.

Using Performance Monitor, you can determine if performance bottlenecks exist on your system.

The following guidelines can be used to determine if a memory bottleneck exists. For each item, an acceptable range or value has been provided.

Pages/Sec	Acceptable range: 0–20
Available Bytes	Minimum of 4MB
Committed Bytes	Less than physical RAM
Pool Nonpaged Bytes	Remains steady, no increase

The following guidelines can be used to determine if a processor bottleneck exists:

% Processor Time	Less than 75 percent
% Privileged Time	Less than 75 percent
% User Time	Less than 75 percent
System: Processor Queue Length	Less than 2
Server Work Queues: Queue Length	Less than 2

The following guidelines can be used to determine if a disk bottleneck exists:

% Disk Time	Under 50 percent
Disk Queue Length	Acceptable range: 0–2

The following guidelines can be used to determine if a network bottleneck exists:

Bytes Total/sec	Function of the number of NICs and protocols used
Network Segment: % Network Utilization	Generally lower than 30 percent, switched networks may be higher

To successfully answer the questions for this objective, you need a firm under-standing of several key terms. For definitions of these terms, refer to the Glossary in this book.

Key Terms

- Performance Monitor

- Network Monitor

- Counters

70-068.05.04.001

Recently, network performance has decreased, and you suspect a bottleneck related to the network. You are preparing to use Performance Monitor to analyze network data.

The required result is to determine the amount of logon validation traffic.

The first optional result is to determine how much data is being transmitted and received.

The second optional result is to determine the percentage of the network bandwidth in use for your local segment.

The proposed solution is to add the Network Monitor Agent and use Performance Monitor to log and analyze data using these counters:

> Server: Bytes Total/sec
> Server: Logon/sec
> Server: Logon Total
> Network Segment: % Network Utilization

What does the proposed solution provide?

A. The required result and all optional results.

B. The required result and one optional result.

C. The required result but none of the optional results.

D. The proposed solution does not provide the required result.

70-068.05.04.001

Recently, network performance has decreased, and you suspect a bottleneck related to the network. You are preparing to use Performance Monitor to analyze network data.

The required result is to determine the amount of logon validation traffic.

The first optional result is to determine how much data is being transmitted and received.

The second optional result is to determine the percentage of the network bandwidth in use for your local segment.

The proposed solution is to add the Network Monitor Agent and use Performance Monitor to log and analyze data using these counters:

> Server: Bytes Total/sec
> Server: Logon/sec
> Server: Logon Total
> Network Segment: % Network Utilization

What does the proposed solution provide?

▶ **Correct Answer: A**

A. **Correct:** Using the Server: Logon/sec and Server: Logon Total counters will help you analyze the amount of logon validation traffic being generated on your network. This will realize the required result. The Server: Bytes Total/sec counter will help determine the amount of data being generated and the Network Segment: % Network Utilization counter will monitor network bandwidth. Using these counters, the optional results will be realized.

B. **Incorrect:** The proposed solution will realize the required result. The Server: Bytes Total/sec and Network Segment: % Network Utilization counters will meet the requirements of both optional results. Therefore, this answer is incorrect.

C. **Incorrect:** Although the required result will be realized, the Server: Bytes Total/sec and Network Segment: % Network Utilization counters meet the requirements of both optional results. Therefore, this answer is incorrect.

D. **Incorrect:** The Server: Logon/sec and Server: Logon Total counters will help you analyze the amount of logon validation traffic being generated on your network. This will realize the required result, making this answer incorrect.

70-068.05.04.002

You use Performance Monitor to check PhysicalDisk: % Disk Time. The value averages 95 percent. What is the recommended bottleneck detection procedure?

A. Check the processor usage.

B. Check to see if the paging file is too large.

C. Check to see if the paging file is too small.

D. Check to see if a memory shortage is causing excessive paging.

70-068.05.04.003

You use Performance Monitor to check PhysicalDisk: Disk Queue Length. The value averages 4. What is the recommended optimization procedure?

A. Add memory.

B. Upgrade the processor.

C. Upgrade the disk subsystem.

D. Upgrade the network subsystem.

70-068.05.04.002

You use Performance Monitor to check PhysicalDisk: % Disk Time. The value averages 95 percent. What is the recommended bottleneck detection procedure?

▶ **Correct Answer: D**

    A. **Incorrect:** Since the disk utilization percentage is so high, you should check to see if there is a shortage of memory. Use of the paging file could be the cause of the high disk usage.

    B. **Incorrect:** The size of the paging file will not affect the amount of disk utilization being generated by the system. If there is a shortage of memory, the amount of disk access will increase. Therefore, you should check the memory requirements.

    C. **Incorrect:** The size of the paging file will not affect the amount of disk utilization being generated by the system. If there is a shortage of memory, the amount of disk access will increase. Therefore, you should check the memory requirements.

    D. **Correct:** Windows NT Server uses a paging file to create additional available memory. As memory requirements exceed the available RAM, the system will page memory into and out of the paging file on the disk. This can cause excessive disk utilization. Therefore, the next step in troubleshooting this problem would be to verify the amount of paging generated by the system.

70-068.05.04.003

You use Performance Monitor to check PhysicalDisk: Disk Queue Length. The value averages 4. What is the recommended optimization procedure?

▶ **Correct Answer: C**

    A. **Incorrect:** The disk queue measures the amount of pending disk I/O requests. The larger the queue, the slower the disk subsystem. Adding additional memory will not increase the performance of the disk subsystem.

    B. **Incorrect:** If the System: Processor Queue Length is consistently greater than 2, the system processor should be upgraded or additional processors added. However, the processor capacity does not affect the size of the disk I/O request queue. This is controlled by the disk subsystem.

    C. **Correct:** If the PhysicalDisk: Disk Queue Length is consistently higher than 2, this means there is disk I/O congestion and the disk subsystem needs to be upgraded to increase performance.

    D. **Incorrect:** An unusually high disk queue length is a result of a slow disk subsystem. Therefore, this subsystem, not the network subsystem, must be upgraded.

70-068.05.04.004

Recently, network performance has decreased, and you suspect a bottleneck related to the network. You want to use Performance Monitor to analyze network data.

The required result is to determine the amount of logon validation traffic.

The first optional result is to determine how much data is being transmitted and received.

The second optional result is to determine the percentage of the network bandwidth in use for your local segment.

The proposed solution is to add the Network Monitor Agent and use Performance Monitor to record these counters:

    Server: Bytes Total/sec
    Server: Logon/sec
    Server: Logon Total

What does the proposed solution provide?

A. The required result and all optional results.

B. The required result and one optional result.

C. The required result but none of the optional results.

D. The proposed solution does not provide the required result.

70-068.05.04.004

Recently, network performance has decreased, and you suspect a bottleneck related to the network. You want to use Performance Monitor to analyze network data.

The required result is to determine the amount of logon validation traffic.

The first optional result is to determine how much data is being transmitted and received.

The second optional result is to determine the percentage of the network bandwidth in use for your local segment.

The proposed solution is to add the Network Monitor Agent and use Performance Monitor to record these counters:

> Server: Bytes Total/sec
> Server: Logon/sec
> Server: Logon Total

What does the proposed solution provide?

▶ **Correct Answer: B**

A. **Incorrect:** Although the required result will be realized, only the requirements of the first optional result will be met. You will need to monitor the Network Segment: % Network Utilization in order to measure network bandwidth.

B. **Correct:** Unless the Network Segment: % Network Utilization counter is used, the second optional result will not be realized. Therefore, this proposed solution meets the needs of the required result and only the first optional result.

C. **Incorrect:** Using the proposed solution, the required result will be realized. In addition, using the Server: Bytes Total/sec counter will return information about the amount of data being generated. This meets the requirements of the first optional result. Therefore, since one optional result will be realized, this answer is incorrect.

D. **Incorrect:** Since the proposed solution includes the Server: Logon/sec and Server: Logon Total counters, the required result of monitoring logon validation traffic will be realized. Therefore, this answer is incorrect.

70-068.05.04.005

Recently, network performance has decreased, and you suspect a bottleneck related to the network. You want to use Performance Monitor to analyze network data.

The required result is to determine the amount of logon validation traffic.

The first optional result is to determine how much data is being transmitted and received.

The second optional result is to determine the percentage of network bandwidth in use for your local segment.

The proposed solution is to add the Network Monitor Agent and use Performance Monitor to record these counters:

    Server: Logon/sec
    Server: Logon Total

What does the proposed solution provide?

A. The required result and all optional results.

B. The required result and one optional result.

C. The required result but none of the optional results.

D. The proposed solution does not provide the required result.

70-068.05.04.005

Recently, network performance has decreased, and you suspect a bottleneck related to the network. You want to use Performance Monitor to analyze network data.

The required result is to determine the amount of logon validation traffic.

The first optional result is to determine how much data is being transmitted and received.

The second optional result is to determine the percentage of network bandwidth in use for your local segment.

The proposed solution is to add the Network Monitor Agent and use Performance Monitor to record these counters:

> Server: Logon/sec
> Server: Logon Total

What does the proposed solution provide?

▶ **Correct Answer: C**

A. **Incorrect:** Using only the Server: Logon/sec and Server: Logon Total counters will meet the required result. Additional counters must be monitored to achieve the requirements of either optional result.

B. **Incorrect:** Using this proposed solution, neither optional result will be realized. Additional counters must be used in order to monitor the amount of data generated or network bandwidth.

C. **Correct:** Using the Server: Logon/sec and Server: Logon Total counters, the amount of logon validation traffic can be monitored. However, this solution does not meet the requirements of either optional result. Therefore, this answer is correct.

D. **Incorrect:** If only the Server: Logon/sec and Server: Logon Total counters are used, the amount of logon validation traffic generated can be monitored. This meets the needs of the required result, making this answer incorrect.

70-068.05.04.006

The performance of your Windows NT Server–based computer has decreased, and you want to use Performance Monitor to identify a possible bottleneck.

The required result is to check for a memory bottleneck.

The first optional result is to determine how much data is being transmitted and received.

The second optional result is to determine the percentage of network bandwidth in use for your local segment.

The proposed solution is to add the Network Monitor Agent and use Performance Monitor to record these counters:

> Server: Pool Nonpaged Failures
> Server: Bytes Total/sec

What does the proposed solution provide?

A. The required result and all optional results.

B. The required result and one optional result.

C. The required result but none of the optional results.

D. The proposed solution does not provide the required result.

70-068.05.04.006

The performance of your Windows NT Server–based computer has decreased, and you want to use Performance Monitor to identify a possible bottleneck.

The required result is to check for a memory bottleneck.

The first optional result is to determine how much data is being transmitted and received.

The second optional result is to determine the percentage of network bandwidth in use for your local segment.

The proposed solution is to add the Network Monitor Agent and use Performance Monitor to record these counters:

> Server: Pool Nonpaged Failures
> Server: Bytes Total/sec

What does the proposed solution provide?

▶ **Correct Answer: B**

A. **Incorrect:** The required result and first optional result will be realized with this solution. However, an additional counter must be used to monitor network bandwidth. Therefore, the second optional result will not be realized, making this answer incorrect.

B. **Correct:** The Server: Pool Nonpaged Failures counter will monitor memory usage and the Server: Bytes Total/sec counter will monitor the amount of data generated. Since these are the only two counters included in the proposed solution, this is the correct answer.

C. **Incorrect:** Using the Server: Bytes Total/sec counter will return information about the amount of data generated. This meets the requirements of the first optional result, making this answer incorrect.

D. **Incorrect:** Since the proposed solution implements the Server: Pool Nonpaged Failures counter, you can determine if a memory bottleneck exists. This meets the required result. Therefore, this answer is incorrect.

Further Reading

Supporting Microsoft Windows NT Server in the Enterprise Training kit. Complete Lesson 3, "Performance Analysis, Forecasting, and Record Keeping," of Chapter 5, "Server Monitoring and Optimization." In this lesson, you will learn how to characterize workload on a server.

Windows NT Server 4.0 in the Enterprise Accelerated MCSE Study Guide. Read Chapter 18, "Server Optimization" to learn more about identifying and managing system bottlenecks.

OBJECTIVE 5.5

Optimize performance for various results.

These results include:

- Controlling network traffic

- Controlling server load

In a Windows NT domain, you can implement a Primary Domain Controller to centralize administration of the domain. However, in a large environment, this can reduce efficiency, since the PDC will need to authenticate all user requests. By implementing Backup Domain Controllers you can share the authentication responsibilities between the PDC and BDCs. In addition, in the case of a wide area network (WAN), a BDC installed locally can both increase logon efficiency and reduce network traffic over the WAN.

In addition to implementing BDCs to increase overall efficiency, you may want to use a master domain model with trust relationships. This can provide an organization centralized overall management while also allowing for decentralized administration of local resources. As organizations grow, the requirements of the corporate network will also grow. These requirements may include not only the need to accommodate more users, but also the need for decentralized management of these users, such as with the emergence of a distributed workforce. As the administration of the network becomes more complex, a master domain model can be used to meet these requirements more efficiently than can a traditional single domain model.

To successfully answer the questions for this objective, you need a firm understanding of several key terms. For definitions of these terms, refer to the Glossary in this book.

Key Terms

- Backup Domain Controller (BDC)

- Master domain model

- Primary Domain Controller (PDC)

- Single domain model

70-068.05.05.001

Examine the network diagram shown below. The required result is that network links must not be saturated with logon validations, users in Los Angeles and Madrid must be able to access resources in Atlanta, and users from Atlanta must be able to access resources in Denver, Houston, and Dover.

The first optional result is to centralize user management.

The second optional result is to allow administrators in all locations to manage access to their own resources.

The proposed solution is to use the single domain model and name the domain Atlanta, place a PDC and one BDC in Atlanta, and place a BDC for the Atlanta domain at each remote location.

What does the proposed solution provide?

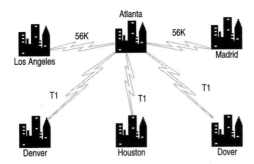

A. The required result and all optional results.

B. The required result and one optional result.

C. The required result but none of the optional results.

D. The proposed solution does not provide the required result.

70-068.05.05.001

Examine the network diagram shown on the previous page. The required result is that network links must not be saturated with logon validations, users in Los Angeles and Madrid must be able to access resources in Atlanta, and users from Atlanta must be able to access resources in Denver, Houston, and Dover.

The first optional result is to centralize user management.

The second optional result is to allow administrators in all locations to manage access to their own resources.

The proposed solution is to use the single domain model and name the domain Atlanta, place a PDC and one BDC in Atlanta, and place a BDC for the Atlanta domain at each remote location.

What does the proposed solution provide?

▶ **Correct Answer: B**

A. **Incorrect:** The proposed solution will realize the required result. In addition, this solution will provide centralized management. However, since a single domain model is being implemented, local administrators will not be able to manage access to their local resources. Therefore, since the second optional result will not be realized, this answer is incorrect.

B. **Correct:** Unless administrators can manage their own resources, the second optional result will not be realized. However, the required result and first optional result will be realized, making this answer correct.

C. **Incorrect:** Using a single domain model with the PDC located in Atlanta will facilitate centralized management. Therefore, since at least one optional result will be realized, this answer is incorrect.

D. **Incorrect:** Installing a BDC for the single domain in each city will limit the amount of logon validation requests sent across the WAN. This meets the required result, making this answer incorrect.

70-068.05.05.002

Examine the network diagram shown below.

The required result is that network links must not be saturated with logon validations, users in Los Angeles and Madrid must be able to access resources in Atlanta, and users from Atlanta must be able to access resources in Denver, Houston, and Dover.

The first optional result is to centralize user management.

The second optional result is to allow administrators in all locations to manage access to their own resources.

The proposed solution is to use the single master domain model and set up the necessary trust relationships, place a PDC and one BDC in Atlanta, and place a BDC for the Atlanta domain in each remote domain.

What does the proposed solution provide?

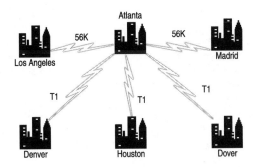

A. The required result and all optional results.

B. The required result and one optional result.

C. The required result but none of the optional results.

D. The proposed solution does not provide the required result.

70-068.05.05.002

Examine the network diagram shown on the previous page.

The required result is that network links must not be saturated with logon validations, users in Los Angeles and Madrid must be able to access resources in Atlanta, and users from Atlanta must be able to access resources in Denver, Houston, and Dover.

The first optional result is to centralize user management.

The second optional result is to allow administrators in all locations to manage access to their own resources.

The proposed solution is to use the single master domain model and set up the necessary trust relationships, place a PDC and one BDC in Atlanta, and place a BDC for the Atlanta domain in each remote domain.

What does the proposed solution provide?

▶ **Correct Answer: A**

A. **Correct:** Installing BDCs in each city will reduce the amount of logon validation traffic. This meets the required result. In addition, using a single master domain model will provide centralized management. Since the proposed solution also includes the creation of trust relationships, local administrators can still maintain their own resources. This meets both optional results.

B. **Incorrect:** The proposed solution meets the requirements of both optional results. Local BDCs will reduce logon traffic, and trust relationships between local domains and the master domain will allow administrators the ability to manage their local resources.

C. **Incorrect:** Although the required result will be realized, the proposed solution meets the requirements of both optional results. Logon validation traffic will be reduced, and administrators can still manage their local resources. Therefore, this answer is incorrect.

D. **Incorrect:** Installing a BDC for the single domain in each city will limit the amount of logon validation requests sent across the WAN. This meets the required result, making this answer incorrect.

70-068.05.05.003

Examine the Server dialog box shown below. Your primary domain controller runs WINS. Which optimization setting should you use for this computer?

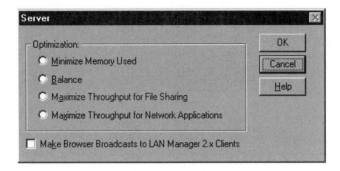

A. Balance

B. Minimize Memory Used

C. Maximize Throughput for File Sharing

D. Maximize Throughput for Network Applications

70-068.05.05.004

Your Windows NT network consists of a single domain with two Backup Domain Controllers. When logging on to the domain, the logon process is slow. Performance Monitor indicates that the average number of logons per second is approximately five.

What should you do to increase logon validation performance?

A. Add another Backup Domain Controller.

B. Add more memory to the Primary Domain Controller.

C. Increase the ReplicatorGovernor value in the Registry.

D. Decrease the ReplicationGovernor value in the Registry.

70-068.05.05.003

Examine the Server dialog box shown on the previous page. Your primary domain controller runs WINS. Which optimization setting should you use for this computer?

▶ **Correct Answer: D**

A. **Incorrect:** Since there will be a number of network requests for name information, selecting Balance would not optimize the server for these requests. Therefore, this is not the correct answer.

B. **Incorrect:** A server that supports WINS can use available memory to process requests more efficiently, as well as manage other server requirements. Minimizing Memory Used would not optimize server performance.

C. **Incorrect:** Supporting WINS requests does not require file access from clients. Therefore, this would not be the best choice for optimizing a server that is running WINS.

D. **Correct:** Since this server is also a WINS server, it will receive a large amount of requests for name information. Therefore, Maximizing Throughput for Network Applications will increase the server's performance in responding to these requests.

70-068.05.05.004

Your Windows NT network consists of a single domain with two Backup Domain Controllers. When logging on to the domain, the logon process is slow. Performance Monitor indicates that the average number of logons per second is approximately five.

What should you do to increase logon validation performance?

▶ **Correct Answer: A**

A. **Correct:** Implementing another BDC can reduce the amount of time required to validate a user. Remember, the location of the BDC can also affect logon performance. Be sure to analyze your network bandwidth when deciding where to locate an additional BDC.

B. **Incorrect:** Since there are additional BDCs already on the network, the slow logons indicate there are too many validation requests based on the available security providers. An additional BDC will help reduce the amount of time required to validate a user.

C. **Incorrect:** The amount of time required to replicate the directory database is not causing the long delay in validating users. The capacity of the domain to handle these requests must be increased by implementing an additional BDC.

D. **Incorrect:** The directory database replication is not the cause for the long validation times. An additional BDC is required to reduce the amount of time users wait to be authenticated.

70-068.05.05.005

Examine the single domain network diagram shown below.

Users in Amsterdam complain that logging on and browsing the network takes too long.

The required result is to decrease logon validations over the WAN.

The first optional result is to decrease DHCP and WINS traffic over the WAN.

The second optional result is to decrease directory replication traffic over the WAN.

The proposed solution is to install a BDC with DHCP and WINS in Amsterdam, change the Pulse parameter to 25, and configure both servers to be Pull partners.

What does the proposed solution provide?

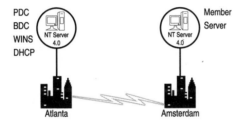

A. The required result and all optional results.

B. The required result and one optional result.

C. The required result but none of the optional results.

D. The proposed solution does not provide the required result.

70-068.05.05.005

Examine the single domain network diagram shown on the previous page.

Users in Amsterdam complain that logging on and browsing the network takes too long.

The required result is to decrease logon validations over the WAN.

The first optional result is to decrease DHCP and WINS traffic over the WAN.

The second optional result is to decrease directory replication traffic over the WAN.

The proposed solution is to install a BDC with DHCP and WINS in Amsterdam, change the Pulse parameter to 25, and configure both servers to be Pull partners.

What does the proposed solution provide?

▶ **Correct Answer: A**

A. **Correct:** A local BDC in Amsterdam will allow user validation to occur locally. This meets the required result. Installing DHCP and WINS on this local BDC will also eliminate the need to cross the WAN for these requests. This meets the requirement of the first optional result. Configuring the Pulse parameter and replication server type will reduce the amount of directory traffic over the WAN. This realizes the second optional result, making this answer correct.

B. **Incorrect:** Installing DHCP and WINS on the new BDC and configuring the replication server as described in the proposed solution meets the requirements of both, not just one, of the optional results.

C. **Incorrect:** Installing DHCP and WINS on the new BDC and configuring the replication server as described in the proposed solution meets the requirements of both of the optional results.

D. **Incorrect:** Installing a BDC in Amsterdam will eliminate the logon validation requests currently being sent over the WAN to Atlanta. In addition, this will reduce the amount of time users wait to be authenticated. Therefore, the required result will be realized, making this answer incorrect.

70-068.05.05.006

Examine the Server dialog box shown below.

Users access a 100-MB database on a server running SQL Server. Which optimization setting should you use to optimize the network performance of this file and print server?

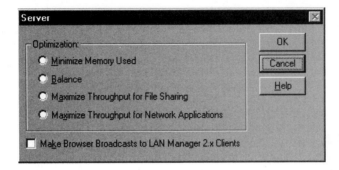

A. Balance

B. Minimize Memory Used

C. Maximize Throughput for File Sharing

D. Maximize Throughput for Network Applications

70-068.05.05.006

Examine the Server dialog box shown on the previous page.

Users access a 100-MB database on a server running SQL Server. Which optimization setting should you use to optimize the network performance of this file and print server?

▶ **Correct Answer: D**

A. **Incorrect:** Since SQL Server responds to network requests, using the Balance optimization would not be the most efficient solution.

B. **Incorrect:** Minimizing the amount of memory used for server functions will decrease performance of this server based on its role supporting SQL Server. Therefore, this answer is incorrect.

C. **Incorrect:** Although this server may provide file and print services, users accessing the SQL Server database will access the data through network requests. The correct optimization setting given this environment is Maximize Throughput for Network Applications.

D. **Correct:** SQL Server provides data through network protocols, such as named pipes. It does not allow users direct access to the database on the local file system. Since this computer is using SQL Server, the correct optimization is Maximize Throughput for Network Applications.

Further Reading

Supporting Microsoft Windows NT Server in the Enterprise Training kit. Complete Lesson 1, "Server Analysis and Optimization Basics," of Chapter 5, "Server Monitoring and Optimization." In this lesson, you will learn about using Performance Monitor for server analysis.

Supporting Microsoft Windows NT Server in the Enterprise Training kit. Complete Lesson 2, "Implementing a Measurement Baseline," of Chapter 5, "Server Monitoring and Optimization." In this lesson, using a baseline to help analyze a system is discussed.

Supporting Microsoft Windows NT Server in the Enterprise Training kit. Complete Lesson 3, "Performance Analysis, Forecasting, and Record Keeping," of Chapter 5, "Server Monitoring and Optimization." In this lesson, you will learn how to characterize workload on a server.

Supporting Microsoft Windows NT Server in the Enterprise Training kit. Complete Lesson 4, "Analyze File and Print Server Performance," of Chapter 5, "Server Monitoring and Optimization." In this lesson, creating and managing a shared file and printer environment is discussed.

Supporting Microsoft Windows NT Server in the Enterprise Training kit. Complete Lesson 5, "Analyzing Application Server Performance," of Chapter 5, "Server Monitoring and Optimization." In this lesson, configuring and managing servers that share applications is discussed.

Supporting Microsoft Windows NT Server in the Enterprise Training kit. Complete Lesson 6, "Analyzing Domain Server Performance," of Chapter 5, "Server Monitoring and Optimization." In this lesson, you will learn about specific server considerations when using a domain model.

Supporting Microsoft Windows NT Server in the Enterprise Training kit. Complete Lesson 1, "Network Analysis and Optimization Basics," of Chapter 6, "Network Monitoring and Optimization." In this lesson, the various types of network traffic that should be analyzed are described.

Supporting Microsoft Windows NT Server in the Enterprise Training kit. Complete Lesson 2, "Analyzing Client Initialization Traffic," of Chapter 6, "Network Monitoring and Optimization." In this lesson, you will learn about analyzing traffic generated by functions such as DHCP and WINS.

Supporting Microsoft Windows NT Server in the Enterprise Training kit. Complete Lesson 3, "Analyzing and Optimizing Client to Server Traffic," of Chapter 6, "Network Monitoring and Optimization." In this lesson, you will learn about analyzing traffic generated by client browsers, DNS, and intranet browsing.

Supporting Microsoft Windows NT Server in the Enterprise Training kit. Complete Lesson 4, "Analyzing Server to Server traffic," of Chapter 6, "Network Monitoring and Optimization." In this lesson, traffic generated by interserver communication, such as WINS or directory replication, is discussed.

Supporting Microsoft Windows NT Server in the Enterprise Training kit. Complete Lesson 5, "Predicting Network Traffic," of Chapter 6, "Network Monitoring and Optimization." In this lesson, guidelines used for predicting network traffic are presented.

Windows NT Server 4.0 in the Enterprise Accelerated MCSE Study Guide. Read Chapter 18, "Server Optimization" to learn more about identifying and managing system bottlenecks.

Troubleshooting

One of the most important aspects of being a Windows NT administrator is the ability to diagnose and troubleshoot problems. This objective covers a number of categories that relate to troubleshooting and supporting a Windows NT server. To help administrators, Windows NT includes a number of tools that can be used to resolve a variety of problems. In various situations, such as operating system installation problems, boot errors, or printing difficulties, you will need to know what tools are available and how to use them effectively.

Sometimes, problems can occur while the operating system is being installed. These are typically the result of hardware conflicts. You should use the Hardware Compatibility List (HCL), available at http://www.microsoft.com/hwtest/hcl, to verify that the hardware used by the computer is compatible with Windows NT Server. Once Windows NT Server is installed, you can begin using various troubleshooting utilities provided by the operating system. However, you should first have a good understanding of how Windows NT interacts with the computer when the operating system boots. This can help you troubleshoot potential problems associated with initialization files or a corrupt kernel.

When preparing for this objective, you will also want to review managing the System Registry. The Registry contains information critical for the proper operation of the system. Windows NT Server provides various tools for checking the state of the Registry and for backing up and restoring it. In addition, tools such as REGEDT32 can be used to view the current state of the Registry and manually edit entries as needed. In preparation for the exam, you should have a complete understanding of the Registry and how to edit entries using REGEDT32.

You will also need to know how to troubleshoot network problems. This includes problems that can arise when resources are shared or dial-up access is provided using RAS. Troubleshooting network problems also includes the effective application of user account permissions. Be sure you understand which privileges and capabilities each permission setting provides. For example, the No Access permission setting will override any other permissions a particular user may have. This is especially important when permissions have been granted through groups and the user is a member of multiple groups.

This objective also includes recovering from a fault-tolerant drive failure. Windows NT supports a variety of fault-tolerance options when configuring system drives. You will need to understand the differences between these options, such as stripe sets with parity and mirror sets. Specifically, you will need to know which tools and steps are required to recreate lost data when an individual drive has been replaced.

Tested Skills and Suggested Practices

The skills you need to successfully master the Troubleshooting objective domain on the exam include:

- **Resolving installation problems.**

  - Practice 1: Use the Hardware Compatibility List to determine if a particular computer is compatible with Windows NT Server.

  - Practice 2: Evaluate a server's hardware configuration using the Windows NT Hardware Detection Tool (NTHQ).

- **Troubleshooting possible configuration problems.**

  - Practice 1: Back up system files and the Registry using the Microsoft Backup utility.

  - Practice 2: Use the REGEDT32 utility to review the contents of the Registry.

- **Managing print devices.**

  - Practice 1: Configure a printer for use on a network.

  - Practice 2: Send a print job to a printer and manually pause the job using the print queue. Review the various features provided to restart and resume print jobs.

- **Implementing Remote Access Service.**

  - Practice 1: Install and configure RAS on a Windows NT Server.

  - Practice 2: Dial into the RAS server from a dial-up networking (DUN) client and use the RAS ADMIN utility, on the RAS server, to monitor the live connection.

- **Troubleshooting advanced problems.**

  - Practice 1: Start the Event Viewer and review the event log for each category: System, Security, and Application.

  - Practice 2: Use Disk Administrator to manage drive and partition configuration. Review the features available for recreating data that might be lost due to a drive failure for both a mirror-set and a stripe-set drive.

Choose the appropriate course of action to take to resolve installation failures.

Although Windows NT Server has been tested successfully on a variety of hardware configurations, noncompliant or faulty hardware can cause problems when first installing Windows NT. To minimize the chances of a hardware compatibility problem, check the HCL before starting the installation process to verify that the computer you are using will work with Windows NT Server. In addition to hardware conflicts, there may also be configuration problems outside the control of the Setup program. One example might be the absence of a PDC when adding a server to a particular domain. In such a case, Setup will function properly, but you will not be able to complete the installation until the PDC is found.

To successfully answer the questions for this objective, you need a firm understanding of several key terms. For definitions of these terms, refer to the Glossary in this book.

Key Terms

- Backup Domain Controller (BDC)

- Primary Domain Controller (PDC)

- Hardware Compatibility List (HCL)

- Windows NT Hardware Detection Tool (NTHQ)

70-068.06.01.001

You are installing Windows NT Server as a BDC in the CORP domain, and you see a message stating that the PDC could not be found. How should you proceed with the installation?

A. Continue with the installation, then physically connect the computer to the domain.

B. Do not continue with the installation until the PDC is connected to the CORP domain.

C. Install Windows NT Server as a PDC, and downgrade the computer to a BDC after connecting to the CORP domain.

D. Install Windows NT Server as a member server, and upgrade the computer to a BDC after connecting to the CORP domain.

70-068.06.01.002

You are installing Windows NT Server as a member server in the CERTIFIED domain, and you see a message stating that the domain could not be found. A computer account has already been created on the PDC.

How should you proceed with the installation?

A. Do not continue with the installation until the computer is connected to the CERTIFIED domain.

B. Install Windows NT Server as a BDC, and downgrade the computer to a member server after connecting to the CERTIFIED domain after installation.

C. Install Windows NT Server as a member of a workgroup, connect to the domain, and join the computer to the CERTIFIED domain after installation.

D. Install Windows NT Server as a PDC, and downgrade the computer to a member server after connecting to the CERTIFIED domain after installation.

70-068.06.01.001

You are installing Windows NT Server as a BDC in the CORP domain, and you see a message stating that the PDC could not be found. How should you proceed with the installation?

▶ **Correct Answer: B**

A. **Incorrect:** In order to create a BDC when installing Windows NT Server, the domain's PDC must be available on the network. You will need to complete the installation once the PDC becomes available.

B. **Correct:** A PDC is required at the time a BDC is configured on a Windows NT server. Once the CORP PDC becomes available, you can complete the installation. Note that this error can also occur if the BDC is using a NIC that is incompatible or not configured correctly.

C. **Incorrect:** You should not create a new PDC only because the current PDC cannot be located. There may be a problem with the new server, such as incorrect network drivers, rather than a problem with the original PDC. In addition, once implemented, a PDC cannot be demoted to a BDC when the original PDC is available.

D. **Incorrect:** A member server cannot be upgraded to a PDC or a BDC unless Windows NT Server is reinstalled. The installation should be paused, or terminated, until the PDC becomes available.

70-068.06.01.002

You are installing Windows NT Server as a member server in the CERTIFIED domain, and you see a message stating that the domain could not be found. A computer account has already been created on the PDC.

How should you proceed with the installation?

▶ **Correct Answer: C**

A. **Incorrect:** Since the computer is a member server, and the computer account has already been created on the PDC, you can complete the installation. When the domain becomes available, the member server can join the domain.

B. **Incorrect:** You cannot downgrade a PDC or a BDC to a member server once Windows NT has been installed. In this case, you should complete the installation using a workgroup and join the domain when it becomes available.

C. **Correct:** In order to complete the installation, you'll need to specify a domain or a workgroup. Since this computer will be a member server and the computer account has already been created in the PDC, you will be able to join the domain at a later time.

D. **Incorrect:** The only way to change a server from a PDC or a BDC is to reinstall the operating system. Since the domain cannot be found, you should configure the member server to join a workgroup. This can be changed once the domain becomes available.

70-068.06.01.003

You attempt to install Windows NT Server on a computer with an ESDI hard disk. When you reboot the computer, a message indicates Fatal System Error:0x0000006b. Which action will most likely resolve this installation failure?

A. Use the NoSerialMice switch in BOOT.INI.

B. Replace the hard disk with a compatible drive.

C. Resolve a possible IRQ conflict with the hard disk.

D. Replace the video adapter card with a compatible model.

70-068.06.01.004

Setup hangs while installing Windows NT Server 4.0 on an Intel-based computer. Which troubleshooting tools will help you resolve this problem? (Choose two.)

A. Hardware Compatibility List (HCL)

B. Microsoft Diagnostics (MSD)

C. NT Hardware Qualifier

D. HARDWARE.TXT

70-068.06.01.003

You attempt to install Windows NT Server on a computer with an ESDI hard disk. When you reboot the computer, a message indicates Fatal System Error:0x0000006b. Which action will most likely resolve this installation failure?

▶ **Correct Answer: B**

A. **Incorrect:** This error is associated with an incompatible hard drive. Windows NT does not support all ESDI drives. Check the hardware compatibility list and upgrade the drive.

B. **Correct:** Windows NT does not support all ESDI drives. If this error occurs, you will need to upgrade the drive to one supported by Windows NT Server.

C. **Incorrect:** This error is the result of an incompatible drive type. Windows NT does not support all ESDI drives. You will need to consult the Windows NT hardware compatibility list and upgrade the drive.

D. **Incorrect:** The fatal system error reported is associated with an incompatible hard disk. You will need to upgrade the drive since Windows NT does not support all ESDI drives.

70-068.06.01.004

Setup hangs while installing Windows NT Server 4.0 on an Intel-based computer. Which troubleshooting tools will help you resolve this problem? (Choose two.)

▶ **Correct Answers: A and C**

A. **Correct:** The Hardware Compatibility List can help you determine what devices might be causing the problem. Be sure that all components are listed on the HCL before installing Windows NT Server.

B. **Incorrect:** Windows NT Server does not support Microsoft Diagnostics (MSD).

C. **Correct:** The Windows NT Hardware Qualifier is a tool used to determine whether current hardware is compatible with Windows NT.

D. **Incorrect:** Windows NT Server does not support the HARDWARE.TXT file.

Further Reading

Supporting Microsoft Windows NT Server in the Enterprise Training kit. Complete Lesson 1, "Overview of Troubleshooting in the Enterprise," of Chapter 7, "Trouble-shooting Tools and Methods." In this lesson, Windows NT Server troubleshooting resources are discussed.

Windows NT Server 4.0 in the Enterprise Accelerated MCSE Study Guide. Read Chapter 20, "Troubleshooting" to learn more about resolving installation problems.

Choose the appropriate course of action to take to resolve boot failures.

When preparing for this objective, you will want to review the process Windows NT uses when booting the operating system. You will need to know which files, such as BOOT.INI and NTLDR, Windows NT uses in the boot process. In addition, you will also want to review how Windows NT supports booting into other operating systems, including MS-DOS.

To successfully answer the questions for this objective, you need a firm understanding of several key terms. For definitions of these terms, refer to the Glossary in this book.

Key Terms

- BOOT.INI

- BOOTSECT.DOS

- NTDETECT.EXE

- NTLDR

- NTOSKRNL.EXE

70-068.06.02.001

While booting a Windows NT Server computer, the following message appears:

```
I/O Error accessing boot sector file
multi(0)disk(0)rdisk(0)partition(1):\bootsect.dos
```

Which Windows NT file needs to be repaired or replaced?

A. NTLDR

B. BOOTSECT.DOS

C. NTOSKRNL.EXE

D. NTDETECT.COM

70-068.06.02.002

While booting a Windows NT Server computer, the following message appears:

```
NTDETECT v4.0 Checking Hardware. NTDETECT failed
```

Which Windows NT file needs to be repaired or replaced?

A. NTLDR

B. BOOTSECT.DOS

C. NTOSKRNL.EXE

D. NTDETECT.COM

70-068.06.02.001

While booting a Windows NT Server computer, the following message appears:

```
I/O Error accessing boot sector file
multi(0)disk(0)rdisk(0)partition(1):\bootsect.dos
```

Which Windows NT file needs to be repaired or replaced?

▶ **Correct Answer: B**

A. **Incorrect:** NTLDR is used by the Windows NT installation program to load the operating system. If the error message presented in the question is displayed, it means the BOOTSECT.DOS file is missing or corrupt.

B. **Correct:** BOOTSECT.DOS is used by the NTLDR program to boot into the MS-DOS operating system. If this message appears, it means the BOOTSECT.DOS file is missing or corrupt.

C. **Incorrect:** The error displayed is associated with a missing or corrupt BOOTSECT.DOS file, not the Windows NT kernel.

D. **Incorrect:** The NTDETECT program is used by Windows NT to detect the current hardware configuration upon startup. The error message displayed is associated with a missing or corrupt BOOTSECT.DOS file.

70-068.06.02.002

While booting a Windows NT Server computer, the following message appears:

```
NTDETECT v4.0 Checking Hardware. NTDETECT failed
```

Which Windows NT file needs to be repaired or replaced?

▶ **Correct Answer: D**

A. **Incorrect:** The NTLDR program is used by the Windows NT installation program to load the operating system. If the error message presented in the question is displayed, the NTDETECT program is corrupt.

B. **Incorrect:** BOOTSECT.DOS is used by the NTLDR program to boot into another operating system, such as MS-DOS. The error message displayed in this question is associated with a corrupt NTDETECT.

C. **Incorrect:** The error message displayed is associated with a damaged version of the NTDETECT program. NTOSKRNL.EXE is the Windows NT kernel, which is not associated with this error message.

D. **Correct:** The error message is associated with a corrupt version of the NTDETECT program. If such an error should occur, the NTDETECT file must be repaired or replaced from the Windows NT Server source disk.

70-068.06.02.003

This message appears when you attempt to boot a Windows NT Server computer:

```
Windows NT could not start because the following file system is missing or corrupt:
<winnt root>\system32\ntoskrnl.exe
Please reinstall a copy of the above file.
```

Which Windows NT files might need to be replaced or edited? (Choose all that apply.)

A. BOOT.INI

B. NTLDR

C. NTOSKRNL.EXE

D. NTDETECT.COM

E. BOOTSECT.DOS

70-068.06.02.003

This message appears when you attempt to boot a Windows NT Server computer:

```
Windows NT could not start because the following file system is missing or corrupt:
<winnt root>\system32\ntoskrnl.exe
Please reinstall a copy of the above file.
```

Which Windows NT files might need to be replaced or edited? (Choose all that apply.)

Correct Answers: A and C

A. **Correct:** The BOOT.INI file is used by the NTLDR application when this program is starting the appropriate operating system. If BOOT.INI becomes corrupt, Windows NT may not be able to locate the kernel, NTOSKRNL.EXE. Check the [Boot Loader] section of BOOT.INI and verify Windows NT is installed in the location specified in [Operating Systems].

B. **Incorrect:** The error displayed is associated with a corrupt or missing BOOT.INI or kernel, NTOSKRNL.EXE. NTLDR uses BOOT.INI to locate the kernel when booting the system. If a BOOT.INI exists, check both the [Boot Loader] and [Operating Systems] sections to verify correct entries.

C. **Correct:** The Windows NT installation program uses the NTLDR program to read the BOOT.INI file and locate the appropriate operating system when booting. If the Windows NT kernel file cannot be found or is corrupt, it will need to be replaced.

D. **Incorrect:** BOOTSECT.DOS is used by the NTLDR application to boot the system into another operating system, such as MS-DOS. This file is not associated with the Windows NT kernel.

Further Reading

Supporting Microsoft Windows NT Server in the Enterprise Training kit. Complete Lesson 4, "Examining the Boot Process," of Chapter 7, "Troubleshooting Tools and Methods." In this lesson, you will learn about the various phases used by Windows NT when booting, such as the initial, boot loader, and kernel.

OBJECTIVE 6.3

Choose the appropriate course of action to take to resolve configuration errors.

This objective focuses on backing up, editing, and restoring the System Registry. Windows NT uses the Registry to store information required by both the operating system and installed applications. If the Registry becomes corrupt, you may be required to reinstall Windows NT. However, there are tools, such as Microsoft Backup, that can be used to create backup versions of the Registry. These versions can then be restored in the event the Registry becomes corrupt.

In most instances, the data required by Windows NT or an application is automatically saved to the Registry during installation. As changes are required, such as when you install and configure new services, most Setup programs will update the Registry without requiring you to manually edit Registry entries.

However, in some cases, particularly during troubleshooting, you may need to create Registry keys, edit existing values, or add new values. Windows NT Server includes the REGEDT32.EXE utility to provide this ability. As a Windows NT administrator, you should have a complete understanding of the Registry, its organization, and the impact manually editing the Registry can have. Mistakes made in editing the Registry manually can cause problems for Windows NT since incorrect data can prevent services from running or even booting correctly. You should always be sure you have a backup of the Registry before directly making any modifications with REGEDT32.EXE.

To successfully answer the questions for this objective, you need a firm understanding of several key terms. For definitions of these terms, refer to the Glossary in this book.

Key Terms

- Event Viewer
- Microsoft Backup Utility
- REGEDIT
- REGEDT32
- Registry
- Remote Command Service (RCMD)

70-068.06.03.001

You have changed the configuration of a computer running Windows NT Server. The computer is a member server in your domain, and the operating system and data are protected by a tape backup.

An error occurs when you attempt to boot the computer, and you suspect a problem in the Registry. How should you proceed?

A. Use Registry Editor.

B. Use the RDISK.EXE utility.

C. Use the REGREST.EXE utility.

D. Use the Microsoft Backup utility.

70-068.06.03.001

You have changed the configuration of a computer running Windows NT Server. The computer is a member server in your domain, and the operating system and data are protected by a tape backup.

An error occurs when you attempt to boot the computer, and you suspect a problem in the Registry. How should you proceed?

Correct Answer: D

A. **Incorrect:** The Registry Editor is a Windows-based program. If the system cannot boot, you will not be able to use the Registry Editor. In addition, if the Registry is corrupt, you will need to re-store the entire Registry from a backup. The Registry Editor will not allow you to fully restore a corrupt Registry, so a recent backup should always be available.

B. **Incorrect:** The RDISK utility is used to create an emergency repair disk that can help restore a system. Normally this is not used to restore the Registry since space limitations on the floppy may prevent the entire Registry from being backed up. This should be used as a last resort when attempting to rebuild a system.

C. **Incorrect:** REGREST.EXE is a tool included on the *Windows NT Workstation Resource Kit* CD. The REGREST utility can be used to restore portions of the Registry, called *hives*. REGREST is not used to restore a previous version of the Registry when the current version becomes corrupt.

D. **Correct:** In order to restore a previous version of the System Registry, you will need to use the Microsoft NT Backup utility.

70-068.06.03.002

You change the configuration of a computer running Windows NT Server as a member server connected to your domain. An error occurs, and you suspect a problem in the Registry. You want to view Registry data for this server on the workstation in your office for troubleshooting purposes.

Which tools can be used to obtain data about the system configuration of the remote server? (Choose two.)

A. Remote Command Service (RCMD)

B. Windows NT Diagnostics (WINMSD)

C. Windows NT Diagnostics command-line utility (WINMSDP)

D. Windows NT Registry Editor (REGEDT32)

70-068.06.03.002

You change the configuration of a computer running Windows NT Server as a member server connected to your domain. An error occurs, and you suspect a problem in the Registry. You want to view Registry data for this server on the workstation in your office for troubleshooting purposes.

Which tools can be used to obtain data about the system configuration of the remote server? (Choose two.)

▶ **Correct Answers: A and C**

    A. **Correct:** The Remote Command Service, which is available in the *Windows NT Server Resource Kit*, provides administrators the ability to create a virtual console on a remote server. The remote server must have the RCMDSVC.EXE service installed and running before the client RCMD.EXE application can be used. You can then run command-line diagnostic tools on the remote server.

    B. **Incorrect:** The Windows NT diagnostic tool, WINMSD, is a Windows-based utility that provides information about a server. WINMSD cannot be run from a remote workstation.

    C. **Correct:** WINMSDP is the command-line version of the WINMSD diagnostic tool. Using a utility, such as RCMD, that creates a virtual console to be opened on a remote server, the WINMSDP utility can be launched on the remote server to begin the troubleshooting process.

    D. **Incorrect:** Although REGEDT32 will allow you to view data from a remote server, it is a Windows NT Server tool and cannot be run from a workstation.

70-068.06.03.003

You see a message in the Event Viewer stating that the redirector failed to load.

The required result is to use the Registry Editor to find services and dependencies related to the redirector.

The first optional result is to configure the computer so it will not become a browser if the master browser fails.

The second optional result is to provide the capability of adjusting the amount of data in a TCP/IP packet.

The proposed solution is to open Registry Editor and look in HKEY_LOCAL_MACHINE\ System\CurrentControlSet\Services\LanmanServer. Observe the values in DependOnGroup, DependOnService, Error Control, Image Path, Start, and Type. Use Registry Editor to set the parameter at HKEY_LOCAL_MACHINE\System\CurrentControlSet\Services\Browser\ MaintainServerList to AUTO.

What does the proposed solution provide?

A. The required result and all optional results.

B. The required result and one optional result.

C. The required result but none of the optional results.

D. The proposed solution does not provide the required result.

70-068.06.03.003

You see a message in the Event Viewer stating that the redirector failed to load.

The required result is to use the Registry Editor to find services and dependencies related to the redirector.

The first optional result is to configure the computer so it will not become a browser if the master browser fails.

The second optional result is to provide the capability of adjusting the amount of data in a TCP/IP packet.

The proposed solution is to open Registry Editor and look in HKEY_LOCAL_MACHINE\ System\CurrentControlSet\Services\LanmanServer. Observe the values in DependOnGroup, DependOnService, Error Control, Image Path, Start, and Type. Use Registry Editor to set the parameter at HKEY_LOCAL_MACHINE\System\CurrentControlSet\Services\Browser\ MaintainServerList to AUTO.

What does the proposed solution provide?

▶ **Correct Answer: D**

   A. **Incorrect:** Information about the redirector is located in LanmanWorkstation. Therefore, looking in LanmanServer will not provide the required result.

   B. **Incorrect:** The correct location in which to view information about the redirector is LanmanWorkstation. Therefore, the required result will not be realized. In addition, the proposed solution does not meet either optional result.

   C. **Incorrect.** The required result cannot be realized by this solution because the proper location in which to look for for information about the redirector is the LanmanWorkstation key, not LanmanServer.

   D. **Correct:** The correct location in the Registry is LanmanWorkstation, not LanmanServer. Therefore, the required result cannot be realized.

70-068.06.03.004

You see a message in the Event Viewer stating that the redirector failed to load.

The required result is to use Registry Editor to find services and dependencies related to the redirector.

The first optional result is to configure the computer so it will not become a browser if the master browser fails.

The second optional result is to provide the capability of adjusting the amount of data in a TCP/IP packet.

The proposed solution is to open the Registry Editor and look in HKEY_LOCAL_MACHINE\ System\CurrentControlSet\Services\LanmanWorkstation. Observe the values in DependOnGroup, DependOnService, Error Control, Image Path, Start, and Type. Use Registry Editor to set the parameter at HKEY_LOCAL_MACHINE\System\CurrentControlSet\Services\Browser\MaintainServerList to AUTO.

What does the proposed solution provide?

A. The required result and all optional results.

B. The required result and one optional result.

C. The required result but none of the optional results.

D. The proposed solution does not provide the required result.

70-068.06.03.004

You see a message in the Event Viewer stating that the redirector failed to load.

The required result is to use Registry Editor to find services and dependencies related to the redirector.

The first optional result is to configure the computer so it will not become a browser if the master browser fails.

The second optional result is to provide the capability of adjusting the amount of data in a TCP/IP packet.

The proposed solution is to open the Registry Editor and look in HKEY_LOCAL_MACHINE\ System\CurrentControlSet\Services\LanmanWorkstation. Observe the values in DependOnGroup, DependOnService, Error Control, Image Path, Start, and Type. Use Registry Editor to set the parameter at HKEY_LOCAL_MACHINE\System\CurrentControlSet\Services\Browser\MaintainServerList to AUTO.

What does the proposed solution provide?

▶ **Correct Answer: C**

A. **Incorrect:** Although the correct location in the Registry in which to find information about the redirector is LanmanWorkstation, the proposed solution does not meet the requirements of either optional result. Setting MaintainServerList to AUTO may result in this computer becoming a browser. In addition, the proposed solution includes no steps to adjust the default TCP/IP packet size.

B. **Incorrect:** The proposed solution does meet the required result, but neither optional result will be realized. Setting the MaintainServerList to AUTO may allow this server to be the master browser. In addition, there are no provisions in the proposed solution to adjust the size of a TCP/IP packet.

C. **Correct:** Using the LanmanWorkstation key, you can find information about the redirector. However, since the proposed solution may result in this computer becoming a browser and does not include steps to affect the TCP/IP packet size, it does meet either optional result.

D. **Incorrect:** Looking in the LanmanWorkstation key, you will find information about the redirector. Therefore, the proposed solution will meet the required result, making this answer incorrect.

70-068.06.03.005

You see a message in the Event Viewer stating that the redirector failed to load.

The required result is to use Registry Editor to find services and dependencies related to the redirector.

The first optional result is to configure the computer so it will not become a browser if the master browser fails.

The second optional result is to provide the capability of adjusting the amount of data in a TCP/IP packet.

The proposed solution is to open Registry Editor and look in HKEY_LOCAL_MACHINE\ System\CurrentControlSet\Services\LanmanWorkstation. Observe the values in DependOnGroup, DependOnService, Error Control, Image Path, Start, and Type. Use Registry Editor to set the parameter at HKEY_LOCAL_MACHINE\System\CurrentControlSet\Services\Browser\MaintainServerList to NO.

What does the proposed solution provide?

A. The required result and all optional results.

B. The required result and one optional result.

C. The required result but none of the optional results.

D. The proposed solution does not provide the required result.

70-068.06.03.005

You see a message in the Event Viewer stating that the redirector failed to load.

The required result is to use Registry Editor to find services and dependencies related to the redirector.

The first optional result is to configure the computer so it will not become a browser if the master browser fails.

The second optional result is to provide the capability of adjusting the amount of data in a TCP/IP packet.

The proposed solution is to open Registry Editor and look in HKEY_LOCAL_MACHINE\ System\CurrentControlSet\Services\LanmanWorkstation. Observe the values in DependOnGroup, DependOnService, Error Control, Image Path, Start, and Type. Use Registry Editor to set the parameter at HKEY_LOCAL_MACHINE\System\CurrentControlSet\Services\Browser\MaintainServerList to NO.

What does the proposed solution provide?

▶ **Correct Answer: B**

A. **Incorrect:** Although the solution meets the required result and the first optional result, no steps are included in the proposed solution to adjust the size of a TCP/IP packet.

B. **Correct:** If you use the LanmanWorkstation key and set the MaintainServerList value to NO, the required result and first optional result will be realized.

C. **Incorrect:** Since the proposed solution sets the MaintainServerList value to NO, the first optional result will be realized, making this answer incorrect.

D. **Incorrect:** Looking in the LanmanWorkstation key will provide information about the redirector. Therefore, the proposed solution will meet the required result, making this answer incorrect.

70-068.06.03.006

You see a message in the Event Viewer stating that the redirector failed to load.

The required result is to use Registry Editor to find services and dependencies related to the redirector.

The first optional result is to configure the computer so it will not become a browser if the master browser fails.

The second optional result is to provide the capability of adjusting the amount of data in a TCP/IP packet.

The proposed solution is to open Registry Editor and look in HKEY_LOCAL_MACHINE\ System\CurrentControlSet\Services\LanmanWorkstation. Observe the values in DependOnGroup, DependOnService, Error Control, Image Path, Start, and Type. Use Registry Editor to set the parameter at HKEY_LOCAL_MACHINE\System\CurrentControlSet\Services\Browser\MaintainServerList to NO. Add a TcpWindowSize parameter to the Registry at HKEY_LOCAL_MACHINE\System\ CurrentControlSet\Services\Tcpip.

What does the proposed solution provide?

A. The required result and all optional results.

B. The required result and one optional result.

C. The required result but none of the optional results.

D. The proposed solution does not provide the required result.

70-068.06.03.006

You see a message in the Event Viewer stating that the redirector failed to load.

The required result is to use Registry Editor to find services and dependencies related to the redirector.

The first optional result is to configure the computer so it will not become a browser if the master browser fails.

The second optional result is to provide the capability of adjusting the amount of data in a TCP/IP packet.

The proposed solution is to open Registry Editor and look in HKEY_LOCAL_MACHINE\ System\CurrentControlSet\Services\LanmanWorkstation. Observe the values in DependOnGroup, DependOnService, Error Control, Image Path, Start, and Type. Use Registry Editor to set the parameter at HKEY_LOCAL_MACHINE\System\CurrentControlSet\Services\Browser\MaintainServerList to NO. Add a TcpWindowSize parameter to the Registry at HKEY_LOCAL_MACHINE\System\ CurrentControlSet\Services\Tcpip.

What does the proposed solution provide?

▶ **Correct Answer: A**

   A. **Correct:** The proposed solution meets the requirements of all results. The LanmanWorkstation key is used to locate information about the redirector, the MaintainServerList is used to specify whether the computer can act as a master browser, and the size of a TCP/IP packet can be adjusted by adding the TcpWindowSize parameter to the Tcpip Registry entry.

   B. **Incorrect:** The proposed solution meets the requirements of both optional results. The MaintainServerList is used to control whether the computer can act as a master browser and the Tcpip entry can be used to set the size of a TCP/IP packet.

   C. **Incorrect:** The proposed solution meets the requirements of both optional results. The MaintainServerList is used to control whether the computer can act as a master browser, and the Tcpip entry can be used to set the size of a TCP/IP packet.

   D. **Incorrect:** Looking in the LanmanWorkstation key will provide information about the redirector. Therefore, the proposed solution will meet the required result, making this answer incorrect.

Further Reading

Supporting Microsoft Windows NT Server in the Enterprise Training kit. Complete Lesson 3, "Modifying the System Through the Registry," of Chapter 7, "Trouble-shooting Tools and Methods." In this lesson, you will learn about using the Registry Editor, and key Registry locations are described.

OBJECTIVE 6.4

Choose the appropriate course of action to take to resolve printer problems.

Depending on the network configuration and printer types in use, a number of possible problems can arise when sharing printer resources. Factors to consider in trouble-shooting a printer problem include the operating system of the computer hosting the printer, the network protocols in use, and the printer drivers installed on the client computers. In addition to troubleshooting configuration problems, this objective also discusses how to resume a print order when a problem occurs. For example, if the paper jams during a print job, you will need to understand how to use the print queue tool to restart or resume the job.

It will also be useful to have a clear understanding of the differences between the terms *print device* and *printer* or *logical printer*. The print device is the actual hardware device used to create the output. The printer, or logical printer, is the software between the computer's operating system and the physical printer.

To successfully answer the questions for this objective, you need a firm understanding of several key terms. For definitions of these terms, refer to the Glossary in this book.

Key Terms

- Data Link Control (DLC)

- Line printer daemon (LPD)

- Logical printer

- Print device

- Printer

70-068.06.04.001

You are adding a network printer to a small Windows NT workgroup. The workgroup has 15 users who all need to print to the local printer attached to a Windows NT 4.0 Workstation computer. Users have complained that they sometimes have problems printing, while at other times they are able to print with no problems.

What is the most likely cause of the problem?

A. An incorrect printer driver is installed on some computers.

B. Windows NT Workstation 4.0 supports only 10 user connections for a printer.

C. The Windows NT Workstation computer does not have enough physical RAM.

D. There is a frame type mismatch between the Windows NT Workstation and the attached printer.

70-068.06.04.001

You are adding a network printer to a small Windows NT workgroup. The workgroup has 15 users who all need to print to the local printer attached to a Windows NT 4.0 Workstation computer. Users have complained that they sometimes have problems printing, while at other times they are able to print with no problems.

What is the most likely cause of the problem?

▶ **Correct Answer: B**

    A. **Incorrect:** If an incorrect printer driver had been installed, users would never be able to success-fully print. Since the problem reported occurs intermittently, the problem cannot be associated with an incorrect printer driver.

    B. **Correct:** Since users are able to print sometimes but not others, the problem may be the limit of Windows NT Workstation. Consider moving the printer to a Windows NT server since Windows NT Server, not Workstation, is designed to support more than 10 concurrent clients.

    C. **Incorrect:** The amount of RAM on the workstation would not be the reason users are experiencing intermittent printing capabilities. Since the number of users attempting to print exceeds the num-ber of concurrent clients supported by Windows NT Workstation, you need to upgrade to Windows NT Server.

    D. **Incorrect:** Since the printer is connected directly to the Windows NT Workstation, the frame type will not affect its ability to support user requests.

70-068.06.04.002

You are the administrator of a network with 5 Windows NT Server 4.0 computers, 2 NetWare 4.11 servers, 30 Windows NT Workstation 4.0 client computers, and 2 UNIX client computers. A local printer attached to one of the Windows NT 4.0 servers is shared with no restrictive permissions.

The Windows NT 4.0 servers are able to communicate with the UNIX client computers using the TCP/IP protocol. The UNIX client computers, however, cannot print to the network printer. All other computers on the network can print to this printer.

How can you resolve this problem so the UNIX client computers can print to the network printer?

A. The LPD program must be installed on the UNIX client computers.

B. The DLC protocol must be installed on the UNIX client computers.

C. A UNIX client computer cannot print to a Windows NT 4.0 Server computer's shared printer.

D. The LPD program must be installed on the Windows NT 4.0 Server computer sharing the printer.

E. The DLC protocol must be installed on the Windows NT 4.0 Server computer sharing the printer.

70-068.06.04.002

You are the administrator of a network with 5 Windows NT Server 4.0 computers, 2 NetWare 4.11 servers, 30 Windows NT Workstation 4.0 client computers, and 2 UNIX client computers. A local printer attached to one of the Windows NT 4.0 servers is shared with no restrictive permissions.

The Windows NT 4.0 servers are able to communicate with the UNIX client computers using the TCP/IP protocol. The UNIX client computers, however, cannot print to the network printer. All other computers on the network can print to this printer.

How can you resolve this problem so the UNIX client computers can print to the network printer?

▶ **Correct Answer: D**

A. **Incorrect:** In order for UNIX clients to print to a network printer, you will need to first install the line printer daemon service on the Windows NT server. The UNIX clients will then require that the line printer remote (LPR) utility be installed.

B. **Incorrect:** Installation of the Data Link Control protocol is required only on the computer acting as a print manager to a Hewlett-Packard printer connected directly to the network.

C. **Incorrect:** Once the LPR utility has been installed on the UNIX client, and the LPD service has been installed on the Windows NT server, UNIX clients will then be able to print to a shared Windows NT printer.

D. **Correct:** The line printer daemon is a service designed to access print commands from clients running the LPR utility (such as UNIX clients). These clients will then be able to access a shared network printer.

E. **Incorrect:** Installation of the Data Link Control protocol is required on a Windows NT server only if that server is managing a Hewlett-Packard network printer that is connected directly to the network via its own NIC. Since the printer is connected directly to the Windows NT server, DLC is not required.

70-068.06.04.003

A user attempts to print a large document, but the print device encounters a paper jam while printing the second page. After clearing the paper jam, how should you print the document from the beginning?

A. Select Resume from the Document menu of the printer.

B. Select Restart from the Document menu of the printer.

C. Stop and restart the Server service at the print server.

D. Stop and restart the Spooler service at the print server.

70-068.06.04.003

A user attempts to print a large document, but the print device encounters a paper jam while printing the second page. After clearing the paper jam, how should you print the document from the beginning?

▶ **Correct Answer: B**

A. **Incorrect:** Selecting Resume will cause the print device to attempt to continue printing the document from the point when the paper jam occurred. The question asks that the document be printed from the beginning, which requires the Restart command.

B. **Correct:** Only by selecting Restart can you print the document from the beginning.

C. **Incorrect:** Since the problem was a paper jam, you do not have to stop and restart the print server. Instead, choose Restart from the Document menu in order to restart the print job from the beginning.

D. **Incorrect:** The Spooler Service does not have to be stopped and restarted in order to start printing the document from the beginning. Instead, click Restart on the Document menu.

Further Reading

Supporting Microsoft Windows NT Server in the Enterprise Training kit. Complete Lesson 6, "Managing Shared Resources," of Chapter 3, "Managing Enterprise Resources." In this lesson, you will learn about the permission settings supported by Windows NT Server.

Windows NT Server 4.0 in the Enterprise Accelerated MCSE Study Guide. Read Chapter 10, "Printing" to learn more about configuring and supporting printers in a non-Windows environment.

Choose the appropriate course of action to take to resolve RAS problems.

Just like Windows 95 and Windows NT Workstation, Windows NT Server can provide connectivity to remote clients via traditional phone lines. However, Windows NT Server provides greater control and security for remote clients. It does this through the Remote Access Service (RAS). RAS is used to specify which users have dial-up rights and how the clients access the network. Administrators can specify which protocols should be used and how they should be configured. For example, when using TCP/IP, clients can request protocol information, such as the IP address to use, the default gateway address, and a DNS server name. This allows administrators to control how the client interacts with the network without having to manually configure each remote client.

However, before a network protocol can be implemented, you must select a connection protocol. By default, the Point-to-Point Protocol (PPP) is used to allow clients to communicate with the server when connecting over a phone line. An alternative to clients connecting over a dial-up phone line is to connect via the Internet. In this case, the more secure Point-to-Point Tunneling Protocol (PPTP) can be used. To help troubleshoot potential problems with these connections, you can enable the creation of a PPP log file to analyze activity on the network. In addition, you can use the DUN Monitor utility, on the client, and the RAS ADMIN utility, on the server, to observe a live RAS session.

To successfully answer the questions for this objective, you need a firm understanding of several key terms. For definitions of these terms, refer to the Glossary in this book.

Key Terms

- Point-to-Point Protocol (PPP)

- Remote Access Service (RAS)

- TCP/IP

70-068.06.05.001

You are logged on to the network through a RAS client using TCP/IP. You attempt to ping across a router, but the attempt fails. What is the most likely configuration problem in the RAS phonebook under TCP/IP settings?

A. An IP Address is selected.

B. IP Header Compression is selected.

C. Default Gateway on Remote Network is selected.

D. Server Assigned Named Server Addresses is selected.

70-068.06.05.001

You are logged on to the network through a RAS client using TCP/IP. You attempt to ping across a router, but the attempt fails. What is the most likely configuration problem in the RAS phonebook under TCP/IP settings?

▶ **Correct Answer: C**

A. **Incorrect:** This setting allows you to give the station an IP address. The ability to ping across a router is not affected by this setting.

B. **Incorrect:** Enabling IP header compression will reduce overhead that is transmitted over the modem. Header compression will not affect whether or not you can ping across a router.

C. **Correct:** This error can occur because a new entry will be added to the client's route table that specifies unresolved IP addresses should be routed to the gateway on the RAS link. However, you must have this option enabled if the client needs to use other Internet applications, such as a Web browser or an FTP client.

D. **Incorrect:** This setting tells the client computer that the RAS server will determine the IP addresses of the WINS and DNS servers. Whether the server provides address information will not affect whether or not the client can ping across a router.

70-068.06.05.002

A Windows NT Server computer is configured to accept incoming calls from traveling employees via RAS. RAS is not authenticating some users, one of whom uses a PPP connection.

The required result is to create a log file for use in troubleshooting PPP connection problems.

The first optional result is to determine the highest level of authentication the dial-up networking (DUN) client will support for the RAS connection.

The second optional result is to choose a tool for use in viewing DUN status and error information.

The proposed solution is to enable the PPP.LOG file by accessing the Registry at HKEY_LOCAL_MACHINE\ SYSTEM\CurrentControlSet\Services\Rasman\PPP, and change the Logging parameter to 1. Adjust the authentication settings for the DUN client by trying the lowest authentication option on each side of the connection, and then increasing the authentication level. Use the DUN Monitor to show the statistics of the next RAS session.

What does the proposed solution provide?

A. The required result and all optional results.

B. The required result and one optional result.

C. The required result but none of the optional results.

D. The proposed solution does not provide the required result.

70-068.06.05.002

A Windows NT Server computer is configured to accept incoming calls from traveling employees via RAS. RAS is not authenticating some users, one of whom uses a PPP connection.

The required result is to create a log file for use in troubleshooting PPP connection problems.

The first optional result is to determine the highest level of authentication the dial-up networking (DUN) client will support for the RAS connection.

The second optional result is to choose a tool for use in viewing DUN status and error information.

The proposed solution is to enable the PPP.LOG file by accessing the Registry at HKEY_LOCAL_MACHINE\SYSTEM\CurrentControlSet\Services\Rasman\PPP, and change the Logging parameter to 1. Adjust the authentication settings for the DUN client by trying the lowest authentication option on each side of the connection, and then increasing the authentication level. Use the DUN Monitor to show the statistics of the next RAS session.

What does the proposed solution provide?

▶ **Correct Answer: A**

A. **Correct:** The proposed solution meets both the required and optional results. Using the Logging parameter, you can choose to begin logging a PPP session. This realizes the required result. Increasing the authentication level from the lowest to the highest while using the DUN Monitor to monitor the connection's statistics will meet the requirements of both optional results.

B. **Incorrect:** Although the required result will be realized by the proposed solution, both optional results will be realized as well. Therefore, this answer is incorrect.

C. **Incorrect:** Starting with the lowest and increasing the authentication level while checking the connection statistics using the DUN Monitor meets the requirements of both optional results.

D. **Incorrect:** Setting the Logging parameter to 1 will enable logging of a PPP session. This meets the required result, making this answer incorrect.

70-068.06.05.003

A Windows NT Server computer is configured to accept incoming calls from traveling employees via RAS. RAS is not authenticating some users, one of which uses a PPP connection.

The required result is to create a log file for use in troubleshooting PPP connection problems.

The first optional result is to determine the highest level of authentication the dial-up networking (DUN) client will support for the RAS connection.

The second optional result is to choose a tool for use in viewing DUN error information.

The proposed solution is to enable the PPP.LOG file by accessing the Registry at HKEY_LOCAL_MACHINE\SYSTEM\CurrentControlSet\Services\Rasman, and creating a Logging parameter with a value of 1. Adjust the authentication settings for the DUN client by trying the lowest authentication option on each side of the connection, and then increasing the authentication level. Use the DUN Monitor to show the statistics of the next RAS session.

What does the proposed solution provide?

A. The required result and all optional results.

B. The required result and one optional result.

C. The required result but none of the optional results.

D. The proposed solution does not provide the required result.

70-068.06.05.003

A Windows NT Server computer is configured to accept incoming calls from traveling employees via RAS. RAS is not authenticating some users, one of which uses a PPP connection.

The required result is to create a log file for use in troubleshooting PPP connection problems.

The first optional result is to determine the highest level of authentication the dial-up networking (DUN) client will support for the RAS connection.

The second optional result is to choose a tool for use in viewing DUN error information.

The proposed solution is to enable the PPP.LOG file by accessing the Registry at HKEY_LOCAL_MACHINE\SYSTEM\CurrentControlSet\Services\Rasman, and creating a Logging parameter with a value of 1. Adjust the authentication settings for the DUN client by trying the lowest authentication option on each side of the connection, and then increasing the authentication level. Use the DUN Monitor to show the statistics of the next RAS session.

What does the proposed solution provide?

▶ **Correct Answer: D**

A. **Incorrect:** The proposed solution does not meet the required result because an incorrect Registry location has been specified. The correct location is HKEY_LOCAL_MACHINE\SYSTEM\CurrentControlSet\Services\Rasman\PPP. In addition, the Logging parameter does not need to be created; it already exists by default.

B. **Incorrect:** You do not need to create the Logging parameter; it exists by default.. In addition, the Registry entry specified in the proposed solution is incorrect. Therefore, the required result cannot be realized.

C. **Incorrect:** The proposed solution references an incorrect Registry location. The Logging parameter is located under HKEY_LOCAL_MACHINE\SYSTEM\CurrentControlSet\Services \Rasman\PPP. Therefore, the required result cannot be realized by this solution.

D. **Correct:** The required result cannot be realized by this solution since an incorrect Registry key location has been specified. In addition, you must set the existing Logging parameter to 1 in order to log a PPP session. The Logging parameter does not have to be manually created.

Further Reading

Supporting Microsoft Windows NT Server in the Enterprise Training kit. Complete Lesson 7, "Managing Remote Access Servers," of Chapter 4, "Connectivity." In this lesson, you will learn about configuring and supporting RAS on a Windows NT Server.

OBJECTIVE 6.6

Choose the appropriate course of action to take to resolve connectivity problems.

System administrators often need to troubleshoot problems that are associated with maintaining the connections between clients on a large network. As a network grows, and more demands are placed on shared resources and security systems, administrators need a good understanding of the problems that can arise. Some of the connectivity problems discussed in this objective are related to unavailable servers, incorrect network protocols, and conflicting user permissions. For example, if a master browser is unavailable, clients will not be able to browse for network resources. When preparing for this objective, you will need to understand how to configure Microsoft clients to act as master browsers or backup browsers. In addition, you should know how to disable a computer's ability to act as a browser.

Besides troubleshooting problems associated with network browsing, administrators also need to know how to configure security. This includes the creation and management of trust relationships between domains as well as the proper application of user permissions within those domains. An incorrectly configured trust relationship, or conflicting user permissions, can cause connectivity problems for users. This, in turn, requires the administrator to troubleshoot the environment. Understanding how security affects access to other domains, and shared resources, will help an administrator quickly locate and resolve the problem.

To successfully answer the questions for this objective, you need a firm understanding of several key terms. For definitions of these terms, refer to the Glossary in this book.

Key Terms

- Global group

- Local group

- Master browser

70-068.06.06.001

A client computer in your domain has received an ERROR_BAD_NETPATH message, and users report that they cannot browse servers on their local network segment. Which methods can be used to resolve this problem? (Choose two.)

A. Establish at least one backup browser.

B. Establish at least one non-browser.

C. Restore connectivity to the master browser.

D. Restore connectivity to the domain master browser.

70-068.06.06.002

Your network environment includes a Windows NT Server domain with 700 users. NWLink is the only protocol in use. You have recently installed Windows NT Server on a Pentium-based computer as a member server. The installation was successful, but the new server is unable to connect to the network.

Which action will most likely resolve this problem?

A. Optimizing the binding order

B. Specifying the correct frame type

C. Specifying NWLink as the default protocol

D. Changing the Server properties to Maximize Throughput for Network Applications

70-068.06.06.001

A client computer in your domain has received an ERROR_BAD_NETPATH message, and users report that they cannot browse servers on their local network segment. Which methods can be used to resolve this problem? (Choose two.)

▶ **Correct Answers: A and C**

    A. **Correct:** The problem reported is associated with a nonexistent master browser. By configuring a backup browser, clients will be able to browse network resources when the original master browser is unavailable.

    B. **Incorrect:** Establishing a computer to never assume the role of a browser will not solve this problem. Computers configured in this manner will never assume the master browser role, even if the master browser becomes unavailable.

    C. **Correct:** In order to correct this problem, a master browser must be present on the network. If the original master browser is unavailable, a backup browser must be available in order to allow clients the ability to browse network resources.

    D. **Incorrect:** A master browser or a backup browser must be available on the network before clients can browse network resources.

70-068.06.06.002

Your network environment includes a Windows NT Server domain with 700 users. NWLink is the only protocol in use. You have recently installed Windows NT Server on a Pentium-based computer as a member server. The installation was successful, but the new server is unable to connect to the network.

Which action will most likely resolve this problem?

▶ **Correct Answer: B**

    A. **Incorrect:** If NWLink is the only protocol in use, the binding order will not affect whether the new computer can access the network.

    B. **Correct:** Since NWLink is the only protocol in use, you must be sure to configure the frame type to match that of the network.

    C. **Incorrect:** Since NWLink is the only protocol in use, you do not have to specify it as the default protocol.

    D. **Incorrect:** Optimizing how the server supports the network will not affect whether it has the basic ability to access the network.

70-068.06.06.003

There are two domains on your Windows NT network. A user logged in to the CERTIFIED domain is unable to access a print device in the POOL domain. You want to simplify network management. What should you do to allow this user to connect to the print device in the POOL domain? (Choose the best answer.)

A. Set up a two-way trust relationship between the domains.

B. Set up another user account for the user in the POOL domain.

C. Set up a one-way trust relationship where the POOL domain trusts the CERTIFIED domain.

D. Set up a one-way trust relationship where the CERTIFIED domain trusts the POOL domain.

70-068.06.06.003

There are two domains on your Windows NT network. A user logged in to the CERTIFIED domain is unable to access a print device in the POOL domain. You want to simplify network management. What should you do to allow this user to connect to the print device in the POOL domain? (Choose the best answer.)

▶ **Correct Answer: C**

A. **Incorrect:** Although this solution will solve the problem, it does not provide the most efficient or secure solution to the problem. Instead, consider using a one-way trust.

B. **Incorrect:** Creating a separate account will require the user to log on to the POOL domain to print. This is not the most efficient solution to the problem.

C. **Correct:** By creating a trust relationship, the user can log on to and access shared resource in the POOL domain. This provides the most efficient solution.

D. **Incorrect:** This solution reverses the trust relationship direction. To provide the ability for users in the CERTIFIED domain to access resources in the POOL domain, the POOL domain must trust the CERTIFIED domain.

70-068.06.06.004

A user is unable to access data in the \LSA folder on a Windows NT Server system. She is a member of the TECHPUB local group and the LOGISTICS local group. NTFS permissions to the \LSA folder are assigned to groups as follows:

> The TECHPUB local group has No Access.
> The LOGISTICS local group has Change permission.
> The EVERYONE group has Read permission.

As the administrator, what should you do to allow her to access the \LSA folder?

A. Remove her user account from the TECHPUB group.

B. Remove her user account from the EVERYONE group.

C. Grant Change permission for the \LSA folder to her user account.

D. Configure the Replicator service to copy the folder to her local hard disk.

70-068.06.06.004

A user is unable to access data in the \LSA folder on a Windows NT Server system. She is a member of the TECHPUB local group and the LOGISTICS local group. NTFS permissions to the \LSA folder are assigned to groups as follows:

> The TECHPUB local group has No Access.
> The LOGISTICS local group has Change permission.
> The EVERYONE group has Read permission.

As the administrator, what should you do to allow her to access the \LSA folder?

▶ **Correct Answer: A**

A. **Correct:** Since the TECHPUB group has No Access permission, regardless of what other access the user has, she will not be able to use the \LSA share. Only after being removed from the TECHPUB group will her other permissions allow her the appropriate access.

B. **Incorrect:** Removing the user from the EVERYONE group, which has permission to the \LSA share, will leave the user in the TECHPUIB group, which has the No Access permission. It is the TECHPUB group that prevents the user from gaining access to the share. Therefore, this answer is incorrect.

C. **Incorrect:** Since the user is in the TECHPUB group, which has the No Access permission setting, no other permissions will allow this user access to the \LSA share. No Access overrides all other permission settings.

D. **Incorrect:** Automating a process of copying files to a local drive is not the most efficient solution. Since the problem is associated with access permissions, you should consider first changing the user's permissions or group memberships to solve the problem.

Further Reading

Supporting Microsoft Windows NT Server in the Enterprise Training kit. Complete Lesson 2, "Examining Windows NT Architecture," of Chapter 7, "Troubleshooting Tools and Methods." In this lesson, the Windows NT architecture and techniques for troubleshooting are discussed.

OBJECTIVE 6.7

Choose the appropriate course of action to take to resolve resource access and permission problems.

Typically, when a user cannot access a network resource, the problem is caused by incorrectly configured security settings. For example, a particular user may be a member of multiple groups, and one of the groups has the No Access permission to a shared folder. In this case, regardless of the other permissions the user may have, even if this includes Full Control, the No Access permission will override these other permissions. Managing user access to shared resources requires careful management of both user permissions and group permissions. When preparing for this objective, be sure to understand which permission settings, such as Change permission and Read Only permission, allow which capabilities. In addition, you should understand the capabilities provided by the default groups, such as Administrators, Power Users, and Backup Operators.

To successfully answer the questions for this objective, you need a firm understanding of several key terms. For definitions of these terms, refer to the Glossary in this book.

Key Terms

- Change permission

- Full Control permission

- Global group

- Local group

- No Access permission

- NT file system (NTFS)

- Read Only permission

70-068.06.07.001

A user on a Windows NT 4.0 domain needs to edit a file on a Windows NT Server 4.0 computer with NTFS partitions. He is a member of the following groups with permissions to the file as shown:

Everyone group (Read Access)
Accounting group (Read Access)

What should you do to allow Change access to the file for this user?

A. Create a new local group with Change permissions to the file, and give the user membership in the group.

B. Change the Everyone group's access to Change access.

C. Change the Accounting group's access to Full Access.

D. Remove the user from both the Accounting group and the Everyone group.

70-068.06.07.001

A user on a Windows NT 4.0 domain needs to edit a file on a Windows NT Server 4.0 computer with NTFS partitions. He is a member of the following groups with permissions to the file as shown:

Everyone group (Read Access)
Accounting group (Read Access)

What should you do to allow Change access to the file for this user?

▶ **Correct Answer: A**

A. **Correct:** Changing the permissions for either of the existing groups is not the most efficient solution. Other users in those groups would then be granted the Change permission. Only by creating a new local group, and providing the appropriate permission, can the user access the file without allowing other users the same rights.

B. **Incorrect:** Although altering the permissions on the Everyone group will allow the user edit capabilities, it will also allow all other users the same rights. Therefore, this is not the most efficient solution.

C. **Incorrect:** Although altering the permissions on the Accounting group will allow the user edit capabilities, it will also allow all other users in this group the same rights. Therefore, this is not the most efficient solution.

D. **Incorrect:** Removing the user from both the Accounting and Everyone groups will deny the user any access to the file.

70-068.06.07.002

User DavidK on a Windows NT 4.0 domain needs to access a directory on a Windows NT Server 4.0 Intel-based computer with NTFS partitions. DavidK is a member of the Engineers global group. He is also a member of the following groups with permissions to the directory as shown:

> Everyone (List Access)
> Accounting group (Read Access)
> Power Users group (Add & Read Access)
> Replicator group (Change Access)

The user needs to change the permission levels for the directory, but is unable to do so. What must you do to allow the user to change permissions for this directory?

A. Create a new local group and add the Engineers global group to the new local group. Assign the new local group Full Control permissions to the directory.

B. Create a new local group and add it to the Engineers global group. Assign the Engineers global group Full Control permissions to the directory.

C. The Accounting group must be granted Full Control permission.

D. The Replicator group must be granted Add & Read permission.

70-068.06.07.002

User DavidK on a Windows NT 4.0 domain needs to access a directory on a Windows NT Server 4.0 Intel-based computer with NTFS partitions. DavidK is a member of the Engineers global group. He is also a member of the following groups with permissions to the directory as shown:

> Everyone (List Access)
> Accounting group (Read Access)
> Power Users group (Add & Read Access)
> Replicator group (Change Access)

The user needs to change the permission levels for the directory, but is unable to do so. What must you do to allow the user to change permissions for this directory?

▶ **Correct Answer: A**

A. **Incorrect:** Only by creating a new local group that has Full Control rights, and adding the Engineers global group, will the user be able to have directory permission change rights.

B. **Incorrect:** You cannot add a local group to a global group. In order to solve this problem, you should add the Engineers global group to a new local group that has Full Control rights.

C. **Incorrect:** Changing the Accounting group to Full Control will allow all members of that group complete control over the directory. This is not the most efficient solution.

D. **Correct:** Introducing Add and Read permission to the Replicator group will not provide the user the necessary rights to change the permission on the directory. For this, the user must have Full Control rights.

70-068.06.07.003

You are the administrator of a Windows NT domain. A user attempts to edit a file in the \DER folder on a Windows NT Server 4.0 computer with NTFS partitions, but is unable to do so. The \DER folder is shared with Full Control permission assigned to the Everyone group.

The user is a member of the following groups with permissions to the file as shown:

> Everyone group (Read Access)
> Accounting group (Read Access)

You want to allow the user to edit the file, but not take ownership of the file. Your supervisor told you to not alter the permissions assigned to existing groups, and to only grant the minimum level of permissions required for each user to perform their task. What should you do?

A. Grant the Change NTFS permission to the user account.

B. Grant the Full Control NTFS permission to the user account.

C. Grant the Change NTFS permission to the Everyone group.

D. Grant the Full Control NTFS permission to the Accounting group.

70-068.06.07.003

You are the administrator of a Windows NT domain. A user attempts to edit a file in the \DER folder on a Windows NT Server 4.0 computer with NTFS partitions, but is unable to do so. The \DER folder is shared with Full Control permission assigned to the Everyone group.

The user is a member of the following groups with permissions to the file as shown:

> Everyone group (Read Access)
> Accounting group (Read Access)

You want to allow the user to edit the file, but not take ownership of the file. Your supervisor told you to not alter the permissions assigned to existing groups, and to only grant the minimum level of permissions required for each user to perform their task. What should you do?

► **Correct Answer: A**

A. **Correct:** By granting the Change permission to the user, no other groups will be affected. In addition, this maintains the minimum level of permissions for each user.

B. **Incorrect:** Granting Full Control will allow the user to change permissions on the directory, including taking ownership. This does not support the requirements specified by the question.

C. **Incorrect:** Although granting the Change permission to the Everyone group will allow the user to edit files in the \DER folder, it does not meet the requirements of the question. The supervisor specified that the permissions currently set for each group cannot change.

D. **Incorrect:** Although Full Control will allow the user the ability to edit files, it also changes the Accounting group's permission settings and provides more rights than are necessary for all users in this group. This is in conflict with the supervisor's requests and is not the most efficient solution to the problem.

Further Reading

Supporting Microsoft Windows NT Server in the Enterprise Training kit. Complete Lesson 1, "User and Group Accounts," of Chapter 3, "Managing Enterprise Resources." In this lesson, you will learn to effectively apply and administer permissions.

O B J E C T I V E   6 . 8

Choose the appropriate course of action to take to resolve fault-tolerance failures.

The fault-tolerance methods covered by this objective include:

- Tape backup

- Mirroring

- Stripe set with parity

Regardless of the type of fault-tolerance, such as RAID, that may be implemented on a server, you will always want to make regular tape backups of critical data. To protect them against a catastrophic event, such as fire, where these tapes are stored is as important as creating them.

In addition to traditional tape backups, Windows NT Server supports data redundancy features, such as mirror sets and stripe sets with parity, that help recover data that is lost when a drive fails. In some cases, a faulty drive can be replaced and the data recovered without taking the computer off the network. Fault tolerance of this sort generally comes at the expense of drive performance. This objective discusses how to respond to drive failures when the data resides on tape, in a mirrored set, and in a stripe set with parity.

To successfully answer the questions for this objective, you need a firm understanding of several key terms. For definitions of these terms, refer to the Glossary in this book.

Key Terms

- Disk Administrator

- Emergency repair disk (ERD)

- Fault tolerance

- Mirror set

- Stripe set

- Stripe set with parity

70-068.06.08.001

You have a Windows NT Server computer with six SCSI hard disks. The system partition is located on disk 0, and disks 1 through 5 are a stripe set with parity. Disk 2 fails, and you replace the failed drive. What should you do next in the Disk Administrator?

A. No further action is required.

B. Choose Regenerate from the Fault Tolerance menu.

C. Choose Extend Volume Set from the Partition menu.

D. Make a new stripe set with parity, and restore from backup.

70-068.06.08.002

You have a Windows NT Server computer with six SCSI hard disks. The system partition is located on disk 0, and disks 1 through 5 are a stripe set with parity. Disks 2 and 3 fail, and you replace the failed drives. What should you do next in the Disk Administrator?

A. No further action is required.

B. Choose Regenerate from the Fault Tolerance menu.

C. Choose Extend Volume Set from the Partition menu.

D. Make a new stripe set with parity, and restore from backup.

70-068.06.08.001

You have a Windows NT Server computer with six SCSI hard disks. The system partition is located on disk 0, and disks 1 through 5 are a stripe set with parity. Disk 2 fails, and you replace the failed drive. What should you do next in the Disk Administrator?

▶ **Correct Answer: B**

A. **Incorrect:** Since the disk that failed was part of a stripe set with parity, you will need to regenerate the data that was contained on the faulty drive. This can be accomplished using Disk Administrator.

B. **Correct:** Since the disk that failed was part of a stripe set with parity, the lost data can be restored using the Regenerate command in Disk Administrator.

C. **Incorrect:** Extending a volume set will not restore lost data on a drive that was part of a stripe set. Instead, you will need to regenerate the data using Disk Administrator.

D. **Incorrect:** One of the main benefits of a stripe set with parity is that it allows the data on a drive that fails to be regenerated when the drive is replaced. This does not require restoring the data from a backup. Instead, use the Regenerate command in Disk Administrator.

70-068.06.08.002

You have a Windows NT Server computer with six SCSI hard disks. The system partition is located on disk 0, and disks 1 through 5 are a stripe set with parity. Disks 2 and 3 fail, and you replace the failed drives. What should you do next in the Disk Administrator?

▶ **Correct Answer: D**

A. **Incorrect:** Replacing the faulty drives will not automatically restore lost data. Since two drives in the stripe set failed, you will need to restore the data from a backup.

B. **Incorrect:** When one drive fails in a stripe set with parity, you can regenerate the lost data using Disk Administrator. However, in this case, two drives needed to be replaced. Therefore, the lost data must be restored from a backup.

C. **Incorrect:** Extending a volume set will not restore lost data on drives that were part of a stripe set. Instead, you will need to restore the data from a backup.

D. **Correct:** Since two drives in the stripe set were lost, the data cannot be automatically regenerated. You will need to create a new stripe set with parity and restore the data from a backup.

70-068.06.08.003

You have created a mirror set that includes the boot partition of your Windows NT Server system. One of the disks in the mirror set fails. After replacing the failed disk, how should you restore the mirror set?

A. Create a new mirror set, then break the original mirror set.

B. Break the original mirror set, then create a new mirror set.

C. Choose Recreate from the Partition menu in Disk Administrator.

D. Choose Regenerate from the Fault Tolerance menu in Disk Administrator.

70-068.06.08.004

A Windows NT member server contains six SCSI hard disks. A tape backup system is used to protect the data on all disks from catastrophic data loss. The disk containing the system partition is mirrored, while the other four disks are members of a stripe set with parity.

If one of the disks in the stripe set fails, what is the quickest way to recover from the failure once the failed hard disk is replaced?

A. Restore from backup.

B. Recreate the stripe set relationship.

C. Repair the stripe set using the ERD.

D. Regenerate the stripe set using Disk Administrator.

70-068.06.08.003

You have created a mirror set that includes the boot partition of your Windows NT Server system. One of the disks in the mirror set fails. After replacing the failed disk, how should you restore the mirror set?

▶ **Correct Answer: B**

A. **Incorrect:** To restore the mirror set, you must first break the original. The steps in this proposed solution are reversed. Therefore, this answer is incorrect.

B. **Correct:** In order to restore a mirror set, you must first break the original. You can then create a new mirror set with the new drive.

C. **Incorrect:** To restore a mirror set, you cannot recreate it from the Partition menu in Disk Administrator. Instead, you must break the original mirror set and create a new one.

D. **Incorrect:** The Regenerate command will restore a drive that was replaced as part of a stripe set. If you have a mirror set with a new drive, you must first break the original mirror set and create a new one.

70-068.06.08.004

A Windows NT member server contains six SCSI hard disks. A tape backup system is used to protect the data on all disks from catastrophic data loss. The disk containing the system partition is mirrored, while the other four disks are members of a stripe set with parity.

If one of the disks in the stripe set fails, what is the quickest way to recover from the failure once the failed hard disk is replaced?

▶ **Correct Answer: D**

A. **Incorrect:** Since you are using a stripe set with parity, you can regenerate the lost data using Disk Administrator.

B. **Incorrect:** You do not have to recreate the stripe set relationship, as you do with a mirror set. Instead, use Disk Administrator to regenerate the lost data.

C. **Incorrect:** You cannot use the emergency repair disk to recover lost data. Since you have implemented a stripe set with parity, you can easily regenerate the data using Disk Administrator.

D. **Correct:** The Regenerate command in Disk Administrator is used to restore lost data on a drive that has been replaced as part of a stripe set.

70-068.06.08.005

A Windows NT member server contains six SCSI hard disks. A tape backup system is used to protect the data on all disks from catastrophic data loss. The disk containing the system partition is mirrored, while the other four disks are members of a stripe set with parity.

If the disk containing the system partition fails, what is the quickest way to recover from the failure once the failed hard disk is replaced?

A. Restore from backup.

B. Repair the mirror set using the ERD.

C. Regenerate the mirror set using Disk Administrator.

D. Break the original mirror set, and then create a new mirror set relationship.

70-068.06.08.006

A Windows NT member server contains five SCSI hard disks. One disk contains the system partition, while the other four store data and applications. A tape backup system and a stripe set with parity are used to protect information stored on the server hard disks.

If the disk containing the system partition fails, what should you do to recover from the failure once the failed hard disk is replaced?

A. Restore from backup.

B. Repair using the ERD.

C. Regenerate the stripe set using Disk Administrator.

D. Break the stripe set, and specify the new system partition.

70-068.06.08.005

A Windows NT member server contains six SCSI hard disks. A tape backup system is used to protect the data on all disks from catastrophic data loss. The disk containing the system partition is mirrored, while the other four disks are members of a stripe set with parity.

If the disk containing the system partition fails, what is the quickest way to recover from the failure once the failed hard disk is replaced?

► **Correct Answer: D**

A. **Incorrect:** Since the drive was part of a mirror set, you will first need to break the original set and then recreate it to recover the lost data.

B. **Incorrect:** You cannot use the emergency repair disk to recover lost data. Instead, since the drive was part of a mirror set, you must break and recreate the mirror set to recover the lost data.

C. **Incorrect:** You use the regenerate command in Disk Administrator to recover a drive that is part of a stripe set.

D. **Correct:** In order to recover the data on a drive that has been replaced as part of a mirror set, you must first break the original mirror set and create a new one.

70-068.06.08.006

A Windows NT member server contains five SCSI hard disks. One disk contains the system partition, while the other four store data and applications. A tape backup system and a stripe set with parity are used to protect information stored on the server hard disks.

If the disk containing the system partition fails, what should you do to recover from the failure once the failed hard disk is replaced?

► **Correct Answer: A**

A. **Correct:** Since the system drive has no fault tolerance associated with it, you will need to recover the lost data from a tape backup.

B. **Incorrect:** You cannot use the emergency repair disk to recover lost data. In this case, you must restore the lost data using a backup.

C. **Incorrect:** You use the regenerate command in Disk Administrator to recover a drive that is part of a stripe set. Since the drive that was lost has no fault tolerance, you must restore the data from a backup.

D. **Incorrect:** Since this drive is not part of a stripe set with parity or a mirror set, you will need to use a backup in order to restore the drive.

Further Reading

Supporting Microsoft Windows NT Server in the Enterprise Training kit. Complete Lesson 2, "Managing Partitions," of Chapter 1, "Planning the Enterprise with Microsoft Windows NT Server 4.0." In this lesson, you will learn about implementing fault tolerance.

OBJECTIVE 6.9

Perform advanced problem resolution.

The tasks covered by this objective include:

- Diagnosing and interpreting a blue screen

- Configuring a memory dump

- Using the Event Log service

Sometimes, you may experience problems that are outside the scope of general troubleshooting tools such as Performance Monitor or Network Monitor. In the case of a critical error, Windows NT Server may present the well-known "blue screen." This error screen can also be presented if a corrupt kernel is found or if there are problems loading device drivers when the computer boots. In addition, while the system is running, you may be presented with an error that generates a memory dump. In most cases, the information contained in the memory dump cannot be easily interpreted by the system administrator. However, this information can be useful when contacting technical support for the application that caused the error. When troubleshooting some of the more advanced problems that can occur with a Windows NT server, the Event Viewer is a useful tool for reviewing potential error messages created by the system or a running application. However, you need to be able to log on to the server in order to run Event Viewer.

To successfully answer the questions for this objective, you need a firm understanding of several key terms. For definitions of these terms, refer to the Glossary in this book.

Key Terms

- DUMPCHK

- DUMPEXAM

- NTDETECT

70-068.06.09.001

You are not able to start a newly purchased Windows NT Server computer. The computer successfully completes the POST, but the system displays a blue screen shortly after the NTDETECT V1.0 Checking Hardware message appears.

What should you do to solve this problem?

A. Check for partition table corruption using DiskProbe.

B. Make sure there are no CHECKSUM errors in the CMOS settings.

C. Use the debug version of NTDETECT to identify the faulty component.

D. Restart using the Last Known Good Configuration and run Windows NT Diagnostics.

70-068.06.09.001

You are not able to start a newly purchased Windows NT Server computer. The computer successfully completes the POST, but the system displays a blue screen shortly after the NTDETECT V1.0 Checking Hardware message appears.

What should you do to solve this problem?

▶ **Correct Answer: C**

    A. **Incorrect:** The DiskProbe utility is used to edit and view drive data. Since the problem is occurring while NTDETECT is checking the computer's hardware, you should first use the debug version of NTDETECT to learn more about the problem that has been encountered.

    B. **Incorrect:** If there were CMOS problems, the system would not be able to start NTDETECT. Since NTDETECT is reporting the problem, you should first use the debug version of NTDETECT to learn more about the problem that has been encountered.

    C. **Correct:** Since the problem is occurring during the hardware detection phase of bootup, the debug version of NTDETECT will provide more detailed troubleshooting information.

    D. **Incorrect:** If the system has not yet started, you will not be able to select the Last Known Good Configuration to run Windows NT Server. Use the debug version of NTDETECT in order to determine the source of the problem.

70-068.06.09.002

One of your Windows NT servers is experiencing numerous STOP screen messages. You have decided to configure server memory dumps to help troubleshoot the problem.

The required result is to write the contents of memory, when a stop screen occurs, to a MEMORY.DMP file that can be used to troubleshoot the problem.

The first optional result is to automatically write an event to the system log when STOP messages occur.

The second optional result is to automatically run DUMPCHK to perform a validity check on the MEMORY.DMP file before restarting the system.

The proposed solution is to open the System icon in Control Panel and click on the Startup/Shutdown tab. Ensure that the Write Debugging Information option is enabled, and ensure that the Write an Event to the System Log option is enabled. Click OK, and allow the computer to restart if necessary.

What does the proposed solution provide?

A. The required result and all optional results.

B. The required result and one optional result.

C. The required result but none of the optional results.

D. The proposed solution does not provide the required result.

70-068.06.09.002

One of your Windows NT servers is experiencing numerous STOP screen messages. You have decided to configure server memory dumps to help troubleshoot the problem.

The required result is to write the contents of memory, when a stop screen occurs, to a MEMORY.DMP file that can be used to troubleshoot the problem.

The first optional result is to automatically write an event to the system log when STOP messages occur.

The second optional result is to automatically run DUMPCHK to perform a validity check on the MEMORY.DMP file before restarting the system.

The proposed solution is to open the System icon in Control Panel and click on the Startup/Shutdown tab. Ensure that the Write Debugging Information option is enabled, and ensure that the Write an Event to the System Log option is enabled. Click OK, and allow the computer to restart if necessary.

What does the proposed solution provide?

▶ **Correct Answer: B**

A. **Incorrect:** Although the solution meets the required result and the first optional result, no provision is included for automatically running DUMPCHK. Therefore, only one optional result will be realized by this proposed solution.

B. **Correct:** By enabling the Write Debugging Information To: feature, the required result will be realized. In addition, the Write an Event to the System Log option will meet the requirements of the first optional result.

C. **Incorrect:** Although the required result will be realized by the proposed solution, the first optional result will be realized as well. The Write an Event to the System Log option will create a viewable entry in the event log that can be opened in Event Viewer.

D. **Incorrect:** By enabling the Write Debugging Information To: feature, the required result will be realized. When a stop screen occurs, the contents of memory will be written to a MEMORY.DMP file. Therefore, this answer is incorrect.

70-068.06.09.003

Every time you restart Window NT Server, you get a message stating that a driver or service failed to start. What should you do to identify the driver or service that is causing the error message?

A. Search the Registry using REGEDIT.

B. Open the system log in Event Viewer.

C. Run DUMPEXAM on the MEMORY.DMP file.

D. Use the /DEBUG switch in the BOOT.INI file.

70-068.06.09.003

Every time you restart Window NT Server, you get a message stating that a driver or service failed to start. What should you do to identify the driver or service that is causing the error message?

▶ **Correct Answer: B**

A. **Incorrect:** Because of the complexity of the Registry, it would not be the best solution to use the REGEDIT utility to identify the driver or service that is causing the error. Windows NT includes features such as the creation of an event log to help troubleshoot problems like this one.

B. **Correct:** Windows NT creates an event log of system activity and reported errors. Use the Event Viewer utility to review the data that has been written to the event log.

C. **Incorrect:** The DUMPEXAM utility is used to examine the results of a memory dump to help troubleshoot a kernel STOP error. Since the problem in the question is associated with a driver or server, you should check Event Viewer for more information about the problem.

D. **Incorrect:** BOOT.INI provides a list of all operating systems that can be loaded by the Windows NT boot program. Using the /DEBUG switch in the BOOT.INI file will activate the Windows NT debugger whenever this operating system starts. It will not provide information about a driver or service that fails to load once the system has been booted. Use the Event Log, which can be opened by Event Viewer, to learn more about the problem.

Further Reading

Supporting Microsoft Windows NT Server in the Enterprise Training kit. Complete Lesson 5, "Examining Stop Screens," of Chapter 7, "Troubleshooting Tools and Methods." In this lesson, you will learn about how to interpret Windows NT stop screens. In addition, the use of advanced tools, such as Kernel Debugger and CrashDump, are described.

Supporting Microsoft Windows NT Server in the Enterprise Training kit. Complete Lesson 2, "Examining Windows NT Architecture," of Chapter 7, "Troubleshooting Tools and Methods." In this lesson, the Windows NT architecture and techniques for troubleshooting are discussed.

Windows NT Server 4.0 in the Enterprise Accelerated MCSE Study Guide. Read Chapter 18, "Server Optimization" to learn more about resolving Windows NT blue screens and interpreting memory dumps.

The Microsoft Certified Professional Program

The Microsoft Certified Professional (MCP) program is designed to comprehensively assess and maintain software-related skills. Microsoft has developed several certifications to provide industry recognition of a candidate's knowledge and proficiency with Microsoft products and technologies. This appendix provides suggestions to help you prepare for an MCP exam and describes the process for taking the exam. The appendix also contains an overview of the benefits associated with certification and gives you an example of the exam track you might take for MCSE certification.

Preparing for an MCP Exam

This section contains tips and information to help you prepare for an MCP certification exam. Besides study and test-taking tips, this section provides information on how and where to register, test fees, and what to expect upon arrival at the testing center.

Studying for an Exam

The best way to prepare for an MCP exam is to study, learn, and master the technology or operating system on which you will be tested. The Readiness Review can help complete your understanding of the software or technology by assessing your practical knowledge and helping you focus on additional areas of study. For example, if you are pursuing the Microsoft Certified Systems Engineer (MCSE) certification, you must learn and use the tested Microsoft operating system. You can then use the Readiness Review to understand the skills that test your knowledge of the operating system, perform suggested practices with the operating system, and ascertain additional areas where you should focus your study by using the electronic assessment.

▶   **To prepare for any certification exam**

1. Identify the objectives for the exam.

   The Readiness Review lists and describes the objectives you will be tested on during the exam.

2. Assess your current mastery of those objectives.

   The Readiness Review electronic assessment tool is a great way to test your grasp of the objectives.

3. Practice the job skills for the objectives you have not mastered, and read more information about the subjects tested in each of these objectives.

   You can take the electronic assessment multiple times until you feel comfortable with the subject material.

Your Practical Experience

MCP exams test the specific skills needed on the job. Since in the real world you are rarely called upon to recite a list of facts, the exams go beyond testing your knowledge of a product or terminology. Instead, you are asked to *apply* your knowledge to a situation, analyze a technical problem, and decide on the best solution. Your hands-on experience with the software and technology will greatly enhance your performance on the exam.

Test Registration and Fees

You can schedule your exam up to six weeks in advance, or as late as one working day before the exam date. Sylvan Prometric and Virtual University Enterprises (VUE) administer all the Microsoft Certified Professional exams. To take an exam at an authorized Prometric Testing Center, in the United States call Sylvan at 800-755-EXAM (3926). To register online, or for more registration information, visit Sylvan's Web site at http://www.slspro.com. For information about taking exams at a VUE testing center, visit the VUE information page at http://www.vue.com, or call 888-837-8616 in the United States. When you register, you will need the following information:

■ Unique identification number (This is usually your Social Security or Social Insurance number. The testing center also assigns an identification number, which provides another way to distinguish your identity and test records.)

■ Mailing address and phone number

- E-mail address

- Organization or company name

- Method of payment (Payment must be made in advance, usually with a credit card or check.)

Testing fees vary from country to country, but in the United States and many other countries the exams cost approximately $100 (U.S.). Contact the testing vendor for exact pricing. Prices are subject to change, and in some countries, additional taxes may be applied.

When you schedule the exam, you will be provided with instructions regarding the appointment, cancellation procedures, identification requirements, and information about the testing center location.

Taking an Exam

If this is your first Microsoft certification exam, you may find the following information helpful upon arrival at the testing center.

Arriving at Testing Center

When you arrive at the testing center, you will be asked to sign a log book and show two forms of identification, including one photo identification (such as a driver's license or company security identification). Before you may take the exam, you will be asked to sign a Non-Disclosure Agreement and a Testing Center Regulations form, which explains the rules you will be expected to comply with during the test. Upon leaving the exam room at the end of the test, you will again sign the log book.

Exam Details

Before you begin the exam, the test administrator will provide detailed instructions about how to complete the exam and how to use the testing computer or software. Because the exams are timed, if you have any questions, ask the exam administrator before the exam begins. Consider arriving 10 to 15 minutes early so you will have time to relax and ask questions before the exam begins. Some exams may include additional materials or exhibits (such as diagrams). If any exhibits are required for your exam, the test administrator will provide you with them before you begin the exam and collect them from you at the end of the exam.

The exams are all closed book. You may not use a laptop computer or have any notes or printed material with you during the exam session. You will be provided with a set amount of blank paper for use during the exam. All paper will be collected from you at the end of the exam.

The Exam Tutorial

The test administrator will show you to your test computer and will handle any preparations necessary to start the testing tool and display the exam on the computer. Before you begin your exam, you can take the exam tutorial which is designed to familiarize you with computer-administered tests by offering questions similar to those on the exam. Taking the tutorial does not affect your allotted time for the exam.

Exam Length and Available Time

The number of questions on each exam varies, as does the amount of time allotted for each exam. Generally, unless the certification exam uses computer adaptive testing, exams consist of 50 to 70 questions and take approximately 90 minutes to complete. Specific information about the number of exam questions and available time will be provided to you when you register.

Tips for Taking the Exam

Since the testing software lets you move forward and backward through the exam, answer the easy questions first. Then go back and spend the remaining time on the harder questions.

When answering the multiple-choice questions, eliminate the obviously incorrect answers first. There are no trick questions on the test, so the correct answer will always be among the list of possible answers.

Answer all the questions before you quit the exam. An unanswered question is scored as an incorrect answer. If you are unsure of the answer, make an educated guess.

Your Rights as a Test Taker

As an exam candidate, you are entitled to the best support and environment possible for your exam. In particular, you are entitled to a quiet, uncluttered test environment and knowledgeable and professional test administrators. You should not hesitate to ask the administrator any questions before the exam begins, and you should also be given time to take the online testing tutorial. Before leaving, you should be given the opportunity to submit comments about the testing center, staff, or about the test itself.

Getting Your Exam Results

After you have completed an exam, you will immediately receive your score online and be given a printed Examination Score Report, which also breaks down the results by section. Passing scores on the different certification exams vary. You do not need to send these scores to Microsoft. The test center automatically forwards them to Microsoft within five working days, and if you pass the exam, Microsoft sends a confirmation to you within two to four weeks.

If you do not pass a certification exam, you may call the testing vendor to schedule a time to retake the exam. Before reexamination, you should review the appropriate sections of the Readiness Review and focus additional study on the topic areas where your exam results could be improved. Please note that you must pay the full registration fee again each time you retake an exam.

About the Exams

Microsoft Certified Professional exams follow recognized standards for validity and reliability. They are developed by technical experts who receive input from job-function and technology experts.

How MCP Exams Are Developed

To ensure the validity and reliability of the certification exams, Microsoft adheres to a rigorous exam-development process that includes an analysis of the tasks performed in specific job functions. Microsoft then translates the job tasks into a comprehensive set of objectives which measure knowledge, problem-solving abilities, and skill level. The objectives are prioritized and then reviewed by technical experts to create the certification exam questions. (These objectives are also the basis for developing the Readiness Review series.) Technical and job-function experts review the exam objectives and questions several times before releasing the final exam.

Computer Adaptive Testing

Microsoft is developing more effective ways to determine who meets the criteria for certification by introducing innovative testing technologies. One of these testing technologies is computer adaptive testing (CAT). This testing method is currently being used on the Windows NT Server 4.0 (70-068) exam. When taking this exam, test takers start with an easy-to-moderate question. Those who answer the question correctly get a more difficult follow-up question. If that question is answered correctly, the difficulty of the subsequent question also increases. Conversely, if the first question is answered incorrectly, the following question will be easier. This process continues until the testing system determines the test taker's ability.

With this system, everyone may answer the same percentage of questions correctly, but because people with a higher ability can answer more difficult questions correctly, they will receive a higher score. To learn more about computer adaptive testing and other testing innovations, visit http://www.microsoft.com/mcp.

If You Have a Concern About the Exam Content

Microsoft Certified Professional exams are developed by technical and testing experts, with input and participation from job-function and technology experts. Microsoft ensures that the exams adhere to recognized standards for validity and reliability. Candidates generally consider them to be relevant and fair. If you feel that an exam question is inappropriate or if you believe the correct answer shown to be incorrect, write or call Microsoft at the e-mail address or phone number listed for the Microsoft Certified Professional Program in the "References" section of this appendix.

Although Microsoft and the exam administrators are unable to respond to individual questions and issues raised by candidates, all input from candidates is thoroughly researched and taken into consideration during development of subsequent versions of the exams. Microsoft is committed to ensuring the quality of these exams, and your input is a valuable resource.

Overview of the MCP Program

Becoming a Microsoft Certified Professional is the best way to show employers, clients, and colleagues that you have the knowledge and skills required by the industry. Microsoft's certification program is one of the industry's most comprehensive programs for assessing and maintaining software-related skills, and the MCP designation is recognized by technical managers worldwide as a mark of competence.

Certification Programs

Microsoft offers a variety of certifications so you can choose the one that meets your job needs and career goals. The MCP program focuses on measuring a candidate's ability to perform a specific job function, such as one performed by a systems engineer or a solution developer. Successful completion of the certification requirements indicates your expertise in the field. Microsoft certifications include:

- Microsoft Certified Systems Engineer (MCSE)
- Microsoft Certified Systems Engineer + Internet (MCSE + I)
- Microsoft Certified Professional (MCP)
- Microsoft Certified Professional + Internet (MCP + I)
- Microsoft Certified Professional + Site Building
- Microsoft Certified Database Administrator (MCDBA)
- Microsoft Certified Solution Developer (MCSD)

Microsoft Certified Systems Engineer (MCSE)

Microsoft Certified Systems Engineers have a high level of expertise with Microsoft Windows NT and the Microsoft BackOffice integrated family of server software and can plan, implement, maintain, and support information systems with these products. MCSEs are required to pass four operating system exams and two elective exams. The Microsoft Windows NT Server 4.0 (70-068) exam earns core credit toward this certification.

MCSE Exam Requirements

You can select a Microsoft Windows NT 3.51 or Microsoft Windows NT 4.0 track for the MCSE certification. From within the track you have selected, you must pass four core operating system exams and then pass two elective exams. Visit the Microsoft Certified Professional Web site for details about current exam requirements, exam alternatives, and retired exams. This roadmap outlines the path an MCSE candidate would pursue for Windows NT 4.0.

Microsoft Windows NT 4.0 Core Exams

You must pass four core exams and two elective exams. You may choose among Windows 95, Windows NT Workstation 4.0, or Windows 98 for one of the core exams. The core exams are as follows:

- Exam 70-067: Implementing and Supporting Microsoft Windows NT Server 4.0

- Exam 70-068: Implementing and Supporting Microsoft Windows NT Server 4.0 in the Enterprise

- Exam 70-064: Implementing and Supporting Microsoft Windows 95, or exam 70-073: Microsoft Windows NT Workstation 4.0, or exam 70-098: Implementing and Supporting Microsoft Windows 98

- Exam 70-058: Networking Essentials

MCSE Electives

The elective exams you choose are the same for all Windows NT tracks. You must choose two exams from the following list.

- Exam 70-013: Implementing and Supporting Microsoft SNA Server 3.0, or exam 70-085: Implementing and Supporting Microsoft SNA Server 4.0 (If both SNA Server exams are passed, only one qualifies as an MCSE elective.)

- Exam 70-018: Implementing and Supporting Microsoft Systems Management Server 1.2, or exam 70-086: Implementing and Supporting Microsoft Systems Management Server 2.0 (If both SMS exams are passed, only one qualifies as an MCSE elective.)

- Exam 70-027: Implementing a Database Design on Microsoft SQL Server 6.5, or exam 70-029: Designing and Implementing Databases with Microsoft SQL Server 7.0 (If both SQL Server exams are passed, only one qualifies as an MCSE elective.)

- Exam 70-026: System Administration for Microsoft SQL Server 6.5, or exam 70-028: Administering Microsoft SQL Server 7.0 (If both exams are passed from this group, only one would qualify as an MCSE elective.)

- Exam 70-053: Internetworking Microsoft TCP/IP on Microsoft Windows NT (3.5–3.51), or exam 70-059: Internetworking with Microsoft TCP/IP on Microsoft Windows NT 4.0 (If both exams are passed, only one would qualify as an MCSE elective.)

- Exam 70-056: Implementing and Supporting Web Sites Using Microsoft Site Server 3.0

- Exam 70-076: Implementing and Supporting Microsoft Exchange Server 5, or exam 70-081: Implementing and Supporting Microsoft Exchange Server 5.5 (If both exams are passed, only one would qualify as an MCSE elective.)

- Exam 70-077: Implementing and Supporting Microsoft Internet Information Server 3.0 and Microsoft Index Server 1.1, or exam 70-087: Implementing and Supporting Microsoft Internet Information Server 4.0 (If both exams are passed, only one would qualify as an MCSE elective.)

- Exam 70-078: Implementing and Supporting Microsoft Proxy Server 1.0, or exam 70-088: Implementing and Supporting Microsoft Proxy Server 2.0 (If both exams are passed, only one would qualify as an MCSE elective.)

- Exam 70-079: Implementing and Supporting Microsoft Internet Explorer 4.0 by Using the Internet Explorer Administration Kit

Note that certification requirements may change. In addition, some retired certification exams may qualify for credit towards current certification programs. For the latest details on core and elective exams, go to http://www.microsoft.com/mcp and review the appropriate certification.

Novell, Banyan, and Sun Exemptions

The Microsoft Certified Professional program grants credit for the networking exam requirement for candidates who are certified as Novell CNEs, Master CNEs, or CNIs; Banyan CBSs or CBEs; or Sun Certified Network Administrators for Solaris 2.5 or 2.6. Go to the Microsoft Certified Professional Web site at http://www.microsoft.com/mcp/certstep/exempt.htm for current information and details.

Other Certification Programs

In addition to the MCSE certification, Microsoft has created other certification programs that focus on specific job functions and career goals.

Microsoft Certified Systems Engineer + Internet (MCSE + I)

An individual with the MCSE + Internet credential is qualified to enhance, deploy, and manage sophisticated intranet and Internet solutions that include a browser, proxy server, host servers, database, and messaging and commerce components. Microsoft Certified Systems Engineers with a specialty in the Internet are required to pass seven operating system exams and two elective exams. The Implementing and Supporting Microsoft Windows NT Server 4.0 in the Enterprise (70-068) exam earns core credit toward this certification.

Microsoft Certified Professional (MCP)

Microsoft Certified Professionals have demonstrated in-depth knowledge of at least one Microsoft product. An MCP has passed a minimum of one Microsoft operating system exam and may pass additional Microsoft Certified Professional exams to further qualify his or her skills in a particular area of specialization. A Microsoft Certified Professional has extensive knowledge about specific products but has not completed a job-function certification. The MCP credential provides a solid background for other Microsoft certifications.

Microsoft Certified Professional + Internet (MCP + I)

A person receiving the Microsoft Certified Professional + Internet certification is qualified to plan security, install and configure server products, manage server resources, extend servers to run CGI scripts or ISAPI scripts, monitor and analyze performance, and troubleshoot problems.

Microsoft Certified Professional + Site Building

Microsoft has recently created a certification designed for Web site developers. Individuals with the Microsoft Certified Professional + Site Building credential are qualified to plan, build, maintain, and manage Web sites using Microsoft technologies and products. The credential is appropriate for people who manage sophisticated, interactive Web sites that include database connectivity, multimedia, and searchable content. Microsoft Certified Professionals with a specialty in site building are required to pass two exams that measure technical proficiency and expertise.

Microsoft Certified Database Administrator (MCDBA)

The Microsoft Certified Database Administrator credential is designed for professionals who implement and administer Microsoft SQL Server databases. Microsoft Certified Database Administrators are required to pass four core exams and one elective exam. The Implementing and Supporting Microsoft Windows NT Server 4.0 in the Enterprise (70-068) exam earns core credit toward this certification.

Microsoft Certified Solution Developer (MCSD)

The Microsoft Certified Solution Developer credential is the premium certification for professionals who design and develop custom business solutions with Microsoft development tools, technologies, and platforms. The MCSD certification exams test the candidate's ability to build Web-based, distributed, and commercial applications by using Microsoft's products, such as Microsoft SQL Server, Microsoft Visual Studio, and Microsoft Transaction Server.

Certification Benefits

Obtaining Microsoft certification has many advantages. Industry professionals recognize Microsoft Certified Professionals for their knowledge and proficiency with Microsoft products and technologies. Microsoft helps to establish the program's recognition by promoting the expertise of MCPs within the industry. By becoming a Microsoft Certified Professional, you will join a worldwide community of technical professionals who have validated their expertise with Microsoft products.

In addition, you will have access to technical and product information directly from Microsoft through a secured area of the MCP Web site. You will be invited to Microsoft conferences, technical training sessions, and special events. MCPs also receive *Microsoft Certified Professional Magazine,* a career and professional development magazine.

Your organization will receive benefits when you obtain your certification. Research shows that Microsoft certification provides organizations with increased customer satisfaction and decreased support costs through improved service, increased productivity, and greater technical self-sufficiency. It also gives companies a reliable benchmark for hiring, promoting, and career planning.

Skills 2000 Program

Microsoft launched the Skills 2000 initiative to address the gap between the number of open jobs in the computing industry and the number of skilled professionals to fill them. The program, launched in 1997, builds upon the success of Microsoft's training and certification programs to reach a broader segment of the work force. Many of today's computing professionals consider the current skills gap to be their primary business challenge.

Skills 2000 aims to significantly reduce the skills gap by reaching out to individuals currently in the computing work force, as well as those interested in developing a career in information technology (IT). The program focuses on finding and placing skilled professionals in the job market today with Microsoft Solution Provider organizations. Microsoft will also facilitate internships between MSPs and students developing IT skills. In addition, Skills 2000 targets academic instructors at high schools, colleges, and universities by offering free technical training to teachers and professors who are educating the work force of tomorrow.

For more information about the Skills 2000 initiative, visit the Skills 2000 site at http://www.microsoft.com/skills2000. This site includes information about starting a career in the IT industry, IT-related articles, and a career aptitude tool.

Volunteer Technical Contributors

To volunteer for participation in one or more of the exam development phases, please sign up using the Technical Contributors online form on the MCP Web site: http://www.microsoft.com/mcp/examinfo/certsd.htm.

References

To find out more about Microsoft certification materials and programs, to register with an exam administrator, or to get other useful resources, check the following references. For Microsoft references outside the United States or Canada, contact your local Microsoft office.

Microsoft Certified Professional Program

To find information about Microsoft certification exams and information to help you prepare for any specific exam, go to http://www.microsoft.com/mcp, send e-mail to mcp@msprograms.com, or call 800-636-7544.

The MCP online magazine provides information for and about Microsoft Certified Professionals. The magazine is also a good source for exam tips. You can view the online magazine at http://www.mcpmag.com.

Microsoft Developer Network

The Microsoft Developer Network (MSDN) subscription center is your official source for software development kits, device driver kits, operating systems, and information about developing applications for Microsoft Windows and Windows NT. You can visit MSDN at http://msdn.microsoft.com or call 800-759-5474.

Microsoft Press

Microsoft Press offers comprehensive learning and training resources to help you get the most from Microsoft technology. For information about books published by Microsoft Press, go to http://mspress.microsoft.com or call 800-MSPRESS.

Microsoft Press ResourceLink

Microsoft Press ResourceLink is an online information resource for IT professionals who deploy, manage, or support Microsoft products and technologies. ResourceLink gives you access to the latest technical updates, tools, and utilities from Microsoft and is the most complete source of technical information about Microsoft technologies available anywhere. You can reach Microsoft Press ResourceLink and find out about a trial membership at http://mspress.microsoft.com/reslink.

Microsoft TechNet IT Home

Microsoft TechNet IT Home is a resource designed for IT professionals. The Microsoft TechNet Web site is designed for anyone who evaluates, deploys, maintains, develops, or supports IT systems. Microsoft TechNet can help you stay on top of technology trends. See the TechNet Web site for more information at http://www.microsoft.com/technet.

Microsoft Training and Certification

You can find lists of various study aids for the training and certification in Microsoft products at http://www.microsoft.com/train_cert.

Self Test Software

Self Test Software provides the Readiness Review online assessment. For an additional fee, Self Test Software will provide test questions for this exam and other certification exams. For further information go to http://www.stsware.com/microsts.htm.

Sylvan Prometric Testing Centers

To register to take a Microsoft Certified Professional exam at any of the Sylvan Prometric testing centers around the world, go online at http://www.slspro.com. In the United States, you can call 800-755-EXAM.

Virtual University Enterprises (VUE)

You can register for a certification exam with VUE by using online registration, registering in person at a VUE testing center, or by calling 888-837-8616 in the United States. Visit http://www.vue.com/ms for testing sites, available examinations, and other registration numbers.

Glossary

A

AppleTalk Apple Computer network architecture and network protocols. A network that has Macintosh clients and a computer running Windows NT Server with Services for Macintosh functions as an AppleTalk network.

AT Scheduler *See* schedule service.

auditing Tracking activities of users by recording selected types of events in the security log of a server or a workstation.

B

Backup Domain Controller (BDC) In a Windows NT Server domain, a computer running Windows NT Server that receives a copy of the domain's directory database, which contains all account and security policy information for the domain. The copy is synchronized periodically and automatically with the master copy on the Primary Domain Controller (PDC). BDCs also authenticate user logons and can be promoted to function as PDCs as needed. Multiple BDCs can exist on a domain. *See also* member server; Primary Domain Controller (PDC).

basic authentication A method of authentication that encodes user name and password data transmissions. Basic authentication is called *clear text* because the base-64 encoding can be decoded by anyone with a freely available decoding utility. Note that encoding is not the same as encryption. *See also* Windows NT Challenge/Response.

browse master *See* master browser.

BDC *See* Backup Domain Controller.

BOOT.INI The file that builds the Boot Loader Operating System Selection menu.

BOOTP *See* Bootstrap Protocol.

BOOTSECT.DOS A hidden system file loaded by NTLDR if another operating system such as MS-DOS is selected. This file contains the boot sector that was on the hard disk before Windows NT was installed.

Bootstrap Protocol (BOOTP) A TCP/IP network protocol, defined by RFC 951 and RFC 1542, used to configure systems. DHCP is an enhancement of BOOTP. *See also* Dynamic Host Configuration Protocol (DHCP).

C

capture filter Functions like a database query to single out a subset of frames to be monitored in Network Monitor. You can filter on the basis of source and destination address, protocols, and protocol properties, or by specifying a pattern offset.

Change permission With this permission setting, users can read and add files and change the contents of current files.

counter A feature of Performance Monitor that allows you to configure the data that is collected and displayed.

D

Data Link Control (DLC) A network protocol used to access special resources such as an IBM AS/400 computer or a Hewlett-Packard network printer.

DHCP *See* Dynamic Host Configuration Protocol.

directory replication The copying of a master set of directories from a server (called an *export server*) to specified servers or workstations (called *import servers*) in the same or other domains. Replication simplifies the task of maintaining identical sets of directories and files on multiple computers because only a single master copy of the data must be maintained. Files are replicated when they are added to an exported directory and every time a change is saved to the file.

Disk Administrator The Windows NT administration utility for managing drives and partitions. You can also use Disk Administrator to regenerate lost data that was part of a fault-tolerant system.

display filter Functions like a database query, allowing you to single out specific types of information. Because a display filter operates on data that has already been captured, it does not affect the contents of the Network Monitor capture buffer.

DLC *See* Data Link Control.

domain A collection of computers that share a common domain database and security policy. Each domain has a unique name.

Domain Name System (DNS) A protocol and system used throughout the Internet to map Internet Protocol (IP) addresses to user-friendly names such as www.microsoft.com. Sometimes referred to as the BIND service in BSD UNIX, DNS offers a static, hierarchical name service for TCP/IP hosts. DNS domains should not be confused with Windows NT networking domains.

domain trusts *See* trust relationships.

DUMPCHK This command-line utility performs a validity check on a kernel mode crash dump. It also displays basic information from the memory dump file.

DUMPEXAM This command-line utility examines and analyzes a MEMORY.DMP file. The results generated by DUMPEXAM are saved to a text file.

Dynamic Host Configuration Protocol (DHCP) An industry-standard TCP/IP protocol that assigns Internet Protocol (IP) configurations to computers.

E

ERD *See* emergency repair disk.

emergency repair disk (ERD) A floppy disk used by the repair process to restore a corrupt Registry. It also includes information about the drive settings managed by Disk Administrator as well as the NTFS partition boot sector.

Event Viewer The Windows NT administration utility for viewing and analyzing the event log.

F

FAT *See* file allocation table.

FAT16 An implementation of the file allocation table that uses larger file clusters. FAT16 is not as efficient as FAT32.

FAT32 An enhancement of the file allocation table that supports larger hard drives (greater than 2 GB) and uses smaller cluster sizes for better efficiency.

fault tolerance Ensures data integrity when hardware failures occur. In Windows NT, the FDISK.SYS driver provides fault tolerance. In Disk Administrator, fault tolerance is provided using mirror sets, stripe sets with parity, and volume sets.

file allocation table (FAT) An area on a disk set aside to reference file locations on that disk.

File and Print Services for NetWare (FPNW) A Windows NT Server component that enables a computer running Windows NT Server to provide file and print services directly to NetWare-compatible client computers.

file-level security Using the NT file system, this security scheme allows administrators to set permissions on individual files.

Full Control permission With this permission setting, users can read and change files, add new ones, change permissions for the directory and its files, and take ownership of the directory and its files.

G

Gateway Services for NetWare (GSNW) Included with Windows NT Server; enables a computer running Windows NT Server to connect to NetWare servers. Creating a gateway enables computers running only Microsoft client software to access NetWare resources through the gateway.

global groups For Windows NT Server, a group in one domain that has access to resources, servers, and workstations outside of its own domain as well as within that domain. In all those places, a global group can be granted rights and permissions and can become a member of local groups. However, it can only contain user accounts from its own domain. Global groups provide a way to create convenient sets of users from inside the domain, available for use both in and out of the domain.

Global groups cannot be created or maintained on computers running Windows NT Workstation. However, if Windows NT Workstation computers participate in a domain, domain global groups can be granted rights and permissions at those workstations and can become members of local groups at those workstations.

GSNW *See* Gateway Services for NetWare.

H

Hardware Compatibility List (HCL) The Windows NT Hardware Compatibility List lists the devices supported by Windows NT. The latest version of

the HCL can be downloaded from the Microsoft Web page (www.microsoft.com) on the Internet.

HCL *See* Hardware Compatibility List.

I

IIS *See* Internet Information Server.

Internet Information Server (IIS) A network file and application server that supports multiple protocols. Primarily, Internet Information Server transmits information in Hypertext Markup Language (HTML) pages by using the Hypertext Transport Protocol (HTTP).

Internetwork Packet Exchange/Sequenced Packet Exchange (IPX/SPX) On Novell NetWare systems, IPX is a network layer protocol used in the file server operating system; SPX is a transport layer protocol built on top of IPX and used in client/server applications.

IPX/SPX *See* Internetwork Packet Exchange/Sequenced Packet Exchange.

L

line printer daemon (LPD) A line printer daemon (LPD) server on the print server receives documents from line printer remote (LPR) utilities running on client systems.

line printer remote (LPR) A client utility used to send print jobs to computers running the line printer daemon (LPD) utility. The LPR is typically used on UNIX clients.

local group For Windows NT Server, a group that can be granted permissions and rights only for the domain controllers of its own domain. However, it can contain user accounts and global groups both from its own domain and from trusted domains.

logical printer *See* printer.

LPR *See* line printer remote.

M

master browser A computer that compiles a list of all available servers on the local network. A single master browser server maintains this list, called the *browse list*. Additional backup browse servers can be used to minimize network traffic.

master domain model In the master domain model, the domain that is trusted by all other domains on the network and acts as the central administrative unit for user and group accounts.

member server A computer that runs Windows NT Server but is not a Primary Domain Controller (PDC) or a Backup Domain Controller (BDC). Member servers do not receive copies of the directory database. Also called a *stand-alone server. See also* Backup Domain Controller (BDC); Primary Domain Controller (PDC).

Microsoft Backup Utility A Windows NT administration utility for backing up files and Registry information to a file on a hard drive or a tape backup system. The Microsoft Backup Utility should be used even when Level 5 RAID fault tolerance has been implemented to guarantee a recovery source in the event of a catastrophic failure.

mirror set A fully redundant or *shadow* copy of data. Mirror sets provide an identical twin for a selected disk; all data written to the primary disk is also written to the shadow or mirror disk. This enables you to have instant access to another disk with a redundant copy of the information on a failed disk. Mirror sets provide fault tolerance. *See also* fault tolerance.

multihomed system A system that has multiple network adapters, or that has been configured with multiple IP addresses for a single network adapter.

N

NET USE The command-line statement to connect to and use a network resource.

NetBEUI (NetBIOS Enhanced User Interface) A network protocol usually used in small, department-size local area networks of 1 to 200 clients. It can use Token Ring source routing as its only method of routing.

NetBIOS An application programming interface (API) that can be used by applications on a local area network. NetBIOS provides applications with a uniform set of commands for requesting the lower-level services required to conduct sessions between nodes on a network and to transmit information back and forth.

Network Administration Tools A suite of Windows NT Server tools, such as User Manager for Domains and Event Viewer, that can be installed on a client system for remote administration of a Windows NT Server. The user using the Network Administration Tools must have the appropriate permissions on the server before these tools will work.

network interface card (NIC) A hardware card installed in a computer so that it can communicate on a network.

Network Monitor A Windows NT administration utility that captures network packet information for later analysis. This tool includes the capability to filter captured packet information, sort captured data, and restrict data that is initially captured.

network printer A printer connected directly to the network via its own network interface card.

NIC *See* network interface card.

No Access permission With this permission setting, users will not be allowed access to a folder or file. This permission overrides any other permissions granted to the user.

NTDETECT.COM This file passes information about the hardware configuration to NTLDR during the boot process.

NTFS *See* Windows NT file system.

NTHQ *See* Windows NT Hardware Detection Tool.

NTLDR The operating system loader. NTLDR must reside in the root directory.

NTLM *See* Windows NT Challenge/Response.

NTOSKRNL.EXE The Windows NT operating system kernel.

P

PDC *See* Primary Domain Controller.

Performance Monitor The Windows NT administration utility for gathering and monitoring system activity. Performance Monitor uses counters to determine what data points should be monitored. As data is collected, it can be displayed in a chart format or a report format. In addition, alerts can be configured to announce when certain conditions, such as low disk space, arise.

PPP *See* Point-to-Point Protocol.

Point-to-Point Protocol (PPP) An industry standard, a part of dial-up networking, designed to ensure interoperability with remote access software from other vendors. It is used in making point-to-point links, especially with dial-up modem servers.

Primary Domain Controller (PDC) The first computer named in a Windows NT Server domain during installation. It contains a master copy of domain information, validates users, and can act as file, print, and application server. Every Windows NT domain is required to have one, and only one, primary domain controller.

print device Refers to the actual hardware device that produces printed output.

print priority Refers to the setting of a print job in a print queue. The higher the print priority for a job, the sooner it will be sent to the printer for output. The print priority can be manually changed on a per-job basis.

print queue Refers to a group of documents waiting to be printed.

printer Refers to the software interface between the operating system and the print device. The printer defines where the document will go before it reaches the print device (to a local port, to a file, or to a remote print share), when it will go, and various other aspects of the printing process.

printer pool Consists of two or more identical print devices associated with one printer.

R

RAID *See* redundant array of independent disks.

RAS *See* Remote Access Service.

RCMD *See* Remote Command Service.

Read Only permission With this permission setting, users will not be allowed to add or change files in a folder. However, they will be able to view the contents of the directory and the files contained therein.

redundant array of independent disks (RAID) A method used to standardize and categorize fault-tolerant disk systems. Six levels gauge various mixes of performance, reliability, and cost. Windows NT includes three of the RAID levels: level 0, level 1, and level 5.

REGEDIT.EXE *See* Registry Editor.

Registry The database repository for information about a computer's configuration. The Registry supersedes the use of separate .INI files for all system components and applications that know how to store values in the Registry.

Registry Editor An application, provided with Windows NT, that is used to view and edit entries in the Registry.

Remote Access Service (RAS) A service that provides remote networking for telecommuters, mobile workers, and system administrators who monitor and manage servers at multiple branch offices.

Remote Command Service (RCMD) A utility that allows command-line statements to be executed on a remote server.

RIP *See* Routing Information Protocol.

roaming user Roaming users are users who need to be able to log on to different computer systems.

router In the Windows NT environment, a router helps LANs and WANs achieve interoperability and connectivity, and can link LANs that have different network topologies (such as Ethernet and Token Ring). Routers match packet headers to a LAN segment and choose the best path for the packet, optimizing network performance.

Routing Information Protocol (RIP) Enables a router to exchange routing information with a neighboring router.

S

SAP *See* Service Advertising Protocol.

schedule service Supports and is required to use the AT command. The AT command can schedule commands and programs to run on a computer at a specified time and date.

Server Manager In Windows NT Server, an application used to view and administer domains, workgroups, and computers.

Service Advertising Protocol (SAP) In the Windows environment, a service that broadcasts shared files, directories, and printers categorized first by domain or workgroup and then by server name.

share-level security A password-protected security scheme that assigns a password to each shared resource. Access to the resource is granted when the user enters the appropriate password. This is a simple security method that is not as secure as user-level security.

single domain model In a single domain model, there is only one domain in which user accounts and groups are managed. A single set of PDCs and BDCs authenticate and control the domain.

stripe set Refers to the saving of data across identical partitions on different drives. A stripe set does not provide fault tolerance; however, stripe sets with parity do. *See also* fault tolerance; stripe set with parity.

stripe set with parity A method of data protection in which data is striped in large blocks across all of the disks in an array. Data redundancy is provided by the parity information. This method provides fault tolerance.

system policy A policy, created by using the System Policy Editor, to control user work environments and actions, and to enforce system configuration for Windows NT, Windows 95, and Windows 98 computers. System policy can be implemented for specific users, groups, and computers or for all users. System policy for users overwrites settings in the Current User area of the Registry, and system policy for computers overwrites the Current Local Machine area of the Registry.

T

TCP/IP *See* Transmission Control Protocol/Internet Protocol.

Transmission Control Protocol/Internet Protocol (TCP/IP) A networking protocol that allows computers to communicate across interconnected networks and the Internet. Every computer on the Internet supports TCP/IP.

trust relationships A link between domains that enables pass-through authentication, in which a trusting domain honors the logon authentications of a trusted domain. With trust relationships, a user who has only one user account in one domain can potentially access the entire network. User accounts and global groups defined in a trusted domain can be given rights and resource permissions in a trusting domain, even though those accounts do not exist in the trusting domain's directory database.

U

User Manager for Domains The Windows NT administration utility for creating and managing user and group accounts.

user profile Configuration information that can be retained on a user-by-user basis. This information includes all of the per-user settings of the Windows NT environment, such as the desktop arrangement, personal program groups and the program items in those groups, screen colors, screen savers, network connections, printer connections, mouse settings, and window size and position. When a user logs on, the user's profile is loaded and the user's Windows NT environment is configured according to that profile.

user-level security When you're using a security provider, such as Windows NT Server, access to network resources is granted on a per-user basis. Both individual user names and groups of users can be given read-only or full access to a network resource. Access is based on a validated user login.

V

volume set A combination of partitions on a physical disk that appears as one logical drive.

W

Windows Internet Naming Service (WINS) A name resolution service that resolves Windows networking computer names to IP addresses in a routed environment. A WINS server handles name registrations, queries, and releases.

Windows NT Challenge/Response (NTLM) A method of authentication in which a server uses challenge/response algorithms and Windows NT security to control access to resources.

Windows NT file system (NTFS) The file system designed for use specifically with the Windows NT operating system. NTFS supports file system recovery and extremely large storage media, in addition to having other advantages. It also supports object-oriented applications by treating all files as objects with user-defined and system-defined attributes.

Windows NT Hardware Detection Tool (NTHQ) Identifies installed hardware and settings for diagnostic purposes.

WINS *See* Windows Internet Naming Service.

Index

MICROSOFT LICENSE AGREEMENT
Book Companion CD

IMPORTANT—READ CAREFULLY: This Microsoft End-User License Agreement ("EULA") is a legal agreement between you (either an individual or an entity) and Microsoft Corporation for the Microsoft product identified above, which includes computer software and may include associated media, printed materials, and "online" or electronic documentation ("SOFTWARE PRODUCT"). Any component included within the SOFTWARE PRODUCT that is accompanied by a separate End-User License Agreement shall be governed by such agreement and not the terms set forth below. By installing, copying, or otherwise using the SOFTWARE PRODUCT, you agree to be bound by the terms of this EULA. If you do not agree to the terms of this EULA, you are not authorized to install, copy, or otherwise use the SOFTWARE PRODUCT; you may, however, return the SOFTWARE PRODUCT, along with all printed materials and other items that form a part of the Microsoft product that includes the SOFTWARE PRODUCT, to the place you obtained them for a full refund.

SOFTWARE PRODUCT LICENSE

The SOFTWARE PRODUCT is protected by United States copyright laws and international copyright treaties, as well as other intellectual property laws and treaties. The SOFTWARE PRODUCT is licensed, not sold.

1. **GRANT OF LICENSE.** This EULA grants you the following rights:

    a. **Software Product.** You may install and use one copy of the SOFTWARE PRODUCT on a single computer. The primary user of the computer on which the SOFTWARE PRODUCT is installed may make a second copy for his or her exclusive use on a portable computer.

    b. **Storage/Network Use.** You may also store or install a copy of the SOFTWARE PRODUCT on a storage device, such as a network server, used only to install or run the SOFTWARE PRODUCT on your other computers over an internal network; however, you must acquire and dedicate a license for each separate computer on which the SOFTWARE PRODUCT is installed or run from the storage device. A license for the SOFTWARE PRODUCT may not be shared or used concurrently on different computers.

    c. **License Pak.** If you have acquired this EULA in a Microsoft License Pak, you may make the number of additional copies of the computer software portion of the SOFTWARE PRODUCT authorized on the printed copy of this EULA, and you may use each copy in the manner specified above. You are also entitled to make a corresponding number of secondary copies for portable computer use as specified above.

    d. **Sample Code.** Solely with respect to portions, if any, of the SOFTWARE PRODUCT that are identified within the SOFTWARE PRODUCT as sample code (the "SAMPLE CODE"):

        i. **Use and Modification.** Microsoft grants you the right to use and modify the source code version of the SAMPLE CODE, *provided* you comply with subsection (d)(iii) below. You may not distribute the SAMPLE CODE, or any modified version of the SAMPLE CODE, in source code form.

        ii. **Redistributable Files.** Provided you comply with subsection (d)(iii) below, Microsoft grants you a nonexclusive, royalty-free right to reproduce and distribute the object code version of the SAMPLE CODE and of any modified SAMPLE CODE, other than SAMPLE CODE, or any modified version thereof, designated as not redistributable in the Readme file that forms a part of the SOFTWARE PRODUCT (the "Non-Redistributable Sample Code"). All SAMPLE CODE other than the Non-Redistributable Sample Code is collectively referred to as the "REDISTRIBUTABLES."

        iii. **Redistribution Requirements.** If you redistribute the REDISTRIBUTABLES, you agree to: (i) distribute the REDISTRIBUTABLES in object code form only in conjunction with and as a part of your software application product; (ii) not use Microsoft's name, logo, or trademarks to market your software application product; (iii) include a valid copyright notice on your software application product; (iv) indemnify, hold harmless, and defend Microsoft from and against any claims or lawsuits, including attorney's fees, that arise or result from the use or distribution of your software application product; and (v) not permit further distribution of the REDISTRIBUTABLES by your end user. Contact Microsoft for the applicable royalties due and other licensing terms for all other uses and/or distribution of the REDISTRIBUTABLES.

2. **DESCRIPTION OF OTHER RIGHTS AND LIMITATIONS.**

    - **Limitations on Reverse Engineering, Decompilation, and Disassembly.** You may not reverse engineer, decompile, or disassemble the SOFTWARE PRODUCT, except and only to the extent that such activity is expressly permitted by applicable law notwithstanding this limitation.

    - **Separation of Components.** The SOFTWARE PRODUCT is licensed as a single product. Its component parts may not be separated for use on more than one computer.

    - **Rental.** You may not rent, lease, or lend the SOFTWARE PRODUCT.

- **Support Services.** Microsoft may, but is not obligated to, provide you with support services related to the SOFTWARE PRODUCT ("Support Services"). Use of Support Services is governed by the Microsoft policies and programs described in the user manual, in "online" documentation, and/or other Microsoft-provided materials. Any supplemental software code provided to you as part of the Support Services shall be considered part of the SOFTWARE PRODUCT and subject to the terms and conditions of this EULA. With respect to technical information you provide to Microsoft as part of the Support Services, Microsoft may use such information for its business purposes, including for product support and development. Microsoft will not utilize such technical information in a form that personally identifies you.
- **Software Transfer.** You may permanently transfer all of your rights under this EULA, provided you retain no copies, you transfer all of the SOFTWARE PRODUCT (including all component parts, the media and printed materials, any upgrades, this EULA, and, if applicable, the Certificate of Authenticity), **and** the recipient agrees to the terms of this EULA.
- **Termination.** Without prejudice to any other rights, Microsoft may terminate this EULA if you fail to comply with the terms and conditions of this EULA. In such event, you must destroy all copies of the SOFTWARE PRODUCT and all of its component parts.

3. **COPYRIGHT.** All title and copyrights in and to the SOFTWARE PRODUCT (including but not limited to any images, photographs, animations, video, audio, music, text, SAMPLE CODE, REDISTRIBUTABLES, and "applets" incorporated into the SOFTWARE PRODUCT) and any copies of the SOFTWARE PRODUCT are owned by Microsoft or its suppliers. The SOFT-WARE PRODUCT is protected by copyright laws and international treaty provisions. Therefore, you must treat the SOFTWARE PRODUCT like any other copyrighted material **except** that you may install the SOFTWARE PRODUCT on a single computer provided you keep the original solely for backup or archival purposes. You may not copy the printed materials accompanying the SOFTWARE PRODUCT.

4. **U.S. GOVERNMENT RESTRICTED RIGHTS.** The SOFTWARE PRODUCT and documentation are provided with RESTRICTED RIGHTS. Use, duplication, or disclosure by the Government is subject to restrictions as set forth in subparagraph (c)(1)(ii) of the Rights in Technical Data and Computer Software clause at DFARS 252.227-7013 or subparagraphs (c)(1) and (2) of the Commercial Computer Software—Restricted Rights at 48 CFR 52.227-19, as applicable. Manufacturer is Microsoft Corporation/One Microsoft Way/Redmond, WA 98052-6399.

5. **EXPORT RESTRICTIONS.** You agree that you will not export or re-export the SOFTWARE PRODUCT, any part thereof, or any process or service that is the direct product of the SOFTWARE PRODUCT (the foregoing collectively referred to as the "Restricted Components"), to any country, person, entity, or end user subject to U.S. export restrictions. You specifically agree not to export or re-export any of the Restricted Components (i) to any country to which the U.S. has embargoed or restricted the export of goods or services, which currently include, but are not necessarily limited to, Cuba, Iran, Iraq, Libya, North Korea, Sudan, and Syria, or to any national of any such country, wherever located, who intends to transmit or transport the Restricted Components back to such country; (ii) to any end user who you know or have reason to know will utilize the Restricted Components in the design, development, or production of nuclear, chemical, or biological weapons; or (iii) to any end user who has been prohibited from participating in U.S. export transactions by any federal agency of the U.S. government. You warrant and represent that neither the BXA nor any other U.S. federal agency has suspended, revoked, or denied your export privileges.

DISCLAIMER OF WARRANTY

NO WARRANTIES OR CONDITIONS. MICROSOFT EXPRESSLY DISCLAIMS ANY WARRANTY OR CONDITION FOR THE SOFTWARE PRODUCT. THE SOFTWARE PRODUCT AND ANY RELATED DOCUMENTATION IS PROVIDED "AS IS" WITHOUT WARRANTY OR CONDITION OF ANY KIND, EITHER EXPRESS OR IMPLIED, INCLUDING, WITHOUT LIMITATION, THE IMPLIED WARRANTIES OF MERCHANTABILITY, FITNESS FOR A PARTICULAR PURPOSE, OR NONINFRINGEMENT. THE ENTIRE RISK ARISING OUT OF USE OR PERFORMANCE OF THE SOFTWARE PRODUCT REMAINS WITH YOU.

LIMITATION OF LIABILITY. TO THE MAXIMUM EXTENT PERMITTED BY APPLICABLE LAW, IN NO EVENT SHALL MICROSOFT OR ITS SUPPLIERS BE LIABLE FOR ANY SPECIAL, INCIDENTAL, INDIRECT, OR CONSEQUENTIAL DAM-AGES WHATSOEVER (INCLUDING, WITHOUT LIMITATION, DAMAGES FOR LOSS OF BUSINESS PROFITS, BUSINESS INTERRUPTION, LOSS OF BUSINESS INFORMATION, OR ANY OTHER PECUNIARY LOSS) ARISING OUT OF THE USE OF OR INABILITY TO USE THE SOFTWARE PRODUCT OR THE PROVISION OF OR FAILURE TO PROVIDE SUPPORT SERVICES, EVEN IF MICROSOFT HAS BEEN ADVISED OF THE POSSIBILITY OF SUCH DAMAGES. IN ANY CASE, MICROSOFT'S ENTIRE LIABILITY UNDER ANY PROVISION OF THIS EULA SHALL BE LIMITED TO THE GREATER OF THE AMOUNT ACTUALLY PAID BY YOU FOR THE SOFTWARE PRODUCT OR US$5.00; PROVIDED, HOWEVER, IF YOU HAVE ENTERED INTO A MICROSOFT SUPPORT SERVICES AGREEMENT, MICROSOFT'S ENTIRE LIABILITY REGARDING SUPPORT SERVICES SHALL BE GOVERNED BY THE TERMS OF THAT AGREEMENT. BECAUSE SOME STATES AND JURISDICTIONS DO NOT ALLOW THE EXCLUSION OR LIMITATION OF LIABILITY, THE ABOVE LIMITATION MAY NOT APPLY TO YOU.

MISCELLANEOUS

This EULA is governed by the laws of the State of Washington USA, except and only to the extent that applicable law mandates governing law of a different jurisdiction.

Should you have any questions concerning this EULA, or if you desire to contact Microsoft for any reason, please contact the Microsoft subsidiary serving your country, or write: Microsoft Sales Information Center/One Microsoft Way/Redmond, WA 98052-6399.

System Requirements

To use the Readiness Review compact disc, you need a computer equipped with the following minimum configuration:

- 486 or higher Intel-based processor (486 must be running in Enhanced mode).

- Microsoft Windows 95, Windows 98, Windows NT 4.0, or later.

- 4 MB of RAM.

- 15 MB of available disk space.

- CD-ROM drive.

- Mouse or other pointing device (recommended).

Register Today!

Return this
*MCSE Readiness Review Exam 70-068
Windows NT® 4.0 Server Enterprise*
registration card today

Microsoft®Press
mspress.microsoft.com

OWNER REGISTRATION CARD

0-7356-0539-4

MCSE Readiness Review Exam 70-068
Windows NT® 4.0 Server Enterprise

FIRST NAME   MIDDLE INITIAL   LAST NAME

INSTITUTION OR COMPANY NAME

ADDRESS

CITY   STATE   ZIP

(   )

E-MAIL ADDRESS   PHONE NUMBER

U.S. and Canada addresses only. Fill in information above and mail postage-free.
Please mail only the bottom half of this page.

For information about Microsoft Press®
products, visit our Web site at
mspress.microsoft.com

Microsoft Press